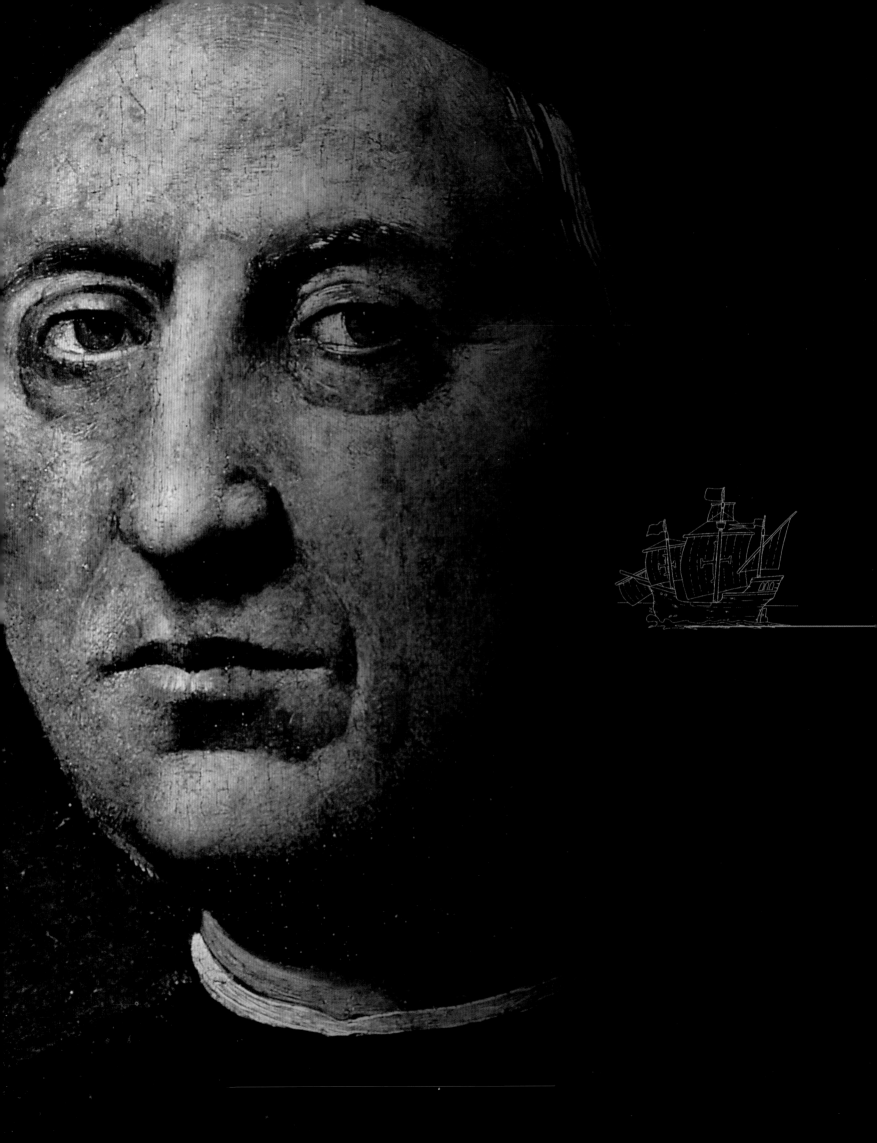

CHRISTOPHER COLUMBUS
and the mystery of the bell of the

SANTA MARIA

WHITE STAR PUBLISHERS

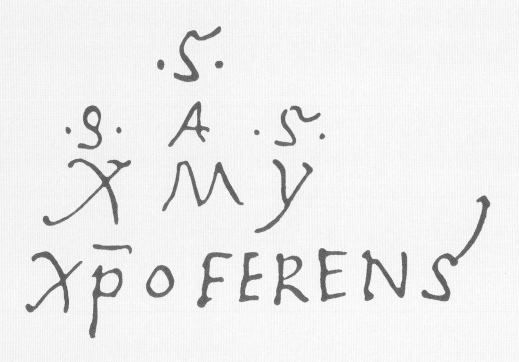

HISTORICAL TEXT

CONSUELO VARELA

TEXT OF "THE BELL FROM THE *SANTA MARIA*"

ROBERTO MAZZARA

EDITED BY

VALERIA MANFERTO DE FABIANIS

EDITORIAL COORDINATION

LAURA ACCOMAZZO
GIORGIO FERRERO

GRAPHIC DESIGN

MARINELLA DEBERNARDI

CONTENTS

PREFACE   PAGE 8

THE MAN   PAGE 10
"BEING BORN IN GENOA..."   PAGE   14
PERSONAL DATA   PAGE   18
HIS FAMILY   PAGE   30
HIS FRIENDS   PAGE   36
ANDALUSIAN NOBLEMEN AND ARAGONESE COURTIERS   PAGE   38
LUIS DE SANTÁNGEL   PAGE   41
HIS FEMALE FRIENDS AND THE SERVANTS   PAGE   43
ITALIAN FRIENDS AND ENEMIES   PAGE   46
COLUMBUS AND VESPUCCI   PAGE   49
FRANCESCO DE' BARDI   PAGE   49
HIS GENOVESE FRIENDS   PAGE   52
A MAN FROM NOVARA: BROTHER GASPARE GORRICIO   PAGE   52
JOHN DAY   PAGE   53

THE SAILOR   PAGE 56
AN APPRENTICE IN THE MEDITERRANEAN   PAGE   60
AN ATTRACTION TO THE ORIENT AND THE ATLANTIC   PAGE   66
TRADING IN THE PORTUGUESE AND SPANISH ATLANTIC   PAGE   74
THE COLUMBUS PROJECT   PAGE   82
THE AGREEMENT AT SANTA FE   PAGE   94
VOYAGES TO THE NEW WORLD   PAGE   98
A SAILOR'S INTUITION   PAGE 134

THE VICEROY — PAGE 146

THE NAVIDAD DISASTER — PAGE 150

COLUMBIAN FOUNDATIONS — PAGE 152

DIFFICULT BEGINNINGS — PAGE 156

RELATIONS WITH INDIGENOUS PEOPLES — PAGE 162

THE FALL OF THE VICEROY — PAGE 164

LEGAL PROCEEDINGS — PAGE 166

THE LAST YEARS — PAGE 170

RETURN TO SPAIN — PAGE 174

DESIRE FOR REDEMPTION — PAGE 176

DESPERATE LETTERS — PAGE 180

HIS LAST VOYAGE — PAGE 182

THE BELL FROM THE *SANTA MARIA* — PAGE 188

A FASCINATION FOR THE ABYSS — PAGE 192

FIRST EFFORTS — PAGE 194

THE *SAN SALVADOR* SHIPWRECK — PAGE 198

INDEX — PAGE 220

BIBLIOGRAPHY — PAGE 223

PREFACE

People talk about Christopher Columbus as if he were someone they knew or who was familiar to them. For a long time, and especially since the 500th anniversary of the First Voyage, when in 1992, in both Spain and Italy, radio and television programs have proliferated with large numbers of speakers energetically expounding upon their knowledge. Everyone knows that Columbus explored the New World, a continent named America only because another Italian, some say his enemy, succeeded in usurping this honor from him. Many people categorically confirm that he died alone, abandoned, and quite poor. On the other hand, others certainly believe that he simply dressed modestly in the humble clothing of a Franciscan friar. The boldest propose bizarre hypotheses that make us blush when comnsidering them. Similar misconceptions about his persona by proponents of the two different views have contributed to creating a false concept in our collective imagination about who he really was – ant this is very difficult to correct. We have much information about Columbus, but there is just as much that we do not as yet have. As far as I'm concerned, this book's intention is humbly to shed light on some of the obscurity surrounding the historical figure that is Christopher Columbus. Not all of the obscurity though, as some of it still proves to be impenetrable today.

Over the last 20 years or so, a good number of documents regarding the many ambiguities has emerged after remaining buried in the Spanish Archives; they now clarify and in some imperceptible ways modify the information we already had. For example, we now have factual data on a large portion of Columbus' financial accounts and definitely know the precise amounts his representatives sent him from the Indies, which demonstrate his profitable financial situation. And yet, when he died in Valladolid, his family had to rely upon Genoese bankers to cover the costs of his burial and their own return to their homes in Seville. We now have the promissory note (with a value of 50,000 Spanish *maravedi*), signed by both his nephew Giovanni Antonio Columbus and his brother-in-law Giovanni de Bardi, who refused to pay the note when it was presented for collection six months later. Seville's diligent notaries public preserved the original draft of this disputed promissory note. We can then assume that the Columbus family paid it a short time later, given that we have no knowledge of any subsequent legal action.

The published registers concerning Columbus' voyages give us a glimpse into who these men were who traveled under his command, though we must note that the list for the second voyage is incomplete. His high standard of living in the New World is apparent considering that, at least from 1493 on, he had at his disposal no fewer than two tailors, Antonio and Bernandino, a confectioner whose name was García, two stewards, one chaplain, and a large group of retainers. These retainers were so numerous that Ferdinand and Isabella had to intervene, forbidding him against such a large contingent.

Perhaps the most revealing document among those showing up in more recent years is a copy of the report of the investigation that the investigating judge Francisco de Bobadilla completed on the Columbus brothers at Santo Domingo in September 1500, which was the cause for their dismissal and return to Spain. It is a document that must be examined carefully and, clearly this shall be accomplished over time.

For the first time, definite confirmation of the admiral's origins in Genoa and his father's weaving business there has materialized in a document other than the official instruments drawn up by Genoese notaries. The Columbus family was not at all indignant because their nationality was mentioned, but because it was reported, or thus rumored, that they were "of humble origins." Other issues, some embarrassing and others perhaps doubtful, appeared in this investigative report without anything else available to substantiate or invalidate them. The Spanish rulers had no other choice than to remove Columbus from his powerful post over the budding colony. It was not due to "envy" on the part of his adversaries, as had been reiterated frequently, but out of pure necessity. Columbus was an excellent admiral yet an awful viceroy and governor.

As I said above, I believe that there are aspects of Columbus' life that prove impossible to decipher. One example among many is his signature. We can hypothesize all we want, but until we have an accurate translation key, it would be rash to suggest outright the meaning of such a strange anagram. The same thing occurs with the cryptic text on the pages of one of his books. Without the code, any effort at decoding it is futile.

I have divided this book into five chapters. The first three regard his persona from three different points of view: the man, the sailor, and the viceroy. These are three aspects of his life through which I've tried to portray the most important characteristics of his personality. Columbus was a versatile man, educated in disparate environments where he had to confront many diverse realities over the course of his lifetime. Sailing along the coasts during his years as a ship's boy and the later difficult crossings over the Atlantic Ocean do not even begin to compare. He then had to adapt to a new lifestyle as a businessman managing part of the colonial venture as well as to his difficult status as viceroy governing a colony in such a distant and unique territory as the New World. In the fourth chapter, I explore his last years when, deprived of strength and good health, he devoted his days to other activities.

I didn't set out to write an intellectual account. My intention was simply that of creating an easy-to-read and pleasant text, accompanied by marvelous illustrations.

THE MAN
chapter 1

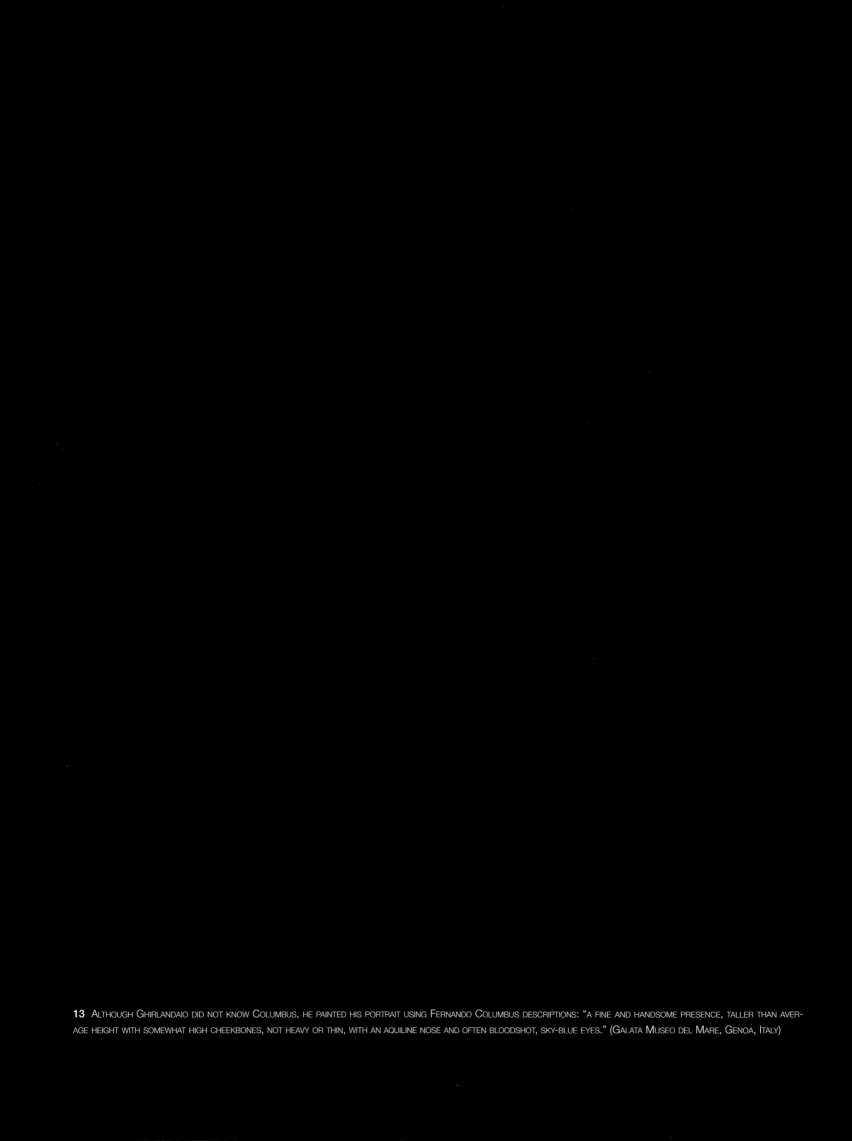

13 Although Ghirlandaio did not know Columbus, he painted his portrait using Fernando Columbus descriptions: "a fine and handsome presence, taller than average height with somewhat high cheekbones, not heavy or thin, with an aquiline nose and often bloodshot, sky-blue eyes." (Galata Museo del Mare, Genoa, Italy)

"BEING BORN IN GENOA..."

One of the mysteries that important historiographers like to discuss, idling away the time with new and bizarre conjectures, is that of the origin and birth date of Christopher Columbus, despite the fact that all chroniclers of that period wrote that he was from Liguria in northern Italy. The origin of these and other researchers' theories is owed first to Columbus himself and then to information provided by his son, Fernando. Columbus contributed to creating an aura of mystery around himself, consigning much needed information to the dark shadows of the past. In his own writings, he mentioned Genoa only a couple of times and notably never wrote a single page in his native language, not even to his fellow countrymen, with whom he always corresponded in Spanish. The only example of his quite disorganized Italian is found in two notes in the margin of one of his

books. There was another occasion when Christopher Columbus wrote that he was born in Genoa and that the bank, which protected the financial interests of his descendants, was none other than the Genoese Bank of San Giorgio. In fact, on 22 February 1498, on the eve of his third voyage to the Indies, Columbus wrote his will, in favor of his firstborn son, Diego. In it he stated, "being born in Genoa, I came to serve [the king and queen] here in Castile." It was a valuable document that unfortunately was preserved only in an official copy.

As if that weren't enough, in a biography about his father, Fernando Columbus confines himself to collecting opinions on diverse hypotheses that were rumored about his father's origins without either clearly favoring any of them or even making an indication of where his father's exact birthplace was. Years later in his own will, he stated peremptorily that his father was "Genoese," without shedding any light on his reasons for this late confession.

Thanks to a deed registered in Genoa in 1478 by Christopher himself, stating he was twenty-seven years old, we can deduce that he was born in 1451, the eldest of five siblings: Giovanni Pellegrino, Bartolomeo, Diego, and Bianchinetta. He was probably born in Quinto, a town in the Moconesi region and a close suburb of Genoa, the city where his parents, Domenico Columbus and Susanna Fontenerosa, lived and where a large part of his modest family originated.

Columbus did not go to the university. We have to make assumptions with respect to the education he received in his homeland. Despite Fernando assuring us that his father studied at the University of Pavia, where he learned about astrology, cosmography, and geometry, it does not appear that the young man attended any center for higher learning yet, undoubtedly, he did attend one of the schools reserved for sons of weavers in his city until he reached the age of majority, when he could devote himself to work.

As for the remainder of his education, it seems not very likely that his parents, who were of humble means, could have financed any literary or scientific studies when they obviously needed everyone to work to support the family. It was in one of these schools, perhaps attending in the late afternoon or early evening, where Columbus learned to write with excellent penmanship, to draw with ease, and

where he revealed an enormous interest in reading, based on his autodidactic training and given that he himself wrote, "I learn everything by experience."

The young man lived in the vicinity of Genoa at least until 1473, practicing diverse professions. Despite what Fernando wrote, wanting us to firmly believe that he didn't ever practice "mechanical or manual arts," Christopher was a weaver like his father and brother Bartolomeo. In those times, artisan families did not ask their children what they would like to do in life because obviously the children would inherit their trades.

Columbus' passion for the universe was awakened to such an extent that a biographer, contemporary to the admiral and also Genoese, in order to distinguish father from son and give the latter more importance, dared to write that while Domenico was a simple weaver of "wool cloth," Christopher was a weaver of "silk." Fantasy about this man even rose to this level! Yet, it was fantasy surpassed only by that of Bartolomé de Las Casas (by turn priest, Dominican monk and historian), who assured us that such were the inaccuracies spread by Agostino Giustiniani in his *Annals of the Republic of Genoa* and the Signory of Genoa said, "that he was able to confirm the truth about what had occurred and had noted Giustiniani's exaggeration in his chronicle," and by decree prohibited the Genoese people from reading it, "having all books and treatises removed so that they could not be accessible to anyone."

14 This engraving was published in the tome, *Liber Chronicarum* by Hartmann Schedel (1493) and depicts the city of Genoa surrounded by the woods and hills that Columbus knew as a child.

16-17 The privileged relationship between Genoa and other powerful republics made its port become one of the most important in the Mediterranean. At the beginning of the 16th century, city administrators experienced an important change in their city thanks to Admiral Andrea Doria who modified its governmental organization, transforming Genoa into a republic led by a doge selected from among aristocrats and elected to a two-year term (Galata Museo del Mare, Genoa, Italy).

ANTIQVÆ VRBIS GENVÆ PICTVRA
TEMPORIS INIVRIA FERE CONSVMPTA
HANC AD EXEMPLVM ILLIVS VETVSTATIS
RETINEDÆ CAVSA P PRES COMMVNIS
EFFINGI MANDARVNT ANNO MDXLVII

CHRISTOPHORO · COLOMBO

PERSONAL DATA

Columbus the man quite often proves to be an unknown personage: no authenticated portraits of him exist, though it is very probable that, imitating noblemen, he could have sat for one of the many painters who frequented the court of his patrons King Ferdinand and Queen Isabella. To appreciate his actual physical appearance, we have to resort to information left by his son Fernando and by Las Casas. In almost in the same words, both report that he had "a fine and handsome presence, and taller than average height with somewhat high cheekbones, not heavy or thin, having an aquiline nose, with often bloodshot, sky-blue eyes" and that as a young man, he had blond hair and beard, even when his hair prematurely turned grey "due to his numerous stresses and anxiety." His biographers tell us that he was a great swimmer, modest in dress and footwear as well as in the amounts he ate and drank, friendly in conversation with strangers and very courteous with people he knew, kind and happy in his behavior, well raised and an enemy to judgment or blasphemy – and only when he was really annoyed did he invoke the name of Seville's patron saint, exclaiming "for the love of San Fernando!"

Other sources indicate that Columbus was preoccupied with his own image. The white hair that his biographers described as spoiling his appearance, must have truly upset him, and consequently he tried to remedy the situation with recipes taken from Pliny's *Historia naturalis* (*Natural History*). In fact, he noted in the margin of this book in his private library: "How to eliminate white hair from the head." Very simply: "the semen from the donkey's genitals make hair thicker and eliminate baldness if sprinkled on the skin after shaving the hair off completely." His first concern should have been

"to keep hair from falling out," for which the Pliny advised using "the dust or ashes from a goat's horn, better yet the ashes from a male goat's horn, add saltpeter (potassium nitrate), tamarind seeds, butter, and oil," a concoction that appeared to "commendably keep hair from falling out any longer."

A delightful scene that Columbus himself recounted of a celebratory banquet aboard the *Santa Maria* on 18 December 1492, provides us with two details about his personal apparel. The first is that he wore colored shoes and the second is that he was in the habit of dressing up, adding a necklace. We would never have imagined this, given that he has always been painted wearing the humble clothing of Franciscan friars. Columbus commented thus at the end of his lunch and pleasant conversation with the cacique (local Caribbean ruler) Guacanagarí: "I noticed that you liked a piece of fabric spread over my bed. I am giving it to you along with some quite beautiful amber beads that I was wearing around my neck, some red shoes, and a water carafe with orange flowers. And, Guacanagarí was so happy with these gifts that he became speechless." The local cacique must have left content. Twelve days later on the occasion of another lunch on dry land with another gift exchange in play, Columbus gave Guacanagarí a second necklace. This time it was a necklace of small colored pearls as recounted by Las Casas: "the admiral removed a cornelian necklace from his neck with delightful colored pearls that looked quite beautiful when the chief put on the necklace."

In this interesting exchange of curios, the cacique also received a silver ring that did not belong to the admiral, but rather to another sailor. It is common knowledge that Columbus did not wear that sort of jewelry and must have asked to borrow it to honor his host who was captivated by the ring when seeing it on the finger of that poor soul. Guacanagarí demonstrated such enthusiasm toward Spanish fashion that Columbus took advantage of this to give him financial and very personal gifts: once a pair of gloves, "for which he demon-

strated much joy and happiness" and when respectfully taking his leave on 2 January 1493, he gave the cacique a shirt that the latter immediately put on.

After so much gift-giving, Columbus must have found himself with an empty closet, given that he soon requested a shipment of clothing and shoes, primarily the latter, which arrived from Spain with a royal consignment note recording that "he has great need for [them]." The compliant colonists' shoes must have worn out quickly in the Indies, so quickly that they must have been the only unusual cargo; in 1494, among lots of other provisions, Antonio de Torres had loaded no fewer than "one hundred twenty pairs of sensible shoes" – for the exclusive use of the admiral's domestic employees.

State gifts proved to be quite frequent in Columbus' relations with the indigenous caciques. On 22 December 1492, just before Christmas Eve, the admiral received an early gift in a splendid belt sent by Guacanagarí. This was a spectacular belt, four fingers wide, handcrafted with white fish bones and stones of many colors, and a mask with a gold nose, ears, and tongue set in the center. Columbus must have shown so much satisfaction in the gift that a few days later, the cacique tried to console him about the sinking of the *Santa Maria* in giving him with an even more valuable mask, this time in a matching set of jewelry that included a gold crown and necklace.

Years later, in August 1498, Columbus arrived on Trinidad on his third expedition. The local cacique came promptly to his ship and asked that he be permitted to welcome and honor the admiral him. In the emotional encounter described by Las Casas, yet another exchange of presents occurred, a custom that was becoming a tradi-

tion. The cacique, wearing a gold crown, took it off with his right hand and, having ceremoniously kissed it, put it on Columbus' head after the admiral first took off "a crimson-colored hat" with his left hand. This is how we learned that Columbus wore the typical pink wool cone-shaped hat that was the only article of clothing that distinguished sailors from other tradesmen in an era when uniforms had not yet been invented.

For Columbus, one of these hats served as a receptacle for chickpeas, which he removed during a voting process on 14 February 1493, when a storm surprised the fleet on its return voyage from the New World to Spain; it proved to be a turning point that added to the problems of the journey.

On different occasions, the caciques bestowed necklaces, crowns, or belts upon Columbus. It is possible that this was a local custom; however there is no doubt that if they were giving him these gifts, it was because they saw him bejeweled and thought that he enjoyed this kind of ornament. For example, none of the chroniclers report the Indies' natives giving Columbus either the gold nose rings or ankle bracelets that it was their custom to wear. Though this side of Columbus that never stands out in any of his biographies, the admiral's taste for ornamentation can be confirmed by a careful reading of an extract from an account in 1500 or 1501, which states that he had a gold wedding ring and necklace with forty-seven links made. This account also highlights the fact that he took advantage of an opportunity to exchange gemstones from his first voyage for precious metal. This was not surprising to those who were familiar with the Genoese hunger for gold.

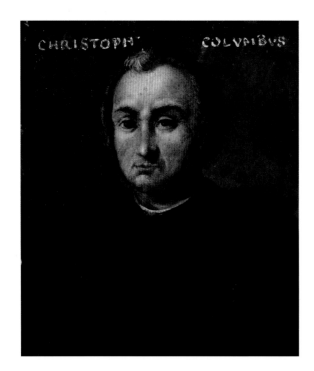

From youth, Columbus was subject to poor health. This was a characteristic that none of his biographers emphasized, even when incidentally mentioning his many ailments. In 1494, after sighting Cuba and Jamaica while skirting the north side of the Hispaniola (as he named what is now Haiti and the Dominican Republic), he suffered a major health crisis. Las Casas says that he suffered a pathological drowsiness that obliged him to stay in bed for five months, after remaining in a state of semi-consciousness for thirty-two days. From that time forward, his aches and pains never ceased. Gout, migraines, dropsy, rheumatism, arthritis were disorders that his doctor, Juan Petit, very probably a Frenchman of modest height, tried to cure him of in Spain.

Particularly troubled by the state of his health, Columbus tried to alleviate his aches and pains with various remedies which he carefully transcribed onto the margins of one of his favorite books. With good reason, he constantly made notes about requisite cures to alleviate "kidney stones" in his copy of Pliny's *Historia naturalis*. Reviewing his writings, we see that he often had complaints about the cold that caused him a lot of pain, primarily in his hands. "My aches and pains do not allow me to write at any time other than nighttime because during the day, my hands are deprived of strength," he wrote to his son, Diego, from Seville on 1 December 1504, excusing himself for not having written more often. And, on the 19th of that same month, he asked Diego to make his apologies to friends to whom he couldn't write, "because of the great pain I feel when using the quill pen." He did not even have the strength to hold the pen in his hand.

After Queen Isabella's death at the end of 1504, Columbus decided to leave Seville to meet with King Ferdinand in Segovia. The route he would have to take on horseback over the ancient Spanish Silver Road was long and tortuous. Because of this, he asked permission to travel by mule, a mount granted only to women and monks in keeping with a royal edict issued in 1494 that aimed at protecting equine breeding. In support of his request, the admiral sent a memorandum about his illness; unfortunately it has been lost. His son, Fernando, recounts that in the last months of his father's life, he couldn't even get out of bed. His body was inflamed from chest to feet and he couldn't even turn over in bed.

COLOMBVS LYGVR NOVI ORBIS REPTOR

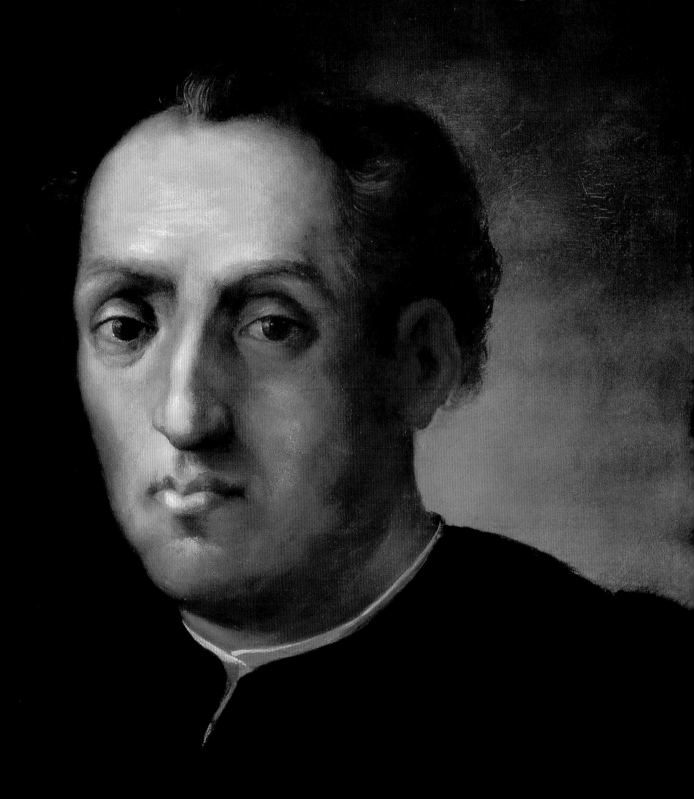

S. LIGVRIS MIRANDA   COLVMBA
RAVIG IN,   ORBEM,

Poor health was perhaps the cause of Columbus' bad moods, despite Las Casas' explicit confirmation that described him as "friendly and generous." On the other hand, the chronicler, Gonzalo Fernandez de Oviedo, who knew Columbus personally, said that he was "kind when he wanted to be and furious when he became angry." Others like Francisco López de Gómara, defined him as "quick-tempered and cruel" or simply "irritable," as his fellow countryman, Girolamo Benzoni, portrayed him resentfully, trying to make it known, yet undoubtedly following what Oviedo said, given that he did not know Columbus personally.

Irascible with those who contradicted him, Columbus was a man who often lost his temper and, like all good Latin men, was contentious. He was proud and conceited, demonstrated by the fact that on at least three occasions, he complained that Ferdinand and Isabella wanted to send bishops to the Indies without first consulting him. He even wondered if the Catholic Queen had mentioned him in her will. Columbus frequently made errors in judgment about the people around him. In reading the memoranda that he sent to the rulers from Isabella settlement on Hispaniola in February 1494, he praises the men that he would confront not a few days later and criticizes those who would always be faithful to him. Among the people from whom Columbus begged pardon there was the example of Juan Aguado, who was briefly sent back to the Indies as investigator and judge, of Brother Bernardo Buil and of Bernal de Pisa, who began to investigate him several days later with.

In addition to the negative, our man also had positive personality traits. For example, he had an insatiable curiosity toward anything that represented innovation and novelty. His descriptions of the Indies and interest in always learning and knowing more stand out in all of his writings, as well as in descriptions of him by his peers. He left a curious example of these aspirations with Peter Martyr d'Angheria. The humanist and historian recounts that Columbus, after savoring an Indies partridge, once asked his cooks to cut into another partridge's stomach so he could find out the source of that delicious flavor. Its reason was neither more nor less the exuberance of the Indies plants: its crop was full of aromatic herbs.

Columbus was a charismatic man, endowed with a great fascination with what he could use to his advantage, and had that certain something that allowed him to be the best promoter of his own ideas as well as himself. Despite having delayed seven years in "selling" his wonderfully clever plan to the Spanish king and queen, he knew how to skillfully convince many other people of something that made no sense, using empty promises. However, this seductive man did know how to conquer his king and queen. If he obtained falcons so that King Ferdinand could hunt or "give them to other princes," he respectfully gave Queen Isabella jewels, gold, and pearls. As a versatile person, he adapted to any circumstances and was capable of transforming his personal failings into triumphs. When on Christmas Day, 1492 he lost the *Santa Maria*, it wasn't his fault or that of his captain, but rather due to the negligent ship boy that fell asleep during his turn on watch. This was a disgrace but really the proof that "because our Lord made the ship run aground here, then here is where He wants me to stay." When he did not find what he had hoped to find in the New World, he searched for an explanation. If the trees did not have fruit, it was because it wasn't the appropriate time and he would have to wait for the right season. If he hadn't seen the wild beasts he was expecting, it was no doubt because "they had run away." If there was not as much gold as he desired, it was because they hadn't yet reached the region where it "its source was located." Despite his complaints and sadness, Columbus managed to convince himself that his situation was always the right one. He died with a clean conscience in having fulfilled his destiny in life. Columbus was a great dreamer with perseverance and an iron will. He thus wrote to Ferdinand and Isabella just before his death: "If I lacked strength and hard work defeated me, the strong will of my spirit never grew weak." This determination allowed him to get where he wanted to go, and is perhaps the most characteristic trait of his personality.

Columbus was a profoundly religious man and perhaps even blessed by God. To demonstrate his piousness, Las Casas tells us that he addressed his letters with the short prayer "Jhesus cum Maria sit nobis in via. We don't question this, even though it proves a bit strange that among about one hundred letters signed by Columbus that we are aware of, just one letter to the Queen Isabella bears that heading. In all other letters as well as that one, he never forgot to affix a cross to which not all of his biographers have noted.

The fact that Columbus was a sober person does not mean that he didn't enjoy the receptions given him by the caciques dining on his ship or visiting him in his home. But food didn't interest him except as a source of sustenance. Like most Europeans he was enthusiastic about the new foods found in the Americas and even described them, though awkwardly, confining himself to comparing their taste to that of chestnuts or carrots, pointing out their "wonderful flavor" or the fact that they were "very different than our own foods." Wild grapes seemed extraordinarily juicy to him and he thought that dates had excellent flavor. Among all these novelties, what he undoubtedly liked the most was bread that was "very white and good," made from the local *ñame* and *ajes* plants, essentials in Indies cuisine. He loaded *ajes* onto his ship when preparing to return to Castile on 13 January 13 1493, perhaps to complement the supplies of bread, cured fish, and game that cacique Guacanagarí gave him so that he would not lack anything on his long return voyage.

Despite having a courtyard full of poultry at his home, Columbus scarcely mentioned them in his writings. He spoke instead about the spit-roasted fish that he had sampled along with the Caribbean seafood that he found bland. Even large snails seemed tasteless, to the point that he informs us that, "they aren't like the Spanish ones." Seasonings were something else all together, he said. Columbus had tried oysters for the first time in the "Gulf of Whales" during his third voyage, even when they were a bit bland, "needing some salt," then proving to be a bit more flavorful. When a particular kind of fish seemed tasty to him, it was because he recalled the seafood with which he was familiar, even taking note of the names of those he appreciated most: tench, salmon, bass, sole, groper (stone bass), prawns, and sardines, very common fish in the Mediterranean diet. To the delight of Columbus and his people, Caribbean fish enjoyed extraordinary virtue: "it doesn't weigh down the body," also particularly digestible, and so healthy that "the doctor prescribed it for those who have stomach ailments."

Columbus liked wine. "In the Indies," he wrote, " there are many types of wine, red and white, and not just made from grapes" that did not have, he said, "unpleasant flavors." All of the chroniclers then began to point out that the Indies people distilled diverse types of alcoholic beverages, each more flavorful than the last: from tplain maize wine "that looks like beer" to the most expensive thus the most appreciated of all" palm juice cooked in water and mixed with spices.

27 At the start of the 19th century in France, diverse Columbus biographies were published, achieving great success (Roselly, Lamartine, Verne) because the man's appearance had been reinvented by period painters and sculptors. This painting by Emile Vassalle (1839), portrays Columbus intent upon taking measurements on a map of the world and making notes (Columbian Library, Seville, Spain).

We are unaware of where Columbus lived. He neither leased nor ever bought a house in Spain. When he arrived at the La Rábida Monastery around 1485, he had to find accommodation in the house his that Portuguese sister-in-law, Briolanja Muñiz, kept at San Juan del Puerto. From that location, he could easily participate in scholarly gatherings held at the Franciscan monastery with Brother Antonio de Marchena and Brother Juan Perez. In Cordova, he had to reside in the home of his companion, Beatriz Enríquez de Arana who was the mother of his son, Fernando. It has been said that during his visits to Seville, he took lodgings in the Carthusian monastery of Santa María de las Cuevas, but that does not seem probable. From 1493 to 1498, he lived in the house that King Ferdinand and Queen Isabella gave to his sister-in-law, Briolanja, in the hamlet of Santa María la Blanca and in 1498 moved to a Francos Road dwelling, which also accommodated Diego and Fernando after the death of the Queen Isabella.

Columbus never built a house in the New World. As a good sailor, what truly gave him pleasure was to live on the ship, thereby avoiding dry land. This was a habit that everyone knew about and maliciously took advantage of, proving that his majordomo, Pedro de Terreros, was the real conquistador of the new continent, given that he was the first to set foot on dry land on 6 August 1498, the man who took firm possession of the territory in the name of King Ferdinand and Queen Isabella. We actually know what Columbus' cabin was like as it was the only one on the whole ship, given that other officials had to wait well into the 16th century to get their own cabins. Situated astern, it was of small size, so tiny that four people could barely fit inside it. Besides a table, the furnishings included only a bed and wardrobe or trunk where he kept his clothes, jewelry, and documents. A crucifix and an image of the Madonna completed the cabin's simple décor.

By rereading Columbus' diaries, it becomes possible to follow his constant movements. During his sojourns in Hispaniola, he frequently had to stay in the fort called La Concepción in La Vega if he did not stay at the Santo Domingo fortress, which was used at that time as a jail or as Columbus brothers' residence. In Isabella, the first city founded in the New World, yet abandoned near the end of 1496, only a very basic abode was available to him.

Columbus lived austerely as demonstrated by the list of furniture and table utensils that were sent out from Spain to him in 1494. For this home, the list only included several tapestries with non-religious landscape themes, two matching glazed doors, four family crests with coat of arms, and several trunks. Four tablecloths, six dozen napkins, six hand towels, various placemats for the sideboard, a simple china service in pewter, two silver cups, a saltcellar, twelve spoons, two candelabra, and six copper jugs were sent for his kitchen. These were very simple pieces of kitchen equipment, clearly indicating what his lifestyle was like in the Indies.

29 THIS IDEALIZED REPRESENTATION DEPICTS THE ARRIVAL OF COLUMBUS AT THE LA RÁBIDA MONASTERY (HUELVA) IN 1485, ACCOMPANIED BY HIS SON, DIEGO. THE PAINTING IS BY ANTONIO CABRAL-BEJARANO (CIRCA 1825/50) (LA RÁBIDA MONASTERY, PALOS, SPAIN).

30 THIS OLD SPANISH PRINT PORTRAYS CHRISTOPHER COLUMBUS IN THE COMPANY OF HIS TWO SONS, FERNANDO AND DIEGO.

HIS FAMILY

Columbus had two sons. During his sojourn in Portugal (where he lived from 1474 to 1485, he married Filipa Muñiz de Perestrello, a Portuguese woman of good family who, during a voyage in 1478 to the island of Porto Santo, gave birth to Columbus' first son, Diego. After his wife had died, Columbus moved to Spain where he married Beatriz Enríquez de Arana of Cordova, with whom he had his second son, Fernando, born in the same city in 1488. Diego became Columbus' successor and the second Admiral and Governor of the Indies while he converted Fernando into one of the greatest bibliophiles of his time. Called the Colombina, Fernando's library contained up to 20,000 volumes and he left it to the Cathedral of Seville after he died; it is still open for public tours today. Despite their well-used condition, the library holds Christopher Columbus's commendable personal book collection, which his son preserved covetously and carefully.

Columbus was an excellent father who complained when he did not receive the correspondence he desired from his sons. His letters to Diego are the only ones that have been preserved, always ending with the memorable phrase, "Your father who loves you more than himself," noting the pride this father had in his eldest son, "take care of your brother [Fernando], who has a good nature and by now is no longer a young lad. Ten brothers would not be too many for you. I never had better friends than my brothers." Columbus was a father who wrote infinite memoirs to his firstborn son, telling him

how to manage his accounts, treat his domestic employees – and added advice for a good marriage. It would be a wedding that he would not participate in, given that Diego happily married the Donna María de Toledo, a cousin of the Duke of Alba, only after his father had already died. Fernando never married, saying "I never had better friends than my brothers"

Columbus, as he stated in a letter addressed to his son, Diego, felt he was getting increasingly closer to his two brothers, Bartolomeo and Diego. We know nothing about the life or even the birthplace of Bartolomeo Columbus, who was ten years younger than Christopher. We may suppose, in light of subsequent events, that his studies and education must have proceeded at the same rate as that of his older brother. For us, his story begins in Portugal where the two brothers settled in Lisbon to dedicate themselves to the business of sea maps and used books. It seems plausible to assume that Bartolomeo arrived in that country along with Christopher in 1479, when both were returning from a rapid voyage to Genoa and very probably must have worked together in association with their Genoese compatriots, participating in some maritime expeditions to Guinea, West Africa.

Everything seems to indicate that Bartolomeo had a good disposition, was more cultured than Christopher, with more desirable personality traits and the more careful appearance of a gentleman, even when descriptions we have of him leave an opposing account. According to his nephew Fernando's version, Bartolomeo did not have a good command of Latin but was an expert in issues surrounding the sea and a master at "accomplishing great feats with navigational maps and other instruments of the trade." Las Casas' account states he suspected, given Bartolomeo's abilities, that he may have been the author of most of the nautical maps and memoirs attributed to Christopher Columbus, an assertion that is really quite impossible to verify.

Apparently, the alliance between the two brothers epitomized the perfect combination. Bartolomeo was tightly bonded to his elder brother whom he adored and aided in presenting their voyaging plans to the European royal courts. Representing his brother, he traveled to England and France. On one voyage to England, Bartolomeo succeeded in obtaining an audience at the court of Henry VII who, according to Las Casas, was so delighted by his conversation that he ended up accepting his proposed plans. Las Casas recounts that Bartolomeo, with the promise of an agreement from the English monarch in his pocket, went immediately in search of his brother in France. At the Court of Charles VIII, among others, Bartolomeo visited Charles' sister, Anne de Beaujeu, probably during the same time when Amerigo Vespucci accompanied his uncle, Ambassador Guidoantonio Vespucci there.

It was there at the French court that Bartolomeo seemed surprised by the news of Christopher's discovery. Bartolomeo's emotions must have been such that Charles VIII himself, moved by this news, also gave him financial aid of 100 escudos so that he could quickly reach Castile to join his brother Christopher. Perhaps, because the news arrived late at the French court or because he had to wait for the slow bureaucratic machine to receive this money as well as a vital safe-conduct, Bartolomeo did not arrive in Spain until the beginning of 1494, after Columbus had already left on his second voyage to the New World. His disappointment was enormous.

In reality, we aren't aware of what mode Christopher used to get back his brothers in Castile. According to Las Casas, it was actually King Charles VIII who gave the news of Christopher's discovery to Bartolomeo in Paris. We will never know how Diego received it. It proves surprising that it was Diego who arrived in time to set sail on 25 September 1493 while Bartolomeo, who was in theory closer to Christopher, was not able to, delayed just a few months.

Reaching Seville, Bartolomeo immediately got into contact with Giannotto Berardi, the admiral's attorney, in whose hands Columbus, thinking that his brother might have appeared at any moment, had left a packet of letters with precise instructions and even a description of the route that he should take to catch up with him. With Berardi's assistance, Bartolomeo prepared thoroughly for the voyage to the Indies and agreed to the financial conditions for the returns that the expedition would be able to provide.

From a family point of view, Bartolomeo's arrival in Spain determined the future training of his nephews, Diego and Fernando. More accustomed than his brother to court controversies, he decided to present himself to King Ferdinand and Queen Isabella in the company of these two children who, at that time in 1494, were welcomed at court as companions to the monarchs' son, the Infante Don John, with their education, wages, food, and dress included.

The Columbus's brothers were two very different people. Bartolomeo, temperamental and a bundle of energy, stirred up more aversion than kindness in his fellow citizens. He was a combative, active, and cultured man, yet at the same time a despot and cruel to his subordinates. Such behavior made him garner harsh judgment from Las Casas who attributed him with being the cause of many of the accusations against Columbus who "could not do anything without him." By contrast, Diego was always a dull man who did not stimulate even minimal commentary from his peers. According to Las Casas, Diego was a virtuous man who dressed quite austerely, almost like a monk. Columbus loved both of them with equal affection, despite the passion that may have blinded him, clearly perceived in a paragraph of instructions that he left his son, Diego, before leaving on his fourth voyage, beseeching him, a young man of barely twenty-four years of age, to take care of his uncle:

"Diego, my brother remains in Cadiz. Please make the necessary arrangements for the money Our Lord will provide for you to support and take care of him because he is my brother, and has always been quite devoted to me. Do this in a way that encourages their Royal Highnesses to bestow upon him the reward of some ecclesiastical title, a canonry or other privilege." Despite the attempts of his family, which included letters of naturalization from his two brothers, Diego did not obtain any clerical privileges and lived exclusively from income that Columbus had left him and later from the charity of his nephews.

Bartolomeo and Diego were Columbus' most faithful supporters and collaborators. When the admiral died, they openly transferred their loyalty to his son Diego, the new admiral who became the head of the family. Their submission to Diego was in keeping with Columbus' instructions, which his brothers accepted with extraordinary loyalty. Columbus believed very strongly in hierarchy, practiced exclusively in his home by the pater familias whose decisions must be obeyed by everyone without dispute. In his will, just as strongly as in the document leaving his estate to his firstborn son, Columbus clearly stated his wishes. Diego was his successor and heir, and everyone was obliged to obey Diego and offer him due respect.

In about 1498, two new members of the Genoese family appeared in the shadow of the admiral: his nephews, Giovanni Antonio and Andrea Columbus. Both came from Genoa and formed a part of the circle of relatives resident in Spain, but they never enjoyed either the glory or the wealth of the other members of the clan and were always considered as loyal servants and domestic help. Giovanni Antonio participated in his uncle's third voyage to the New World as captain of one of his vessels and on his uncle's fourth voyage Andrea traveled in the role of squire.

34 FEW PORTRAITS OF BARTOLOMEO COLUMBUS EXIST AND NONE OF THEM HAVE BEEN AUTHENTICATED. IN THIS ONE, AN ANONYMOUS ENGRAVER REPRESENTS HIM IN THE CLOTHING OF A GOVERNOR, A POST TO WHICH HIS BROTHER, CHRISTOPHER, AP-POINTED HIM IN 1494 (NATIONAL LIBRARY, MADRID, SPAIN).

35 COLUMBUS' YOUNGER SON, FERNANDO, WAS BORN IN CORDOVA IN 1488. ACCOMPA-NYING HIS FATHER AS HIS SECRETARY ON THE FOURTH VOYAGE TO THE NEW WORLD, THE YOUNG MAN WROTE THE HISTORY OF THE ADMIRAL FOR THE PURPOSE OF RAISING HIS STATUS AND EMPHASIZING HIS WORK. A GREAT BIBLIOPHILE HIMSELF, FERNANDO LEFT A LIBRARY CONTAINING 20,000 VOLUMES. HE DIED IN SEVILLE IN 1539 (COLUMBIAN LI-BRARY, SEVILLE, SPAIN).

When necessary, the two nephews were called to attend to family issues, whether to attend a funeral, collect on a promissory note, act as representatives, or to give testimony. The Columbus family accepted few others into its intimate circle and, perhaps to distinguish themselves, modified their last name to "los Colón," while Giovanni Antonio and Andrea kept "Columbus," even when official documents did not identify them as either a part of the Colón or the Columbus family.

Besides being more convenient to use in Castile, the modified Spanish name also represented a surprising sign of things to come. Las Casas was already writing that the surname his hero had adopted in Castile was the most appropriate one for him, and his reference is clear: *colón* means more or less the "inhabitant of a new land" and Columbus had become this twice. Thanks to his endeavors, Heaven was becoming populated with new Christians and he was also the first to enable the Spanish to found "colonies" that were nothing other than "new populations coming from another place, settling and integrating into the native populace of these enormous lands, building a new, large, formidable, and prominent Christian Church and happy republic."

In every home there must be a woman with the role of mother. Columbus resolved his status of widower with wisdom. His sister-in-law Filipa's sister Briolanja Muñiz was always with his family. Married but with no children, the Portuguese woman was the person with the highest social status in the family, coming from the household of the influential Marquise of Montemayor and her son, Don Alvaro, later belonging to the domestic staff of the Dukes of Medina Sidonia. Briolanja ("Donna Violante" to foreigners), devoted herself to the lives of the families she served, and was for many years available to help in the domestic life of the Colón family.

When Columbus left Portugal in 1485 and arrived in Andalusia for the first time Briolanja was married to Miguel Muliart, a native of Burgundy. She lived in San Juan del Puerto, very near to Huelva and the La Rábida Monastery.

Diego remained in her care at her home; Columbus would never forget this favor. In April 1493, upon his return from his first voyage to the Indies, Columbus obtained permission from the monarchs for the couple to be awarded a house in Seville that had belonged to a Jew who had been deported. That house in the Santa María de la Blanca quarter was where the admiral's sons had played as children when they went to visit family there.

After Muliart died, Columbus was anxious to find a new husband for Briolanja: it was to be a rich and trustworthy man who also happened to be his new attorney, the Florentine merchant, Francesco de' Bardi. In fact, Briolanja had long been present in the Columbus family environment and it was she who took care of the children in Spain when Columbus was away on his voyages; she went to visit them at court when away from Seville, where she normally resided. All the members of the Columbus clan gathered in Briolanja's home when they needed to do so, not just Columbus' nephews, who did so on many occasions, but also Columbus' brothers, his domestic staff, and his friends. And Diego Mendez, the domestic employee who in 1504 would save the admiral's life, sent salutations to "the lady of the house" in every one of his letters addressed to Don Diego. For such reasons, it was no surprise that Briolanja accompanied Don Diego Columbus and Donna María de Toledo, when in 1509, they set off for the Indies as governors and that the entire family remembered her in their wills, making financial provision for her. While Beatriz Enríquez de Arana wasn't the admiral's favorite, and was only remem-

bered in Admiral's will, her close relatives were modestly rewarded. In fact, Diego de Arana, first cousin to Beatriz, accompanied Columbus on his first voyage as senior magistrate with a stipend of 24,000 Spanish *maravedí*. When Columbus retuned to Spain, Diego remained in Hispaniola as captain of the island and of the Navidad Fortress, commanding 39 men who remained in the New World because, after the *Santa Maria* sunk, there was not enough room in the other two ships for everyone to return to Castile. Before leaving, the admiral did not forget to recommend to cacique Guacanagarí "that you give great attention, especially to Diego de Arana, Pero Gutiérrez and Rodrigo de Escobedo who are staying here as delegates," so that they would be protected by them there. Unfortunately, Diego only dedicated himself to chasing women and discussing his exploits with subordinates, and his death was not very dignified as it seems that he drowned after an offended native man pursued him.

Among the men remaining at Navidad Fortress, was the master physicist, Juan, much loved by the crew and whom all the rarely unanimous chroniclers refer to as a very warm person. He was also from Cordova, a distant relative of the Aranas and a closer relative of the Sbarroia pharmacists, the Genoans who had welcomed Columbus during his sojourn at Cordova.

Beatrice's brother, Pietro de Arana, joined Columbus on his journey to the New World as captain of a ship on his third voyage. Records show that Pietro decided to marry and remain on the island of Hispaniola, in the city of Puerto Plata.

HIS FRIENDS

To understand the conduct and lifestyle of people, nothing is more telling than the observation of their family environment and scrutiny of their friends. Often, it is enough to know the qualities of the people normally surrounding a man or a woman to discern in all likelihood what that person's attitudes about life may be. Family cannot be chosen: one is irreversibly born in one home environment or another. What truly makes each person human is what makes them closer to or more separate from their family and friends, according to their similarities or interests. We have just barely glimpsed some members of the Columbus family who have felt united or separated. Let's now take a look at who his friends were, the men he personally chose.

Columbus was a solitary man with few friends. So few that it sometimes proved extremely difficult to distinguish between his intimate friends and those who simply formed his circle of acquaintances, servants, or domestic staff. With a difficult yet versatile personality, he had the rare ability to alienate all those around him, many times justifiably so and at others for no reason at all. Life progressively tainted his character until he seemed an intolerable and unbearable man. Despite that, Columbus could count on his most loyal friends and most bitter enemies just like everyone else.

As he lived in Spain, Columbus logically had a number of friends and acquaintances among Spanish men. Many were allied to him because of their commercial and court interests while others for religious reasons or for the prestige. Ultimately, others were simply his personal friends or faithful supporters. Columbus battled against the incredulity and indifference of many and the suspicion of not just a few. Despite all that, there were still the loyal followers and even enthusiastic admirers that he recognized from the beginning.

Accompanied by his son, Diego, Columbus reached the La Rábida Monastery in 1485; it housed a long-established Franciscan order with seafaring and charitable traditions. The friars did not just look after sailors requiring guest quarters but also provided a valuable center of technical assistance for them. Mariners of the Huelva region met there to discuss current events and geographical progress occurring at the time and to familiarize themselves with different theories.

On frequent occasions over seven years, Columbus got to know Brother Antonio de Marchena, a monk and very well-known courtier who was probably the person who put him into contact with the monarchy and leading Andalusian noblemen. He also made friends with the prior, Brother Juan Perez. It was Perez who wrote to Queen Isabella, soliciting an interview for his friend, accompanying him to Granada, helping him to obtain permission to set sail, and later signing related agreements on behalf of Columbus. The latter openly acknowledged that both these men were his "steadfast friars" because they never abandoned him.

37 THE PUBLICATION OF COLUMBUS' WRITINGS IN THE WORK BY M. FERNANDEZ NAVARRETE, *VIAJES QUE HICIERON POR MAR LOS ESPAÑOLES DURANTE EL S. XV (SEA VOYAGES MADE BY THE SPANISH IN THE 15TH CENTURY)* ENCOURAGED PAINTERS AND SCULPTORS TO REPRODUCE THE LIFE AND WORK OF THE ADMIRAL IN DIVERSE STYLES. COLUMBUS WAS IN VOGUE AT THAT TIME. E. CANO DE LA PEÑA CREATED THIS PAINTING IN 1856 (SENATE BUILDING, MADRID, SPAIN).

38 PEOPLE SAID THAT IT WAS CARDINAL MENDOZA (1428-1495) WHO INTRODUCED COLUMBUS AT COURT. FRIEND TO POPE ALEXANDER VI, HE COLLABORATED IN THE MOST IMPORTANT DECISIONS DURING THE REIGN OF THE CATHOLIC KING AND QUEEN, INCLUDING THE INSTITUTION OF THE INQUISITION, THE RECONSTRUCTION OF THE DIOCESES CONQUERED BY ISLAM, AND THE DEPORTATION OF JEWS.

ANDALUSIAN NOBLEMEN AND ARAGONESE COURTIERS

His biographers report that when Columbus had just arrived in Castile, he made contact with the Dukes of Medina Sidonia and Medinaceli who initially offered to sponsor his endeavors. The most current historiography debates this as a more or less empty hypothesis. Was it, as Gómara asserts, Brother Antonio de Marchena who submitted a letter of introduction so that the aristocrats would agree to receive Columbus or was it Brothers Antonio and Alessandro Geraldini, Genoans like the future admiral, who obtained the interview for him? Or, was it Columbus himself, backed by the letters of his best-known Portuguese friends, who appeared at their door, demanding to be heard? The answers to these questions are not really important. The undeniable fact is that Columbus persistently knocked at these persons' doors only after being refused an interview by Ferdinand and Isabella in about 1491. Columbus did not have any great success with Don Enrique de Guzman, the Duke of Medina Sidonia, to whom he first offered his proposal. Las Casas recounts the aristocrat's refusal may have occurred for three reasons. First, because Don Enrique could not recognize the enormous importance of the project, secondly, because he did not understand it and lastly, because he was obliged to assist Ferdinand and Isabella in the War of Granada and did not dare to further augment their expenditures on a shaky venture. It seemed that this was the primary reason for the duke taking such a stance. After his failure with the Duke of Medina Sidonia, Columbus turned to Don Luis de la Cerda, the first Duke of Medinaceli, as Las Casas recounts in detail. Don Luis was so impressed by Columbus' theories that he decided not just to support his endeavors, but also to provide for his expenses until his first departure. Such is the account that the same aristocrat gave in his letter of April 1493 to the "Great Cardinal" Don Pedro Gonzalez de Mendoza. The aspiring discoverer had succeeded in convincing the duke who then prepared himself to communicate to Queen Isabella his desire to participate in this project of voyaging to the Indies. We are certain of one thing: the Duke of Medina Sidonia did not even contribute one Spanish *maravedí* toward Columbus' endeavors. We know very little about Columbus' relationship with Medinaceli, to whom he wrote a letter about his joyous return when reaching Lisbon after his first voyage. In addition, Don Enrique de Guzman didn't live long enough to witness Columbus' return: he died in August 1492. Columbus did not maintain contact with Medinaceli but did so with Don Juan de Guzman, third duke of Medina Sidonia, to the extent that he was almost related by marriage to him had the matrimony of Diego Columbus with one of the aristocrat's daughters taken place, as suggested by Columbus before his death. That Columbus had a series of Aragonese courtiers in his favor is patent. Their deep friendship ensured him an advantage. Three of them were Aragonese knights and were the men closest to Columbus: Juan de Coloma, Juan Cabrero, and Gabriel Sanchez. The future admiral met all three of them at court before his great discovery. In his *Memoranda of Damages* (ca. 1501) Columbus himself informs us repeatedly of the intervention of Juan de Coloma (the king's secretary) in the draft of his Agreement with Ferdinand and Isabella. These documents were written in the third person with some legal terms included, and therefore required an impersonal voice. The admiral offers his proposal here: "Stating that at the time when he came before their Royal Highnesses with the Indies venture, requesting many things through one of his memoranda, Brothers Juan Perez and Mosén Coloma handled it for him, planning along with him how it would occur. First, they would appoint him Admiral of the Indies, conceding all duties therein, as detailed by said contract, and that he as admiral would enjoy the same rewards and income as in

his office as First Admiral of Castile." If it weren't for the Aragonese aristocrat's crucial intervention promoting Columbus' wishes, these opportunities would never have been offered to him. In two letters to his son, Diego, on December 1 and 21, 1504, Columbus quotes Juan Cabrero, chamberlain at the royal court. The admiral was preoccupied because he had not yet received the money that the Crown owed him for his most recent voyage to the Indeis. He was so poor, he wrote, "I am reduced to living from loans," given that the small amount of money he had already obtained had been used to pay the salaries of the people who had accompanied him. In the hope that Diego could help him at court, he asked him to inform of his precarious financial situation the bishop Brother Diego de Deza "who was the cause by which their Royal Highnesses acquired the Indies, then detained me in Castile when I was already at the point of departure, as well as the chamberlain." Juan Cabrero was, with the post he held, one of the closest men to the monarch and, along with his wife, María Cortés, lady-in-waiting to Queen Isabella, made this couple one of the most influential in the kingdom. The King gave important *encomiendas* (a territory grant with the obligation of evangelizing the indigenous populations living there and the revenues drawn from exploiting their work) to Cabrero, first in Hispaniola and later in Puerto Rico "for contributing to the achievement of the Admiral's endeavors," a statement that confirmshis intervention in Columbus' negotiations. The third Aragonese courtier close to Columbus was no less a person than the Treasurer-General of Aragon, Gabriel Sanchez. The only trace the admiral left of his relationship with the Treasurer-General is the letter that he sent Sanchez from Lisbon upon returning from his first voyage, indicating a certain friendship. It is probable that Columbus had distanced himself from the Treasurer after the assassination of the inquisitor, Pedro de Arbues in 1495, after which event disgrace fell upon the Sanchez family. First-generation Jewish converts to Catholicism everywhere were accused or implicated in crimes. It is understandable to presume that Columbus and his family

may have forgotten to mention this well-placed Aragonese official's possible offer in their writings even when it was essential to them. Columbus owes the Aragon people much more than traditional historiography recognizes. As the historian Juan Gil demonstrated, the news of his discovery arrived at other European royal courts in good part due to the court of King Ferdinand. While Gabriel Sanchez was an Aragonese, so was Guillermo Coma, author of the Latin account of Columbus' second voyage, as well as Jaime Ferrer de Blanes, a cosmographer who felt great admiration for the navigator. Moving to Barcelona in 1488, Jaime Ferrer became so famous that just after Columbus returned from his first voyage, the "Great Cardinal" Don Pedro Gonzalez de Mendoza requested his presence and it was perhaps in the home of the prelate where Ferrer made Columbus' acquaintance. Two years later, Ferrer contacted the king and queen, expressing his opinion on the Treaty of Tordesillas (1494), which created a border dividing the New World into geographical zones belonging to Spain and Portugal. Ferrer also asserted his admiration for Columbus' geographical theories, extolling their virtue to such an extent that the Catalan cosmographer was urgently called in for consultation. Once his interview was completed, Ferdinand and Isabella ordered Ferrer to communicate with the admiral about their objective to have both of his theories scientifically confirmed. Columbus and Ferrer maintained an erudite correspondence of which we only know Ferrer's part. In the missive, Ferrer expounds upon his own experiments and research, expressing not just enthusiasm for Columbus but also defining him as the new St Thomas the Apostle. When reading his letter, Columbus likely thought about advancing toward the latitude of Sierra Leone where the Portuguese had already found gold, and to follow this parallel toward the meridian of Hispaniola. It was a route that the admiral followed on his third voyage and that other fleets would follow for many years to come. In fact, influenced or not by this letter, Columbus demonstrated his trust in the existence of gold deposits in warm regions, also where Ferrer asserted that men were black.

LUIS DE SANTÁNGEL

Luis de Santángel, a merchant of Valencia, was another Aragonese who demonstrated keen foresight in recognizing the Columbus project as a promising venture and deciding to support it. Don Luis was a skilled negotiator and, despite being royal scribe for Don Fernando, turned to the queen, who was more responsive to Columbus' proposal. The Kingdom of Castile thus participated in some of the rights that, for the same reasons could be exploited by the Crown of Aragon. Fernando, just as Las Casas did, recounts his own version of the conversation between Santángel and the queen. Luis de Santángel, knowing that his action "went beyond the norms or limits of his duties," presented himself to the queen with the desire to "inform her about what was in his heart." As pointed out by both Fernando and Las Casas, it is important to report that his arguments referred to an invented conversation, but one with a still undeniable basis in truth. First, the venture seemed to have a solid foundation and the admiral, a judicious and learned man, was ready to participate in the financing as well as the venture himself. Second, if the voyage did not in fact deliver the anticipated results, the small amount that Columbus would receive (2500 ducats) was nothing compared with the enormous returns that it could obtain if successful. With a minimum investment, the two monarchs would appear as magnanimous and generous magnates for "having sought out the secrets and grandeur of the universe." These were the typical arguments of Luis de Santángel, a Jewish merchant who clearly recognized the venture's potential and consequently dealt with it from a financial viewpoint. However, there was one element added in order to touch Queen Isabella's sensitive heart: if Columbus' theory were accurate, then the numbers of souls converted to the True Faith would be unimaginable. Unable to resist such persistent reasoning, the queen urgently called for Columbus and ordered him to initiate all necessary preparations, including his signature on their Agreement and determination of the amount of money necessary to accomplish the voyage. Another issue that has provided for every kind of interpretation was the alleged offer from Queen Isabella: she was "ready to find an advance, pledging her own jewels to secure the amount of money required to build such a fleet." The queen had already committed a large part of her jewelry collection to the cities of Valencia and Barcelona to pay the costs for the conquest of Baza, a key city of Granada still held by the Arabs, and could not continue to pledge her valuables as collateral. It is probable that she forgot this during her conversation with Santángel or that, according to another possibility that seems more logical, Queen Isabella decided not to commit them as payment, given her celebrated admiration for jewelry. This could be the real truth, even though there's no evidence to confirm it. What is certain and documented is that it was Santángel who advanced the money, withdrawing it not from his own personal fortune but from the government treasury. The two million Spanish *maravedí* necessary to equip the three caravels (light European 14th to 17th century sailing ships) that Columbus had requested was easily collected. The very same Luis de Santángel advanced one *cuento* (a million) and even paid the 140,000 Spanish *maravedí* in a salary advance to Columbus as captain of the expedition. Columbus raised 500,000 Spanish *maravedí*, exactly twice of the eighth part of the total that he was required to cover according to the Agreement, due to the loan he obtained from his associate, Giannotto Berardi. By means of a fine imposed by the Crown, the inhabitants of the city of Palos contributed 360,000 *maravedí* to the expedition, which represented the transport cost of two of the caravels (an average of 60 tons each, at a cost of 3000 *maravedí* per ton) made available to Columbus.

Columbus also had Castilian supporters at court, people with greater social prestige than the Aragonese, but not as close in friendship to the admiral. Despite being cited neither by Las Casas nor by Fernando, the Duke of Medinaceli's letter to the "Great Cardinal" in 1493 clearly indicated that Alonso de Quintanilla, the Treasurer-General of Castile, advised moving forward with the expedition. But Oviedo, if we trust him, refers to even more substantial news. Columbus often made an appearance at the home of Alonso de Quintanilla who, moved by his misfortune, provided Columbus with food and helped him with other necessities. According to Oviedo, it was Quintanilla who introduced Columbus at court. This information must be accurate as Gómara also confirmed it, ensuring that Quintanilla "gave him food to eat from his own pantry and listened attentively and pleasantly to his promises of unexplored new lands." The key is this: Columbus engaged him in conversation and received nothing more than his support in exchange, which he would not have received any other way. Columbus was like a son to him so Quintanilla recalled only good memories from the past, ignoring memories of years of hunger, and forgetting the deprivation that Columbus must have suffered in his birthplace. Las Casas recounts that "Great Cardinal" Don Pedro Gonzalez de Mendoza once accommodated the admiral at his table, ordering that he be served covered dishes as a great gentleman and asked his permission before speaking. It was the first time that Columbus ever received such attention and was so completely taken with it as to request that he be served in the same way at his own table from that day forward. Deemed worthy of good treatment by Mendoza, with whom we don't believe the admiral had a closer relationship than social protocol required, Columbus must have certainly appreciated his deference, given that it was common knowledge that the cardinal's meals, whether in covered dishes or not, were the most succulent and exquisite in the kingdom. Columbus was honored not just by Don Pedro but by many other gentlemen delivering flattery in order to know firsthand the most anecdotes about his voyages, primarily about the first two when his reputation was no longer in doubt.

Reviewing the names of Castilians with whom Columbus maintained constant contact, we can see that only on rare occasions did he have financial or legal relationships, and with very few individuals. He sent Doctor Zapata, a member of the Council of Castile, the Porras files (the two Porras brothers claimed that Columbus had intended to abandon them on Jamaica) so that the Council would support him after adequate review. He appeared before the king's Finance Minister, Juan Velazquez, on January 18, 1505 to solicit compensation, as well as before Doctor Cea, "a person that I wish to honor," whom he needed to persuade (as he wrote to Diego on 25 February 1505) to intervene in the liberation of two prisoners whose names we do not know but who must have been the admiral's domestic employees.

42 UPON RETURN FROM HIS FIRST VOYAGE, COLUMBUS WROTE IDENTICAL LETTERS FROM LISBON TO VARIOUS ADDRESSEES, TELLING THEM ABOUT HIS "DISCOVERY." THIS ONE WAS SENT TO LUIS DE SANTÁNGEL. THE IMPORTANCE OF THIS LETTER IS EVIDENCED BY A SURPRISING NUMBER OF PUBLISHED VERSIONS THAT WERE PRODUCED IN THE 15TH CENTURY: TWO IN SPANISH, NINE TRANSLATIONS INTO LATIN, THREE ITALIAN VERSIONS EXECUTED BY GIULIANO DATI, AND ONE IN GERMAN (NATIONAL LIBRARY, MADRID, SPAIN).

HIS FEMALE FRIENDS AND THE SERVANTS

Columbus did not limit his affections exclusively to men. Even among the so-called weaker sex, he had admirers. A good conversationalist, he had to enliven many of the dialogues of noblemen's wives or of government officials whom he literally chased to get their signatures on requisite documents, as well as the women who were a part of Queen Isabella's inner circle. Thus it was clear that women of many backgrounds supported him with their friendship. Despite his constant visits to Gaspar de Gricio, the royal secretary did not seem to condemn his horrible Latin and Columbus had much contact with his sister, Beatriz Galindo, instructor of classical languages to Queen Isabella. Beatriz could very well have consulted with Columbus on how he could correct his questionable language skills.

More realistic than the flirtation with Beatriz de Bobadilla, called the Cazadora (the "Huntress"), was the friendship between Columbus and another Beatriz de Bobadilla, the influential Marquise of Moya, the lady with the most influence and authority inside the queen's chamber. The Catholic rulers' court abounded with indiscretions and the rumor must have circulated that it was Bobadilla who convinced Queen Isabella of Columbus' project's feasibility. It was a story that was picked up in detail in the intriguing poetic composition, *On the Wonderful Discovery of the New World*, by Alvar Gomez de Ciudad Real. This was the first epic poem written about Christopher Columbus. It was a randomly adapted memoir, created within the circle of direct descendants of the marquise, eager to single themselves out, like everyone who knew Columbus, as contributing to the voyages to the Indies. Given the relationship between the admiral and Francisco de Bobadilla in 1500, it seems appropriate to quote, "if a Bobadilla had denied Columbus his task, then a Bobadilla was the primary reason for giving it to him in the first place." This quip has never been contradicted, and it is more than certain that Donna Beatriz, always quite close to the queen as well as being wife to Andres Cabrera (with whom we know Columbus had a definite friendship), intervened on behalf of the navigator. Columbus' friendship with Donna Juana de la Torre, who was tutor to the Infante Don John, and also the sister of Captain Antonio de Torres, appears to have developed into a deep affection for the admiral. On at least three occasions, she herself took on the task of preparing rose honey to soothe Columbus during his long voyages, and we gain some information from the accounts presented by Gonzalo de Baeza, the royal treasurer. Columbus wrote a very long letter to Donna Juana in the autumn of 1500 when he was returning from the Indies in chains, in which he informs her not just of his desire that she be his patron at court, but also of his profound respect for her and the friendship she offered in return for his. Certainly, Donna Juana "supported him where she could in audience with the Queen," and must have mediated on more than one occasion, defending her friend to the courtiers.

Columbus doubtlessly had a series of domestic employees and servants who were always loyal to him, among whom Jeronimo de Aguero is clearly identified as the private tutor to his sons, but his most faithful servant was Diego Mendez de Segura, a Portuguese by origin. Two other key people in Columbus' circle were Collantes and Zamora, the admiral's normal couriers, people whom he must have completely trusted, given his habit of converting the messenger of written documents into one of spoken messages.

Dª BEATRIZ D. BOVADILLA
PRIMª MARQVESA D MOYA
CAMARERA MAYOR DE LA
REYNA DOÑA YSABEL.
Nacio Año de 1440 Murio Año d 1511

Columbus always had foreign friends. Among these were his Florentine lawyers; thus we can speculate that he did not trust the Spanish very much. However, things had not always exactly like this.

For the execution of the first and second voyages, Columbus apparently had a Florentine lawyer named Giannotto Berardi. At the onset of preparations for this third voyage, Amerigo Vespucci actively intervened, as did Francesco de' Bardi, who was Columbus' lawyer from 1505 onward. However, once Berardi died, Ferdinand and Isabella tried to select the admiral's agents in the New World from among the people originating in the kingdom of Castile and León. While a Genoan, Rafael Cattaneo, maintained the accounts for the third voyage to the Indies, a change in governor in 1500 with Bobadilla's arrival meant a change in the factor (chief agent). The responsibility was now given to Alonso Sanchez de Carvajal. Carvajal, who had already accompanied the admiral on the second and third voyages, now had the responsibility of following up on all the family's business in those distant lands. Not only did he have to be present and near the inspector when gold was melted and marked, but he also had to receive the 10 percent due to the admiral and also the income deriving from the 8th part of all revenues, due to Columbus by virtue of the Agreement. When Carvajal returned to Spain, he was replaced by Pedro de Llanos, who was later replaced by Alonso de Hervas, Columbus' last factor on Hispaniola.

Columbus' house-steward, Diego Tristan, managed the admiral's financial interests on the expeditions and it was he who dealt with the fleet accountant, Ximeno de Briviesca, who was charged with verifying expenditures. Because of this, when Tristan accompanied Columbus on the fourth voyage to the New World, the Admiral was concerned that someone would replace his accountant in Castile. And for such a task, no one could be more suitable than his own nephew, Giovanni Antonio Columbus, who had already gained experience in the Indies and, more than anyone else, knew how to address complicated administrative questions. Juan Enero aided Giovanni Antonio in his duties, fulfilling the role of administrator when preparing for his employer's last voyage to the New World.

44 IT WAS ALSO DUE TO HIS FRIENDSHIP WITH BEATRIZ DE BOBADILLA, MARQUISE OF MOYA AND AN ESPECIALLY INFLUENTIAL WOMAN WITH QUEEN ISABELLA, THAT COLUMBUS COULD SUCCESSFULLY PRESENT HIS VOYAGE PROJECT TO THE ROYAL COURT OF THE CATHOLIC RULERS (MUNICIPAL MUSEUM, MADRID, SPAIN).

ITALIAN FRIENDS AND ENEMIES

Columbus' difficult personality led him to alienate many people. Perhaps in a number of cases, it had to do with envy on the part of Spanish citizens seeing a foreigner making his name known. For example, there are clear instances of animosity among those people who accompanied him in roles that today we would describe as "political trustees," men such as Brother Buil or the Porras brothers, responsible for the administration of the fourth voyage, or the civil servants in the Contractation House, people whom Columbus exhausted with demands and with accounts that were delivered in bad shape, late, or not at all. His cosmographic ideas achieved little success within the advisory council for the Cathedral of Seville. The first to attack him was Bernardino Carvajal from Rome, a cardinal appointed by Pope Alexander VI. In the speech that he made as Ferdinand and Isabella's ambassador on 19 June 1493, to the pope, the cardinal praised the work performed by the monarchs to whom Christ had shown "other unknown islands toward India." This was a clear allusion to his displeasure toward Columbus. While new lands were on the route to ward "India," they had nothing to do with the admiral's Indies. The prebendary of the cathedral, Don Francisco de Cisneros and the canonical founder of the University of Seville, Don Rodrigo Fernandez de Santaella, asserted themselves against Columbus' theories. The former accused the navigator of not having sailed across the Indian Ocean, and the latter, in his Spanish translation of Marco Polo's account of his travels to and in China, tried to demonstrate that Columbus' regions of Ophir and Tarsus had nothing to do with the mythical mines of King Solomon, as Columbus had maintained.

Columbus' peers accused him of wanting to hand over the Indies to a group of his fellow-Genoans. It is indeed true that he put his brothers in key administrative posts and, as there was no royal prohibition, he could well settle a good number of foreigners in the New World, and it was probably in part his intention to do. As an immigrant living among the Spanish, Columbus would logically make close friends among any local Italians, and during his years of residence he had close relationships with many of the

Italian residents in Spain. The Florentine merchant, Simone Verde, wrote a couple of letters to his fellow countrymen, recounting Columbus's voyages; Columbus himself provided information to assist the scholar Peter Martyr of Anghiera, a humanist invited to the Spanish court, to write his *Decades of the New World*. Niccolò Oderigo, Genoa's ambassador to the Catholic monarchs, was another fellow-townsman with whom Columbus maintained a correspondence, and there were also other Italians who were close personal friends or simply acquaintances of Columbus.

Francesco de' Medici il Popolano ("the Younger").

Columbus, Berardi, and Vespucci were all in Santa Fe, in Granada, at the start of 1492. Rapid preparation of the fleet and subsequent events seem to indicate that it was Berardi who lent Columbus the 500,000 Spanish *maravedí* that he invested in his venture. From 1493, Berardi began to give up his own endeavors in order to exclusively devote himself to the Columbus's interests as the admiral had designated him as his personal representative. As Columbus' factor and with the help of Amerigo

Though Columbus had worked in Portugal for the Spinola, Di Negro, and Centurion families, he did not go to their homes when arriving in Seville. He went instead to the home of Giannotto Berardi, of Florence, who, like him, had lived in Portugal, working for the most part for Bartolomeo Marchioni. This great merchant, originally from Florence, had been resident in Lisbon and was responsible for managing the slave trade at this point of the route that continued via Seville to Valencia. Columbus found in Giannotto a person who was committed to new experiences with which his local Genoese compatriots were unfamiliar at that time. Additionally, Berardi had just been appointed to represent the Medici family in their business affairs in Andalusia. It was Amerigo Vespucci who informed Columbus about Berardi's new post with Pier

Vespucci, Giannotto handled the preparations for his second voyage and also his business affairs during the admiral's absence. Gianotto received the first shipment of American slaves from Columbus, destined for sale in Castile, then presented the accounts to Bartolomeo when he arrived in Seville in 1494. He had even created a system for the exploitation of the newly conquered lands in a proposal request for an exclusive shipping monopoly. Twelve caravels heading toward the Indies would depart in three groups of four during the months of April, June, and September. Up to January 1496, Berardi had not been able to put his hands on the registries of the first fleet that became shipwrecked in the Strait of Gibraltar. He was also unable to salvage much from these shipwrecks, and his death followed soon after his complete bankruptcy.

46 LEFT THIS RENAISSANCE PORTRAIT REPRODUCES THE PHYSICAL APPEARANCE OF POPE ALEXANDER VI. IN THE MOST WELL KNOWN PAPAL BULLS IN 1493 (*INTER CŒTERA, EXIMIŒ DEVOTIONIS* AND *DUDUM SIQUIDEM*), THE MERIDIAN DIVIDING THE AREAS OF INFLUENCE FOR THE TWO POWERS INVOLVED IN THE CONQUEST WAS ESTABLISHED AT 100 LEAGUES FROM THE AZORES AND CAPE VERDE (VATICAN ART GALLERY, VATICAN CITY).

46 RIGHT CARDINAL CISNEROS PERSONALLY TOOK CARE OF ORGANIZING THE EVANGELISM OF THE NEW WORLD BY PLANNING DIVERSE MISSIONARY EXPEDITIONS. IN CONFLICT WITH COLUMBUS, HE CONTRIBUTED TO HIS DISMISSAL AS VICEROY OF THE INDIES (COMPLUTENSIAN UNIVERSITY, MADRID, SPAIN).

47 CANON RODRIGO FERNANDEZ DE SANTAELLA (1444-1509), FOUNDER OF THE UNIVERSITY OF SEVILLE, SHOWED A SLIGHT DISAGREEMENT WITH COLUMBUS WHO HE CRITICIZED IN HIS TRANSLATION OF *IL MILIONE* (THE MILLION) BY MARCO POLO WITHOUT EVER EVEN QUOTING HIM (PARLIAMENT LIBRARY, MADRID, SPAIN).

COLUMBUS AND VESPUCCI

After Berardi's death, Vespucci could not take responsibility for the equipping and provisioning of Columbus' third fleet, as he no longer had the means. After liquidating his accounts with Columbus, Amerigo decided to set sail for the New World. He first worked on the 1499 fleet, captained by Alonso de Hojeda, in the service of Portugal.

Columbs and Vespucci did not meet again until 1504, in Seville. Their friendship must have been a warm one as noted in Columbus' letter to his son in February 1505. Out of work at that time, Vespucci was called to the royal court. Columbus decided to support him and wrote to his son, asking him to take care of Vespucci: "Amerigo Vespucci is quite a good man yet fate has not been as good to him as it has to many others. Though reasonably expected to, his hard work has not favored him in any way."

Columbus was not at all aware that Vespucci had made an important voyage for which he would receive the royal recognition that had previously been denied him. From that time forward, the Florentine remained available to Ferdinand and Isabella, starting a growing career that would lead him to the appointment of First Chief of Navigation of the Contractation House. Columbus did not see this as such a prominent position, neither did he know that his friend's name would be the one given posthumously to a continent first reached by Columbus himself.

FRANCESCO DE' BARDI

Piero Rondinelli, who was also a resident of Seville, wrote a letter in 1502 to his fellow Florentines, advising them to invest in the business affairs of their countryman, Francesco de' Bardi, "Whoever has the means," he wrote, "should take the risk." Rondinelli explained that the financial interest Columbus offered should not be looked upon with contempt because it amounted to a return of between 150 percent and 200 percent, or even more, and it was guaranteed by his business activities in the Indies. Francesco de' Bardi's entrance onto the scene could be nothing but spectacular and colorful at that point as it was he who had married the lively Briolanja. As one can imagine, the Portuguese woman's life changed completely. After this new union, she acquired a small property in Tomares, a town near Seville, moved into her new home, and surrounded herself with all of the luxury and extravagance that her new financial situation permitted her. Francesco was devoted to consolidating the family's affairs after his marriage; he was not just Columbus' factor, but also one of his most trusted men. Columbus made his last provision on behalf of Bardi, just before he died in Salamanca, authorizing him to collect in Columbus' name all his income deriving from the New World, a proxy that Diego approved just a few days after his father's death.

HIS GENOVESE FRIENDS

Of the sixteen Genoans who Columbus mentioned in his writings, eleven were bankers. Despite this, and because of the way in which he wrote of them, we can still sense differences between them. Some seemed to be stereotypical royal bankers; such was the case with the Centurion family. It was these bankers who appropriated the two million *maravedí* that the Crown contributed to Columbus' third voyage. The financial companies of Francesco Doria, Francesco Cattaneo, Gaspare Spinola, and Francesco de Riberol also financed the admiral's endeavors. Among these men, Columbus maintained a truly friendly relationship with Riberol, who also responsible for dispatching to Genoa the copies of the *Book of Privileges* that Columbus intended for Ambassador Niccolò Oderigo and the Bank of San Giorgio so that, based on the book's content, his sons' financial interests were managed by the recipients to provide for his living expenses. In May 1502, when Pope Julius II was elected, the admiral asked Riberol to handle Brother Gaspare Gorricio's pending trip to Rome to defend his interests to the new pope.

In 1492, Francisco Pinelo was co-director with Luis de Santángel of the Santa Confraternita's treasury, which funded Columbus' voyage. And, as royal banker, he participated one year later in financing the second fleet. Columbus and Pinelo maintained a constant and friendly relationship in those times.

Columbus also had two Genoese servants, Marco de Bargali who participated as a squire on the third voyage and Bartolomeo Fieschi who accompanied him on the fourth. We are unaware of what their relationships were like afterward.

A MAN FROM NOVARA: BROTHER GASPARE GORRICIO

Among the members of the monastery of Santa María de las Cuevas, a Carthusian house in Seville, Brother Gaspare Gorricio, an Italian monk who originally came from Novara, was a distinguished man and had reached Spain a few years before Columbus' discovery, along with his brother and etcher, Francisco Gorricio. Even though we do not know exactly when his friendship with Columbus began, we can confirm that from at least 1498, they maintained a fluid correspondence and that their friendship intensified after the end of 1500, when Columbus returned to Spain relieved of his position. During the post-1500 years, Brother Gaspare aided Columbus in editing the *Memoranda of Damages* that the admiral was preparing in order to present his complaints to Ferdinand and Isabella. Brother Gaspare very probably also intervened in the cataloguing of Columbus' *Book of Privileges* as the two men shared common goals. Without the collaboration of Brother Gaspare, Columbus would not have been able to prepare the *Book of Prophecies*, an anthology of biblical passages and writings of Catholic theologians, unifying all of the texts that the admiral believed would validate his geographical theories and confirm his discoveries.

Brother Gaspare kept Columbus' personal documents in his own cell, which became the repository for the Columbus family archive. In the monastery of Santa María de las Cuevas, Columbus and the monk edited the wills of Bartolomeo Columbus, the Second Admiral Don Diego, and Donna Maria when they readied themselves to depart for the Indies in spring 1509. In 1507, Brother Gaspare had accompanied Bartolomeo Columbus to Rome in accordance with Columbus' long-term wish that the monk present himself to the pontiff on his behalf. We know very little of that conversation that occurred when Brother Gaspare hand-delivered Columbus' *Book of the Indies* to Pope Julius II and requested the Holy Father's permission to establish a monastery in the New World, named for St Bruno. It was a proposal that presumably never came to fruition; nothing is known to have ever materialized from it. As a family friend, Brother Gaspare also took charge of receiving Columbus' body from Giovanni Antonio Columbus when it was transported from Valladolid to Seville in 1509.

JOHN DAY

In the autumn and winter of 1497, Columbus received letters from John Day, an English merchant from Bristol and proprietor of a ship that sailed between the cities of Lisbon and Sanlúcar de Barrameda. Day began his letter by announcing the delivery of *The Milion* of Marco Polo to his friend, excusing himself for not being able to find Nicholas of Lynn's book, *Inventio Fortunata*, another volume that Columbus had originally requested from him. It is not surprising that Columbus had asked an unfamiliar foreigner traveling through Europe for any book that he could not find in Spain. When Columbus set sail on his third voyage to the New World months later, he didn't forget to include this book in his baggage; he demonstrated this by quoting Marco Polo from that time forward.

Columbus received one of these letters a few weeks after the voyage of John Cabot. The letter confirms the voyage's occurrence and, more importantly, fixes the exact date of Cabot's exploration, confirming that there were no later voyages toward modern-day North America until 1497. This is the only document that deals with Cabot's failed expedition prior to this date. Since it could not have happened any other way, Day added a series of news items that he presumed would be of interest to his friend. These included initial taking possession of the new lands and describing their characteristics, as well as noting the annual compensation of £20 that Henry VII gave John Cabot for his discovery. The letter also announces that the English were already preparing a new expedition of at least ten or twelve ships for the next year. As a novelty, Day describes the abundance of codfish, which were considered fine cuisine in those times.

The warm friendship between the two is apparent in a farewell letter when the Englishman assures Columbus that he will continue to give him progress reports and try to send him a map of the territory discovered by Cabot.

ergimul · regnum ·

nitur regnum ergimul q̄ est in p̃uincia mag̃ tanguth q̄
regnum magno kaam ſbiectū eſt Ibi ſunt xp̄iani neſtori
ni ydolatre et alij ſectato2es legis machometti Multe ci
uitates et caſtra mlta ſunt ibi v̄ſus ſyrochū inter o2ientalē
et meridionalē plagā itur ad p̃uinciā talchay p2ius tn̄ in

talchay

uenitur ciuitas ſinguy magno kaam tributaria ybi ſilr̄ ſūt
xp̄iani neſto2ini ydolatre et alij ſectato2es leg̃ machomet
ti Ibi ſunt boues ſilueſtres pulcherrimi grādes velut ele
phantes pilos bn̄t p co2pus vndiq̄ albos p2eter do2ſū et i
bi .ſ. in do2ſo nigros bn̄t pylos longitudinis palmo2 triū
Multiq̄ ex bob̃ iſtis domeſtici ſūt et domiti et ad defe
rendum maxiā onera aſſueti: Alij aūt alligant ad aratra
qui p2e mirabili fo2titudine mltum opis in aratura t̄re in
b2eui pficiunt tp̄e: In hac p̃te muſcatū habetur meli⁹ q̄
eſt in mūdo quod ab aiāli quodā habetur Eſt eni tale ani
mal quoddā pulch2 valde magnitudinem bn̄s gatte Pi
los groſſos vt ceruus et pedes vt gatta Dentes aūt qua
tuo2 ſc̄3 duos ſuperius et duos iſeri⁹ longitudinis triū di
gito2um Hoc animal iuxta vmbilicum int carnem et cutē
veſicam habet ſanguine plenā Et ille ſanguis eſt muſcatū
de quo tantus odo2 exalat et de hijs eſt ibi mltitudo max
ima Incole regionis illi⁹ ydolatre ſunt et libidinoſi ſecta
to2es legis machometti et nigros pilos habētes Uiri im
belles ſūt ſ pilos ſolum bn̄t circa labia et naſū habent puū
et nigros capillos bn̄tes: Mulieres pulch2e ſunt et albe
valde Uiri vxo2es quer̄t pulch2as magis q̄ nobiles Nā
nobilis et magn⁹ vir vxo2ē accipit pauperē ſi pulch2a eſt τ
mater illi dotē dat Negociato2es mlti et artifices ibi ml
ti ſunt Habet aūt p̃uincia in lōgitudine dietas xxv. et eſt
fertilis valde . ibi ſūt fagiani in duplo maio2es q̄ in ytalia
et bn̄t caudas lōgitudinis dece vl noue palmo2 .aut octo
ſiue nouem ſiue ſeptem ad minus Eciā faſſiones qui i mg̃
nitudine noſtris ſunt ſimiles Multas alias aues bn̄t pul

cherrimas diuersa℞ spe℞ pennas hn̄tes pulchras diuerß
et pulcherrimis coloribȝ variatas

De p̄uincia egrigaya Capl'm lxiiij.

Ein de p̄tn̄sactis octo dietis vltra p̄uinciā ergymul
ad orientem occurrit prouincia egrigaya In q̄ sunt
ciuitates ml'te et opida Est ciuitas de p̄uincia magna tā
guth c⁹ p̄ncipalior ciuitas est colatia Incole ydolatre sūt
p̄ter aliquos xp̄ianos nestorinos qui tres ibi basilicas ha
bent Sunt aūt s̄biecte magno kaam: In ciūtate colacia fi
unt panni qui dicunt̄ zambelotti de lana alba et pulchrio
res camelo℞ pil' pulchriores qui fiunt i mundo qui ad pro
uincias alias per negociatores deferūtur.

De prouincia tenduch et og et magog et cyagomo℞ Ca
pitulum sexagesimūquintū:

Versū relicta p̄uincia egrigaya p̄uenitur ad orienta
lem plagā ad p̄uinciam tenduch vbi sūt ciuitates et
ml'ta castra vbi manere ꝯsueuerat rex ille magn⁹ i orbe no
minatissim⁹ qui dicebatur a latinis p̄sbiter iohānes: Est
aūt p̄uīcia illa magna kaā tributaria Est tn̄ ibi rex vn⁹ de
p̄genie illi⁹ regis qui adhuc presbit̄ iohānes dr̄. cui nomē
est georgi⁹ Dn̄s magni kaam p⁹ mortē illi⁹ reg̃ qui a chyn
chys in p̄lio occisus fuit filias suas ill' regibȝ tradidert̄ vx
ores Et lȝ quidā sint ibi ydolatre et aliqui q̄ viuāt iuxta le
gem miserabil' machometti maior tn̄ p̄s populi p̄uincie fi
dem xp̄ianā tenet et hij xp̄iani in tota patria dicūt̄ et dn̄i
natur inter eos tn̄ gēs quedā ē q̄ habet hoīes pulchriores
et in negociationib⁹ sagaciores que i tota p̄uincia alibi va
leant repiri In illis p̄tibus sunt regiones que dn̄r gog et
magog Gog in lingua sua noīant vng magog v̄o mūgul
In hijs locis seu partibȝ sunt regiones in quibus reperit̄
lapis lasuli ex quo fit asurium peroptimū In hac p̄uicia

egrigaya pro·
colatia ciuitas·
hic fiunt zambelotti
· tenduch pro·
·gog et magog·
presbiter Iohannes
gog magog
li lapis·

THE SAILOR
chapter 2

58-59 With the *Pinta* and the *Nina* (both caravels) and the *Santa Maria* (a carrack), and a crew of 90 men, Columbus successfully undertook his voyage of exploration (Museum of America, Madrid, Spain).

60-61 In 1485, Francesco Pagano created this view of Naples port, known as the *Tavola Strozzi*. On February 6, 1502 from Granada, Columbus wrote a letter to the Catholic King and Queen telling them about his experiences at sea. In one of the paragraphs, he describes in detail the way he must have executed the voyage from Spain to Naples, according to the season, demonstrating his own experience with that navigational route (Museo di Capodimonte, Naples, Italy).

62-63 In his voyages through the Mediterranean, Columbus toured the islands of Sardinia and Sicily. On diverse occasions, he cited them in his writings recalling the abundance and quality of Sicilian grains or bragging about a spectacular feat he had accomplished. "I can confirm that in one night alone with your ship, I covered the distance between Cape Carthage in Sardinia and the port of Tunis (National Library of France, Paris, France).

AN APPRENTICE IN THE MEDITERRANEAN

The Genoa where Columbus lived the for first 23 years of his life was the most important port of a powerful and expanding republic whose economy was based on maritime trade. Enormous riches reached this port, ensuring the merchants considerable incomes administered by the eminent Bank of San Giorgio. In 1502, Columbus charged this same with the task of safeguarding his interests, and those of his sons and other heirs.

According to Columbus, whom we have no reason to doubt, he frequented a good many ports as a younger man, despite having only spoken of those of Naples, Marseille, and Hyères, also demonstrating knowledge of Cape Creus in Catalonia, the Gulf of Narbonne, Sardinia, and the Barbary Coast.

We possess little documentation on this phase in the life of the future admiral so we must refer back to any indications he made in his letters and other reports. In later years, he edited some of his writings, which resulted in a loss of data and some unintentional errors. Despite that, there is evidence that some errors were intentional, given that the shrewd Genoan left in writing exclusively what he was interested in documenting. We must also keep in mind the *History of the Admiral* written by his son, Fernando who kept a copy in Italian, the chronicles of those who accompanied him on his voyages, and the *History of the Indies* by Bartolomé de Las Casas. This Dominican monk was a great family friend and thus could consult the Columbus family archive.

As the Genoan chronicler, Antonio Gallo, described in his compatriot's *History* in 1506, Columbus very quickly left family activities behind to dedicate himself to the sea. He wrote that "at a tender age" (14 years old) he entered the maritime trades.

The young man's first voyages must have been accomplished as a ship's boy to the crew on one of the ships that sailed between Genoa and other ports on the Tyrrhenian coast. Perhaps he sold the cheese and wine that his father had for sale in Savona, a city to which he moved the family in about 1470. From that date forward, the young Columbus would no longer appear in any official documents as a weaver or wool-maker, but as an employee of a commercial shipping company.

As a sailor, he subsequently sailed along the coasts of Corsica and Sardinia. Without question, the island that struck him the most was Sicily, which was under Aragonese rule at that time. On 29 October 1492 he recalls it as a big island (it is the largest in the Mediterranean), later asserting that Cuba was still larger: "The island is full of very beautiful mountains . . . as high altitude as in Sicily." And, one year afterward, off Jamaica on 24 April 1493, he returns to the same comparison and notes, "it is quite large . . . larger than Sicily." Columbus did not admire only the island's size but also its fruitfulness. He compared this to that of Andalusia when, in February 1493, he wrote to Ferdinand and Isabella, proclaiming how well the European seeds he had left behind had sprouted: "We are convinced . . . that this land will not be less fertile than Andalusia and Sicily." In fact, both Sicily and Andalusia were granaries that provided for a large part of Europe. At Mt Etna, he made a marginal note to this effect in his copy of *Imago Mundi*, a treatise on cosmography by Pierre d'Ailly (1351-1414), which greatly influenced him.

Sardinia insula aput latinos sed greece Sardonisos vocatur
SEPT
CCIDENS
asono
S. Rapaira
longon sardo
porto ternno
sarton
Coro
rosan
santa pancho
cap caualli
cap falcalli
allequor
maraggio
S. luglius
Capt tomin
bossa
organei
saline
capt S. marri
malenue tre
arestan
Aquilastro
Portu neapolis
albatas sera
argeteca
sanctus reseus
eliza
capt salli
marsadomo
trapani
solla
antiocol
Callerj
morrem
fuligmano
marsina
talar
carbonaro
toro

ORIENS

MERIDIES

Map labels (Sicily):

- Strongoli
- Dianu
- hiresia
- lippari olim pheritides
- salfine
- ful...tanus
- henricus
- male de fan ro
- martela
- messina
- melazo
- eltron
- ulifera f.
- S. aleze
- danda zo
- mos gibel
- lastha letta
- tauermona
- Patri
- aterno
- Cap. horlandi
- timetus fl.
- S. nicolaus de arcona
- iaci
- mos pelle lamora
- rol grin Pareno
- Catunia
- raroma
- petra de roma
- nirosia
- pantach fl.
- s. maria de gmione
- gerani
- cirla fl.
- labesca
- lagosta
- Castellu bonu
- Cisalu
- Siracula
- mona lus fl.
- petralia
- tasonura na
- palaonia
- talab fl.
- potentia
- tosa
- petralia lisogana
- lontine
- olata nol tore
- talasth uenetta
- rastoram
- minio
- fur
- nine
- Pulizi
- meza fl.
- ortus
- soirir
- ralata ge rone
- Cap. passer
- coriglio ne
- thieza
- spoza f.
- rassarata
- castellu ueteranu
- hymera fl.
- terra noua
- realis
- talirata
- butera
- fossuis fl.
- Gergenti
- cotriga
- satta
- Gergeti
- pt cc inde trazta namff
- Pantalanea

Come l'Ammiraglio giunſe alla Corte : &
l'eſpeditione, che per lo ſuo ritorno
all'India i Re Catolici gli die-
dero. Cap. LXIIII.

Giunto l'Ammiraglio in terra di Caſtiglia,
ſubito cominciò ad ordinar la ſua partita per
la città di Burgos ; doue fu ben riceuuto da' Re
Catolici, che ſi ritrouauano quiui per celebrar le
nozze del ſereniſſimo Principe don Giouanni, loro
figliuolo, il qual tolſe per moglie Madama Mar-
gherita d'Auſtria, figliuola di Maſſimiliano Im-
peratore, che allhora gli era ſtata condotta, & era
ſtata riceuuta ſolennemente dalla maggior parte
de' Baroni, & dalla migliore, & più illuſtre gen
te, che mai in Spagna foſſe ueduta inſieme. Ma
cotai particolarità, & grandezze, benche io foſſi
preſente, per eſſer paggio del ſuddetto Principe,
altrimenti io non racconterò : sì perche non è coſa
appartenente alla noſtra hiſtoria, come perche i
Croniſti delle loro Altezze hauranno hauuto que-

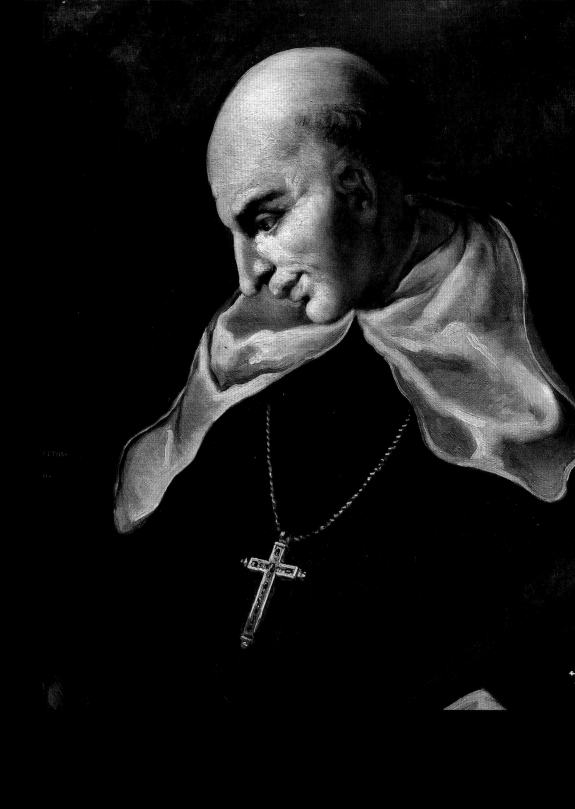

64 The first edition of the *History of the Admiral* written by his son, Fernando, was published with Alonso de Ulloa's Italian translation in Venice in 1571. The Spanish version was not published until 1749 (General Archive of the Indies, Seville, Spain).

65 To draft his *History of the Indies*, Bartolomeo de Las Casas was able to consult the Columbus family archive. Thanks to the transcriptions that the Dominican monk completed by hand, we have knowledge about many documents that had been lost, such as Columbus' diaries from his first and second voyages (General Archive of the Indies, Seville, Spain).

67 For its strategic and commercial importance, the island of Chios was much sought-after by nearby maritime powers. In 1204 after the conquest of Constantinople during the crusades, it became a part of the Latin Empire. Much later, it came under possession of the Republic of Genoa and in 1566, was conquered by the Ottoman Empire (Galata Museo del Mare, Genoa, Italy).

AN ATTRACTION TO THE ORIENT AND THE ATLANTIC

Columbus knew and navigated through many bodies of water, "I have sailed over the entire Levant (Orient) and West." In that era, he was not wrong even though his claim was an obvious exaggeration. The admiral's quote probably referred to the island of Chios in the north Aegean, then held by Genoa and controlled by a shipping association called the Magona whose members subsequently assumed the surname, Giustiniani. Chios, the island that his contemporaries knew as the place of "one thousand scents," was the portal to the Orient and the land of spices. To be precise, Chios smelled of mastic, a characteristic scent that Columbus could never forget. A resin that still supports a major part of the economy on the island today, mastic is extracted through a small incision in the trunk of the lentisk tree. Its therapeutic quality, as a remedy already described by Dioscorides, was effective in fighting rheumatism and was an excellent purifier of the blood, signifying a much sought-after product. The Genoan Magona controlled it with an ironclad monopoly and in Columbus' time, the members garnered 50,000 ducats per year from this product alone.

It has been said that Chios was where Columbus' obsession with the Orient was awakened. This information could be true, yet in any case, whenever he cited this island in his writings, he praised its wealth and carefully considered the financial benefits that his rulers would gain with little effort through his own far-distant island discoveries. This was reason enough to validate the commercial promise of his voyages of discovery. Columbus did not hesitate to assure Ferdinand and Isabella that the resins found in the Antilles were similar to the mastic of Chios. Despite not having yet found the promised gold, trees similar to the lentisk were growing in the new lands, and Columbus had already extracted their resin to transport back to Castile, well preserved inside a wooden box.

Columbus did not clarify in writing the exact date of his voyage to Chios, however we can hypothesize that it occurred between 1474 and 1475, years for which we have documentation on two Genoese expeditions to the island. The first fleet, which sailed from Savona on 25 May 1474 was composed of merchants and weavers in addition to sailors. The second, which left from Genoa in September 1474, had a different mission; it was a fleet bringing reinforcements to an island that the Turks were then threatening.

Everything seems to indicate that Columbus took part in the second armada, given that two of the ships in the fleet were the property of Paolo di Negro and Niccolò Spinola, two important Genoese merchants with whom the young man would have had many brief contacts that continued later in Lisbon, Madeira, and England. The heirs of both appeared in his will.

To reach Chios, Columbus sailed across the Ionian Sea, rounded the Peloponnesus, sailed north through the Cyclades, sighting the island of Samos and the coast of Asia Minor before reaching his final destination, the islands in the Aegean Sea. This was his celebrated route toward the Orient.

In June 1495, Columbus wrote a letter to the Ferdinand and Isabella telling them he had once navigated the route to Tunisia as a privateer and captain in the fleet of René of Anjou, adding that he survived a naval battle during the voyage. This is one of the many episodes in the life of Columbus, as discussed by his biographers, that today seem well founded in fact. There is no doubt about the naval battle, based on knowledge of various attacks perpetrated by René of Anjou's fleet and by the Genoese

against the Catalans before 1479. While the distance between Sardinia and Tunisia as indicated in his letter seems to be too long for him to have sailed it in a single night, as he asserted, it is possible that with particularly favorable climatic conditions he did so.

Another issue that has confused researchers is Columbus' description of himself as self-appointed "captain." He was too young for such a role at that time; perhaps the simple sailor was just putting on airs! Anyhow, many years later no one would have remembered what rank he had held during that expedition?

The Mediterranean was Columbus' first institute of higher learning. It taught him how to sail as he clearly distinguished the winds and knew from memory whether the directions of currents would allow him to dock in specific ports. He met many pirate ships at least once in this enclosed sea, sailing furtively around the Gulf of Lion. On at least one occasion Columbus found it handy to utilize the method of "altering the compass needle" in order to deceive the pirate sailors. It was an odd system that would be very useful to him in the future when the crew would mutiny during his first voyage, allowing him to resort to the same trick.

Columbus' language during this period was called "Eastern," generally meaning from the eastern side of the Mediterranean. A kind of *petit negre* as described more accurately by a sailor from Majorca when in 1636, during a trial in Mexico City, a group of Catalan and Ital-ian sailors were accused of really being French and of trying to scout new lands to the detriment of Spain. Our man, Andres Falcon, originally from Majorca stated: "Despite that the accused has confessed to being from Majorca, he writes in Italian that he was raised by and has sailed his whole life with Italians. He left his homeland when he was ten years old, and learned to read and write while at sea. He speaks Italian very well and speaks the Majorcan language only very poorly. He speaks no other languages except a little bit of Spanish."

Columbus' spoken and written language in those times must have been very similar to that one. Perhaps he knew a few words in French that he could have learned when he was in service to René of Anjou. It's very probable that he had learned to write while at sea, on the ships or in the offices of his superiors, and that he then knew no Portuguese or Spanish.

Columbus returned Spain with his baggage. Tragic situations certainly weren't lacking in his existence and a dramatic episode soon radically changed his life and distanced him from his birthplace. This particular situation dealt with a shipwreck off the Portuguese coast while Columbus was sailing from Genoa toward England as part of a commercial fleet composed of five ships belonging to his superiors, the Spinola-Di Negro business organization. Off Cape St Vincent, a French armada broke up the convoy and after a nasty battle Columbus was obliged to swim all the way to the coast of the Algarve.

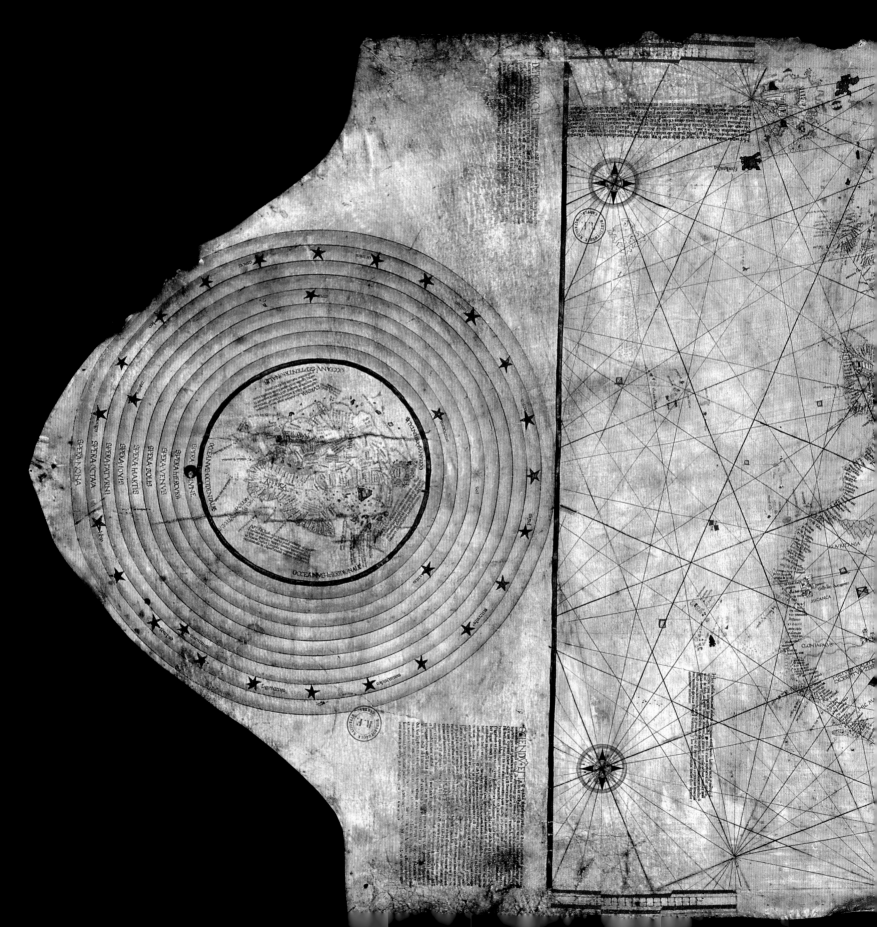

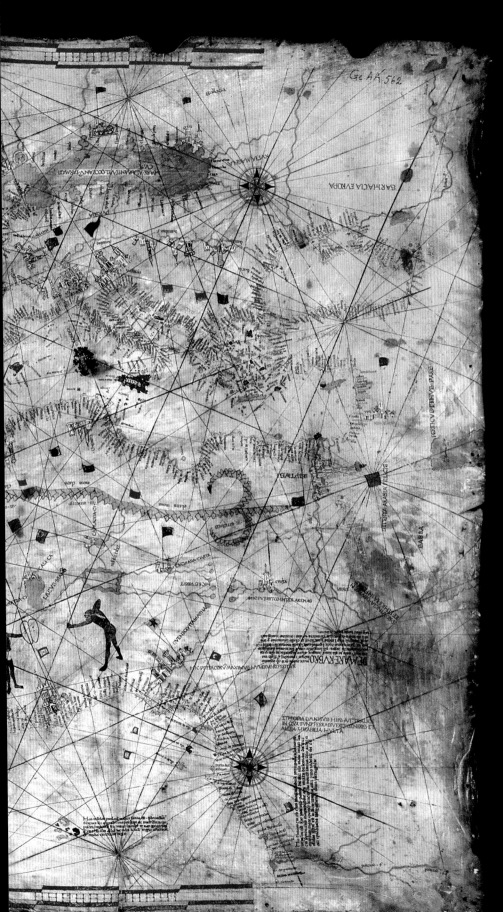

Surely Columbus repeatedly recounted this novel-worthy episode to his son who rushed to include it in his *History*.

With the intention of making the event sound more romantic, Fernando portrayed his father as part of the fleet of Columbus the Younger (George Paleologue de Bissipat) without realizing that the French privateers' attack against the four Venetian galleys returning from Flanders had taken place in 1485, a date when Columbus was already in Spain, the earlier battle having occurred on August 13, 1476. On one side, the antagonists were French pirates with Guillaume de Casenove, alias Columbus the Elder, and on the other, Genoese ships with which the future admiral sailed. This confusion in names and a mistaken date still narrate historical fact, summarized as follows: father's ship endured a dramatic fire, and was bound with chains on the enemy ship when enemy sailors began to bourd so the only solution was to jump in the water... to die there rather than endure the flames; the Admiral being a great swimmer... grabbed an oar that he found, using it sometimes to stay afloat and swimming at other times... [he reached] land, and even then he was so tired and drenched by the water that it took him many days to recover.

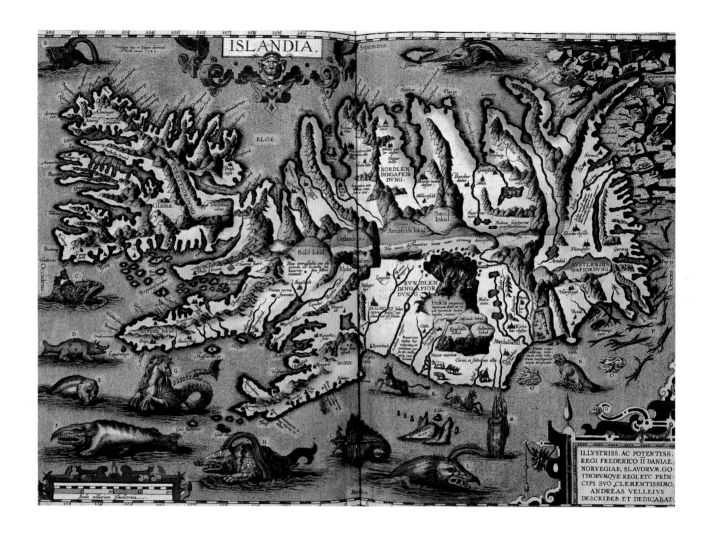

After his adventurous swim to shore, the shipwrecked Columbus eventually went to Lisbon, a city where his Genoese employers had a branch office. From then on, his life would completely change.

From the Algarve, Columbus continued his path toward Lisbon in order to meet with his employers, the Centurions and the Di Negros, the Genoese firm for which he was working. Lisbon fascinated him. In those years, the city was a wonderful cosmopolitan urban center where interesting and lucrative maritime endeavors were growing and Columbus' Genoese compatriots were not at all strangers to these goings-on.

Facing the Mediterranean Sea, from the city's well-known coastline, from its concrete confines, from the currents and winds learned and remembered by dint of enduring them on their voyages, the Atlantic played in the minds of 15th-century sailors like an as yet unknown ocean with infinite boundaries. The cartography of that era represented it as populated by a rosary of islands more or less near the continent, some fantastic and imaginary, others quite real and conveniently located. The legends that accompanied these maps and navigators' tales were lacking in bookish culture that contributed to creating an aura of fantasy and attraction around this great unknown.

Even when both sides of the Atlantic, the northern and the southern (Portuguese), were spatial frontiers that man innately wanted to cross, and both seemed disturbing and attractive, the Portuguese Atlantic seemed much more tempting than the northern Atlantic with its harsh winters and very long nights. But also the northern Atlantic was an ocean which could be crossed, susceptible to being larger at times. Both sides of the Atlantic were strange and mysterious: the initial discoveries were made during "fishing expeditions"; then they were motivated by a yearning for the conquest of new lands. Both fishing voyages and voyages of discovery used much the same navigational techniques, whether among offshore islands or along the American continent's northern or more southern shores. But whether to the north or the south, the routes to America were found and recorded by two Italians: Christopher Columbus and John Cabot.

As he would have expected, Columbus' employers gave the young man the job of continuing his interrupted voyage from Genoa to England that destiny had previously frustrated. Having just arrived in Portugal at the start of 1477, he had to set sail again on a commercial voyage from Lisbon to Iceland, after making stopovers at the ports of Bristol, in England and Galway, in Ireland.

To make the journey from Bristol to Iceland, vessels then required between twelve and fourteen days with favorable weather. Leaving the channel at Bristol, they rounded Cape Mizen to then stop over at Galway, Ireland's most secure and important west coast port, and, from there, they entered the gulf to the north, on the open sea for more or less two weeks until reaching their final destination.

We have information on this voyage from Columbus himself; he left us a testimonial about its dangers in one of his letters to Ferdinand and Isabella, and in a note in the margin of his copy of *Historia Rerum*, by Aeneas Silvius Piccolomini, who became Pope Pius II. On this voyages he first noticed the difference between the Atlantic and Mediterranean tides, a phenomenon that always surprised Mediterranean sailors that weren't familiar with the tidal differences.

He also had an opportunity to hear the language used by the sailors of the North Atlantic that (as demonstrated by M. Mollat) mixed English and Celtic nautical terms with Dutch shipping, Germanic military and Spanish, Portuguese, and Italian institutional and legal terms.

In addition, Columbus inadvertently offers us two particularly interesting dates in his text. First, he strictly confirms having sailed 100 miles north of the island of Thule. Then, as we know, Thule represented the northernmost limit of the known world to early cultures; thus his assertion proves that he was indeed a person who had explored beyond this boundary.

Secondly, Columbus reported a curiuos fact: "Men from Catai (ancient China)," he writes " came to the East. We have seen many remarkable things, especially in Galway, Ireland, where a man and woman amazingly held on to pieces of wood as they were dragged along by a storm." Written subsequent to reported facts, this note may indicate that at this time the future admiral had an inkling of the possibility of making a voyage to the west, in the opposite direction to that taken by those unfortunate men with differences of race. This too may have been the first time Columbus felt attracted to the polar regions. Thus, some of the his biographers definitely believed that this letter of 1500 reporting these earlier events implied this thought pattern and that Columbus still considered upon nothing less than going to discover the North Pole.

What proves true is that this voyage to the North Atlantic was the impetus for Columbus to reestablish himself in Lisbon – and from that date forward, he would reside in Portugal until 1485.

70 This map of Iceland was published in the *Theatrum orbis terrarum* by Abraham Ortelius (1592). Columbus made a voyage to "Islandia" in 1477. It was probably during that voyage that he began to think about making an expedition from the East to the West (Bodleian Library, Oxford, United Kingdom).

Maps of the North Sea and Atlantic Ocean in Columbus' time frequently included representations of imaginary islands or animals.

72 Cartographers frequently decorated the edges of their maps with diverse motifs. In this one, the mapmaker pointed out the different climate zones (fourth, fifth, sixth, and seventh), adorning them with wind roses and the typical ships that navigated the western ocean. In the 15th century, the Atlantic Ocean still represented an unknown body of water, in good part as yet unexplored (National Library of France, Paris, France).

73 Maps of the North Sea and Atlantic Ocean in Columbus' time frequently included representations of imaginary islands or animals (National Library of France, Paris, France).

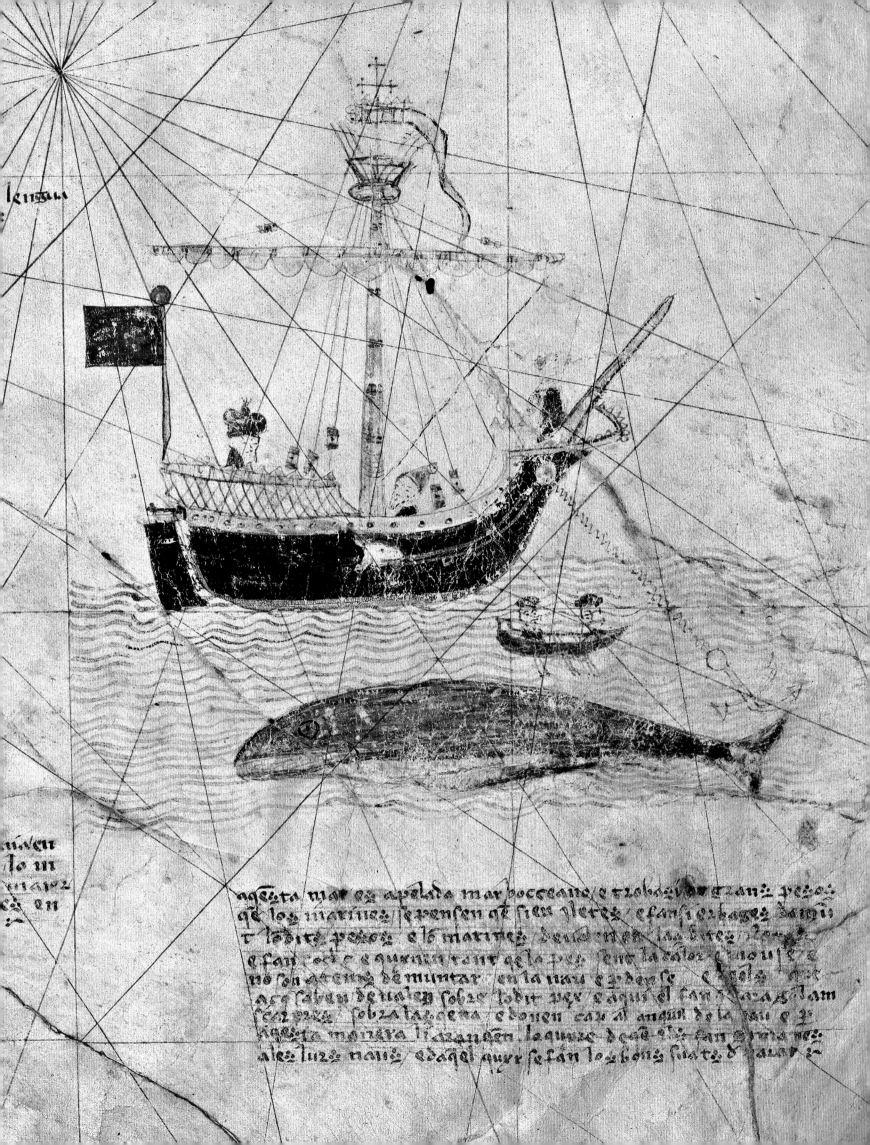

TRADING IN THE PORTUGUESE AND SPANISH ATLANTIC

It is difficult to make a living from a career as a bookseller and Columbus had to make this new endeavor work in concert with his passion for the sea, doubtless for him the most attractive calling. In Lisbon, he drew nearer to the geographical theories in vogue. We must remember that in 1477, the Portuguese were committed to much more promising voyages than the navigators of the North Atlantic nations were making. The Portuguese had already long abandoned voyages across the Atlantic Ocean in search only of cod and whales.

In Lisbon Columbus met Martín Behaim, the first man to create a globe, which was to happen later, when Christopher lived in Castile. Behaim had committed himself to studying the navigation of the high seas. In Portugal, he was able to view the letters of the physician-mathematician Paolo dal Pozzo Toscanelli, who had an interest in voyages to the west. These Behaim copied; he also probably maintained a correspondence with Toscanelli. Columbus himself tells us that he knew the astronomer, *maese* (master) José and thought very highly of him. In all of that and without making any erudite hypotheses about responsibility for correspondence with the Florentine physician or other authors, what seems apparent is that Columbus consulted many experts, interviewed sailors, and made notes about their experiences, voyages, and impressions in documents that are now lost but that certainly must have existed, knowing the navigator's devotion to the written word.

On his voyages as a merchant with the company of Ladislao Centurion and Paolo Di Negro, Columbus listened to seamen's accounts of voyages, learned to read navigational charts, met people of other races, and encountered new products. He witnessed the slow return of fleets that had gone beyond known boundaries and that had, above all, been successful at returning to new places after encountering previously unknown populations. Many of these were simple military explorations that had returned spectacular financial benefits despite ships being destroyed when engulfed by endless dense fog, costing these expeditions dearly. In Lisbon, Columbus married Filipa Muñiz Perestello, with family connections to colonizing captains, not to sailors as erroneously reported on various other occasions. In any case, the contact with these seafaring adventurers revived Columbus' spirit and his eagerness to "know more," a precious motto that the future admiral never abandoned. Once married, Columbus moved for a brief period of time to Porto Santo Island. A small and almost deserted islet, quite close to the island of Madeira where his father-in-law, Bartolomeo Perestrello, had been the captain-major but had already died. There, he could neither consult maps nor instruments, nor even navigational charts, yet he must have been fascinated with the frequent appearance of strange objects, primarily large carvings made from unknown wood, sculpted in a singular manner, that had washed up on shore. The Gulf Stream still transports vegetation from the Antilles onto the shores of Porto Santo. From Porto Santo, Columbus often sailed to Madeira. The sugar business attracted Genoese merchants and Columbus arrived on the island in 1478, one year after his voyage to Iceland. These sugar ventures failed and, one year later in August 1479, Columbus had to go to Genoa to present his accounts to his employers. This was the last time he saw his birthplace.

75 COLUMBUS SET SAIL FROM THE CANARIES ON THREE OF HIS FOUR VOYAGES TO THE NEW WORLD. HIS FIRSTBORN SON, DIEGO, WAS BORN ON THE ISLAND OF PORTO SANTO. ON THIS MAP FROM 1463, WE CAN SEE THE WESTERN COASTLINES OF SPAIN, PORTUGAL, AFRICA, AND THE CANARIES (BRITISH LIBRARY, LONDON, UNITED KINGDOM).

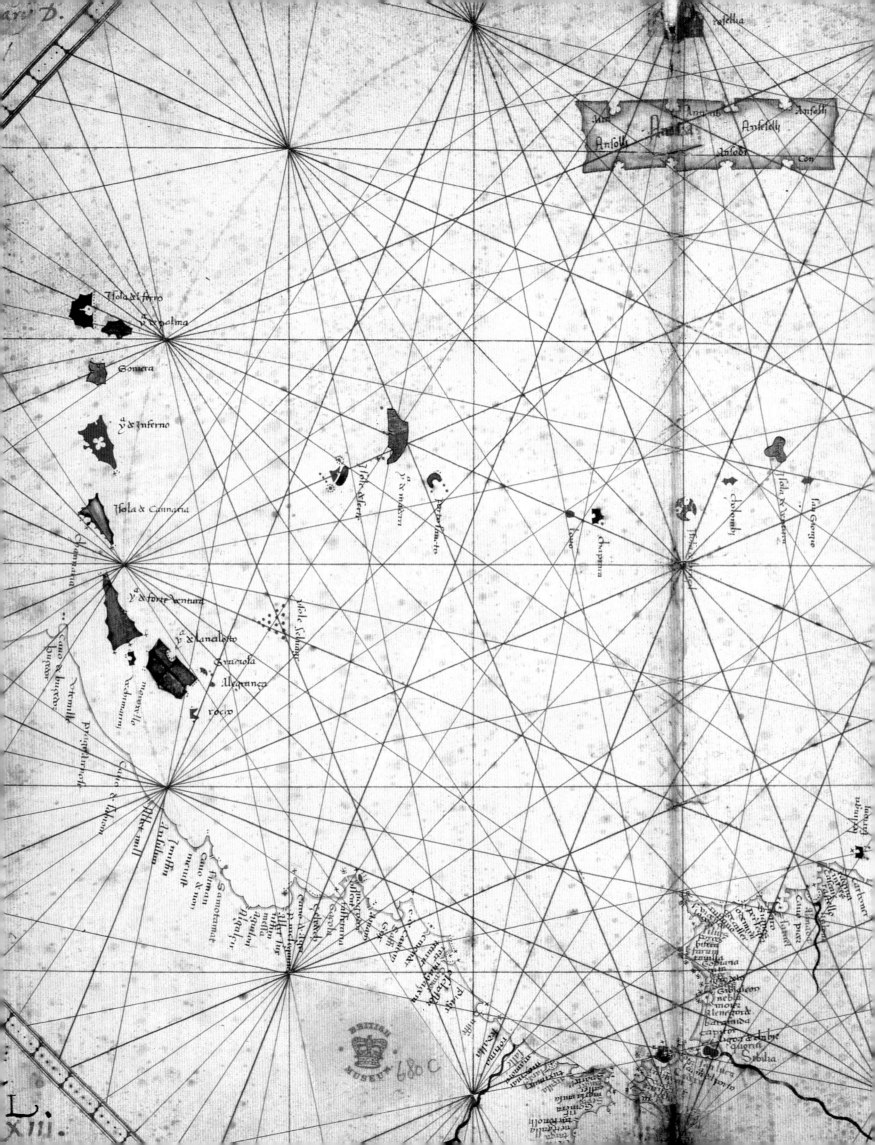

S. GEORGII *Oppidum* MINA *nuncupatum, quod L.*
II *Anno salutis, 1482 in Genea ædificatum est, qu*
fectum apportant, recipientes à Christianis, rubrum, ac
similes ipsis gratas, conuenientesque merces.

um Regum

Pagus.

S. Georgij

The king of Portugal's troops were advancing down the African coast and, on their voyage toward India, they explored and took possession of the parts of western coast of the African continent. Gold, spices, and the slave trade produced immense wealth for merchants who obtained royal concessions to practice mercantile trading. By prohibiting a free market to merchants, the Crown received repeated license fees while risking very little. Besides the Centurion-Spinola-Di Negro merchant-interests that were participating, there was also the Florentine businessman, Bartolomeo Marchioni, who maintained a close relationship with Giannotto Berardi who would in later years be the wheeler-dealer involved in Columbus' first two voyages to the New World. Columbus got to know the African continent along with them.

Though Columbus never mentioned their number or dates, it was during these voyages that he no doubt gained experienced places and events very pertinent to his maritime training. Of the places visited and documented during these voyages, he exclusively cites the coast of Malagueta, where he sighted mermaids and the fortress of San Jorge de la Mina, founded in 1841 and mistakenly thought to be situated at the equator. In addition to a profound knowledge of the Portuguese system of colonization, which would highly influence his political plans in the Indies, he came into contact with a new sailing practice that would prove quite useful to him in the future. On these various voyages, he learned to navigate with a head wind or to sail close hauled, to measure the height of the sun with the astrolabe, or even to barter with curios, a first attempt at a technique that would provide many good results much later in the New World.

On three occasions Columbus made notes in the margins of one of his favorite books, the *Imago Mundi*, written by Cardinal Pierre d'Ailly; the notes were about his experiences in Guinea, based on his geographical theories.

76-77 From the time when the Portuguese founded the fortress of San Jorge de la Mina, its port became a essential enclave on the route they thought would lead them from Lisbon to India. From la Mina, they brought gold and African slaves to Portugal. On one occasion, Columbus wrote to his rulers, confirming that the slaves from the New World could be sold in Europe at greater profits than those coming from Guinea (British Library, London, United Kingdom).

78-79 A detail from the Cantino World Map (1502) depicts the San Jorge de la Mina Fortress founded by the Portuguese in 1480. Visiting it at least once, Columbus cites this enclave on more than one occasion (British Museum, London, United Kingdom).

montes claros em affica:

Rey organo oqual
ey nobre umuito Rico

terra del Rey de nubia oqual
Rey sempre trate continuada
mente guerra conel prello fua
oqual Rey he monzo xenuyto
apemigno de castrios

lloa:

muito ouxe este
e ap em nahua
ia portugall z muitos
xdeof zdole 9 be
capo z estei

Castello damina.

sorente principe doni manuell Rey de portugall cada anno doze cara
belas cam pura trazecadacarabro byla co onera xxb nyll pesos
douro bal cada pesso quinhentos llaas rimos traem umytos
espoos z pumer ta ro su ntra a conf as de muyto
pzoneita

"Africa is twice the size of Europe . . . the southern and northern regions are populated by infinite numbers of people who are not deterred by the very high temperatures. It is beneath the equinoctial point where the days are always twelve hours and where I stopped over at His Royal Highness the King of Portugal's fortress. There, I found myself in a temperate zone." "The Torrid Zone is not uninhabitable . . . rather, it is quite populated."

"Sailing frequently from Lisbon at midday when setting off for Guinea, I diligently observed the route . . . and thus measured the height of the sun with the quadrant and other instruments many times, checking that it agreed with Alfraganus' measurements or that each degree corresponded to 56 and 2/3 miles. Based on such reasoning, I have faith in this measurement. As a result, I would say that the perimeter of the earth, at the length of the equinoctial circle is 20,400 miles. Physicist and astrologer, Master Giuseppe, noted the equivalent as did many others. . . . It is so blatantly obvious to whomever uses the navigational charts, to take a measurement of the distances from north to south, over the Ocean and not land, beginning from England or Ireland in a straight line south to Guinea.

As a great new finding, Columbus noted the habitability of the torrid zones where he had probably never been before, forgetting that the Portuguese had already possessed complete knowledge of these meteorological conditions in subequatorial areas for at least twenty years. By just degrees, he miscalculated the location of the San Jorge de la Mina Fortress that, as had already been demonstrated by Duarte Pacheco in his *Esmeraldo De Situ Orbis*, was situated at 5° 30' north of the equator, being the longitude of the equinoctial circle. His determination in supporting his own hypotheses to the bitter end allowed him to achieve his voyage of exploration. Only God knows how many times a false premise has led to a genius discovery!

Years later, while describing the New World about which he was dreaming, the comparison with Guinea occurred to Columbus:

"There are a large number of palm trees there that are different from those in Guinea and from our own." He found the he bounty of the American river waters was extraordinary: "and they are not like the rivers in Guinea, which are all toxic," and the men, despite being so close to the equinox line "are not negroes as in Guinea," and even the loin cloths worn by natives recalled those used by the African women, "they wear small cotton handkerchiefs that are handmade and elaborately embroidered with colors and decorations like those in Guinea, quite close to those worn at the rivers in the mountains of Liao." Even the names Columbus bestowed upon the Indies were clearly drawn from those of Africa: Cabo do Monte, Cabo Verde, Cabo Roxo, Cabo das Palmas, Rio do Ouro, Porto Santo, and even a Valle del Paraíso.

The future admiral's language about the New World also seemed full of words used in connection with Africa. The people of the Indies weren't *pretos* (dark skinned), had *corredíos* (straight) hair, ate *inhames* (a tuber) and *faxoes* (beans), and sailed on *almadías* (rafts). As Juan Gil reminds us, Columbus' sailor language was a mixture of Castilian terms like *encabalgar el cabo* for *doblar el cabo* (round the cape), words of Mediterranean origin that had already appeared in Portuguese texts like *treu, papafigo* (types of sails), *gisola, colla* (consistent wind), *balços de viento* that Columbus called *baltos* (gusts of wind), *dar reguardo* (pay attention), and Portuguese-isms like *marea ingente* (*enchente*, rising sea levels), *pozo* (*pouso*, in the sense of seabed), and *turboadas* (a term that he learned during his voyages to Mina).

Another phenomenon characteristic of the Atlantic and thus unknown to this Mediterranean man was *macareo*, a meeting of different tides that produced very high waves. Even Columbus must have endured a *macareo* while sailing with the Portuguese, an infrequent incident that the admiral would have to confront again while navigating through the Orinoco River delta.

ꝗ durat vnus dies in vno loco per vnū mēsem Jn alio per duos Jn alio
per tres vel pl9. ꝓporcionaliter est lōgior illa nox hyemis. Sexta ē
ꝙ illi qui habitarēt recte sub polo haberēt per mediū ānī Solē sup orizō
tem ꞇ ꝯtinuū diē ꞇ per aliud dimidiū cōtinuam noctē Et ita si vocemus
diē totū tēpus quo Sol ē super orizōtē nō haberēt toto āno nisi vnū
diem ꞇ noctē. Et sicut dictū est de ista medietate terre que ē vers9 poluz
articū siꝉiter itelligendū est de alia medietate ꝟsus ātarticū ꞇ habitatori
bus ei9 Et hec ōnia sine alia ꝓbatione exēplariter patēt ī spa materiaꝉ.

De quantitate terre habitabilis · Capitulū octauū

AD inuestigandū quātitatem habitationis terre itelligendū est ꝙ ha
bitatio dupliciter ꝯsideratᵘ. Vno mō respectu celi. s. ꝙntuz propter
Solē pōt habitari/ ꞇ ꝗ̃tum nō. ꞇ de hoc super9 generaliter ē satis dictū
Alio mō ꝯsideratᵘ respectu aque. s. ꝗ̃tum aꝗ̃ īpediat. ꞇ de hoc nūc ē cōside
randuz. De quo varie sunt opiniones sapientū· Nā Ptholomeº libro de
dispōne spere. vult ꝙ fere sexta pars terre ē habitabilis propter aquā· ꞇ
totū residuū ē coopertū aꝗ̃. Et ita ī Algamesti libro ii. ponit ꝙ habita
tio nota nō ēnisi in quarta terre. s. in qua habitamᵘ Cui9 lōgitudo ē ab
oriēte ī occidēs· ꞇ ē medietas eꝗnoxialisEt ei9 latitudo ē ab equinoxiali
ī polū· ꞇ est ꝗ̃rta coluri. Sz Aristotiles in fine libri celi ꞇ mūdi. vult ꝙ
pl9 habitetᵘ ꝗ̃ quarta· Et Auerroys hoc cōfirmat Et dicit Aristotilesꝙ
mare paruū est iter finē Hyspanie a pte occidētis/ ꞇ iter principiū Jndie
a parte orientis· Et nō loquitᵘ de Hyspania citeriori/ ꝗ nūc hyspania cō
muniter nominatur. sed de Hyspania vlteriori que nunc Africa dicitur.
de qua certi auctores loquuntur. vt Plinius Orosius ꞇ Ysidorus. Jn
super Seneca libro quinto naturalium dicit ꝙ mare est nauigabile ī pau
cis diebus si ventus sit conueniens. Et Plinius docet in naturalibus li
bro secūdo. ꝙ nauigatum est a sinu Arabico vsꝗ̃ ad gades Herculis nō
multum magno tempore. vnde ex hiis ꞇ multis aliis rationibᵘ de quibus
magis tangam cum loquar de Oceano cōcludunt aliqui apparēter ꝙ ma
re non ē tantuz ꝙ possit cooperire tres quartas terre. Accedit ad hoc auc
toritas Esore libro suo quarto· dicentis ꝙ sex partes terre sunt habita
te ꞇ septima est cooperta aquis. cuius libri auctoritatez sancti habuerūt
in reuerētia. ꞇ veritates sacras per eum confirmarunt. Et ideo videtᵘ ꝙ
licet habitatio nota Ptholomeo et eius sequacibus sit coartata ifra ꝗ̃r
tam vnam plus tamen est habitabile. Et Aristotiles circa hoc plus potu
it nosse auxilio Alexandri· Et Seneca auxilio Heronis. qui ad inuestigā
dum dubia huius mundi fuerunt solliciti. Sicut de Alexandro testātur
Plinius libro octauo. et etiam Solinus· Et de Herone narrat Seneca
libro de naturalibᵘ. Vñ illis magis videtᵘ credendū ꝗ̃ Ptholomeo vꝉ eti
am ꝗ̃ Albategni ꝗ adhuc min9 pōit ēe habitabile· videꝉ solū duodecimā
ptem· sz deficit in ꝓbatiōe sicut posset ostēdi/ sed breuitatis causa transeo

THE COLUMBUS PROJECT

On several occasions, Columbus had to explain his cosmographic theories before a commission of experts, first in Portugal and later in Castile. We know the names of the majority of doctors that took part in the examining commissions however, we do not know all of their responses, so we do not know the full breadth of subject matter or complete line of reasoning that Columbus submitted to the commissioners. Despite no chronicler ever mentioning it, we can assume that he limited himself to defending the "world is round" theory, that land lay over water, and that he offered some scholarly citations in support of his models.

We can briefly summarize the geographical knowledge that inspired the Columbus project, based on two premises. The first, certainly supported by humankind, is that the world is round; the second is Columbus' lower than correct assessment of the distance between Europe and Asia. Given that the world is round, nothing would prevent him from reaching the East by sailing from the West. Given the error in his second theory on the distance between Europe and Asia, the voyage would be shorter than it actually was. Columbus had calculated that the earth was 20,400 miles at its equatorial circumference; in fact is 6,214 miles more, for a total of 26,614 miles.

The admiral had based "his" distance on a series of calculations made by geographers who had preceded him. In his calculations Toscanelli had reduced thesurface extent of oceanic waters by 160 degrees. Of these 160 degrees, 20 had already been accounted for (the Canaries and Azores) and 15 corresponded to the average distance between the Chinese mainland and Cipango (the poetic name that Marco Polo used for Japan), resulting in 160 –20 –5 = 125 degrees. Marino di Tiro had also confirmed such a distance when he attributed oceanic mass to about 120 degrees. Without erring on the high or low side, Columbus deducted those regions included between Europe and the Canaries from di Tiro's 120 degrees, moving Cipango farther east. So, he reduced "his" distance by 45 to 50 degrees. He concluded his theory with the biblical prophet Esdras' supporting evidence, ensuring that only one seventh of the earth was covered by water. In effect, one seventh of the 360 degrees in the earth's circumference is equal to 51 degrees, which was just the distance that Columbus believed extended from the Canaries to the Indies. Columbus must have then converted the degrees to nautical miles. Based on such reasoning, he clearly adopted the theories of Alfragranus who, followed by Toscanelli and d'Ailly, maintained that 56.66 miles corresponded to 1 degree. However, he made another error in estimating each mile at 4.86 feet, instead of about 6.5 feet, the value that Alfraganus gave the mile. Reducing the value of the mile consequently reduced the distance between the Canaries and the Levant (Orient) by no less than 2400 miles with respect to the 3000 that Toscanelli had calculated.

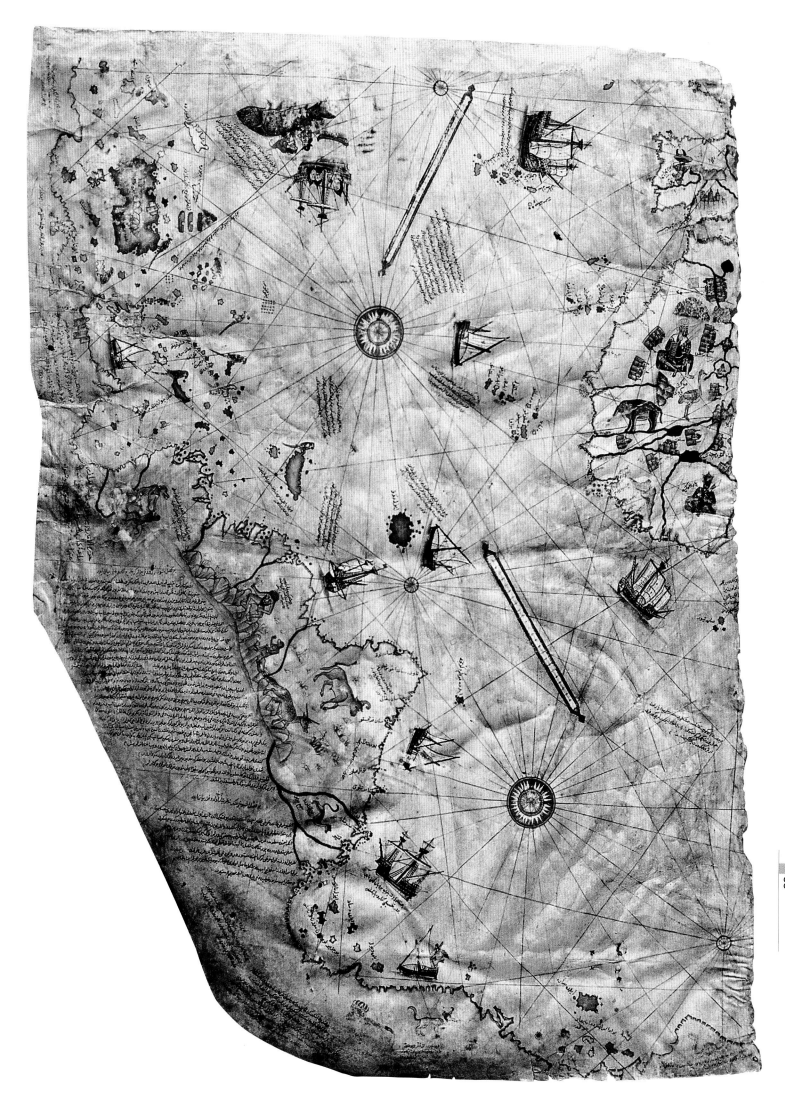

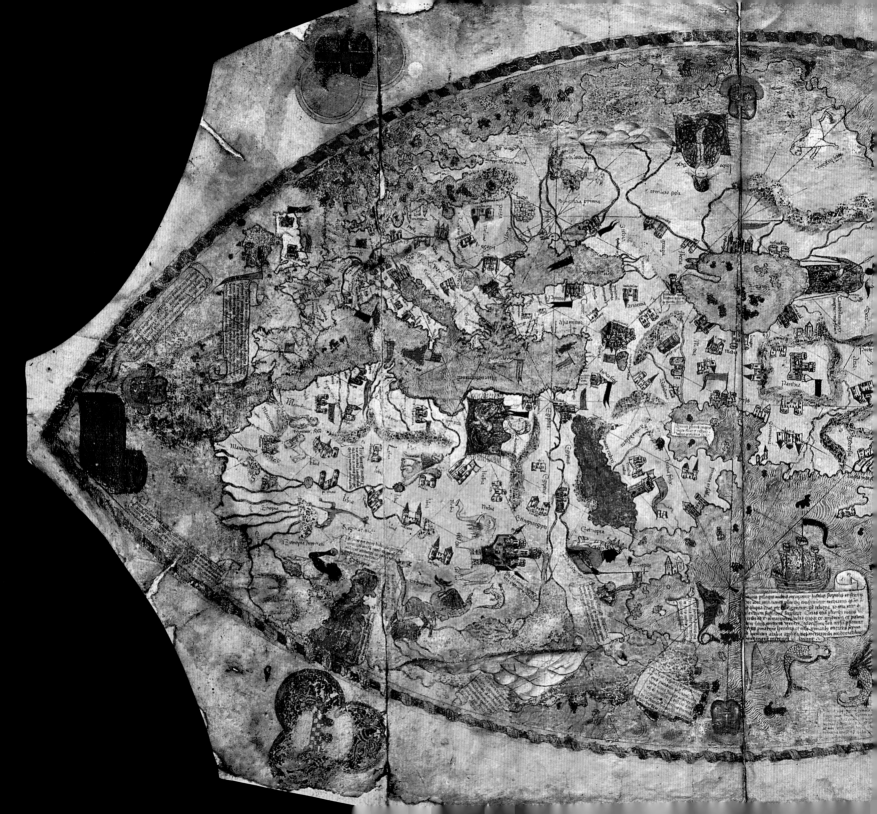

As noted, Columbus adapted his numbers to his own requirements and his calculations were not only wrong, but were very different from those of the official theories. We can assume that his theories would have clashed with the opinions of the doctors.

Nonetheless, we must recognize the fact that though Columbus erred in his geographical calculations, it does not mean that all of his observations were off the mark. Based on his own knowledge or instincts, Columbus always hit the mark in matters of route, voyage duration, winds, tides and currents, maneuvers, the ability to dodge or chase storms, and with regard to meteorological forecasts. Not a true astronomer, Columbus was nevertheless still a good reader of the starlit skies that he always relied upon to navigate, as demonstrated by his discovery of the North Star's movement that no one before him had been able to document.

84-85 ACCORDING TO SOME, THIS COPY MADE BY AN ANONYMOUS ITALIAN IN 1457 ACCURATELY REPRODUCES TOSCANELLI'S PLANISPHERE, THE ORIGINAL NOT HAVING BEEN PRESERVED. THE EXTENSION OF AFRICA TO THE SOUTH POLE DIVIDES THE EARTH WITH TWO LARGE OCEANS. SO TO REACH THE WEST, IT WAS NECESSARY TO SAIL FROM THE LEVANT (EAST). ERRING ON THE LOW SIDE, THE DISTANCE SEEMED TO MAKE THE VOYAGE POSSIBLE (BIBLIOTECA NAZIONALE, FLORENCE, ITALY).

86-87 KNOWN AS THE CATALAN WORLD MAP (CIRCA 1450), AN ANONYMOUS ILLUSTRATOR COMBINED LITERARY SOURCES WITH EMPIRICAL DATA. A RELIGIOUS ELEMENT TAKES THE SHAPE OF A CIRCLE IN THE DRAWING OF HEAVEN LOCATED IN AFRICA (BIBLIOTECA ESTENSE, MODENA, ITALY).

87 WORLD MAPS BASED ON CHRISTIANITY INCLUDED A SERIES OF PLACES CITED IN THE BIBLE, SUCH AS THE GARDEN OF EDEN OR THE REGIONS OF *TARSUS* AND *OPHIR* (SORIA CATHEDRAL, BURGO DE OSMA, SPAIN).

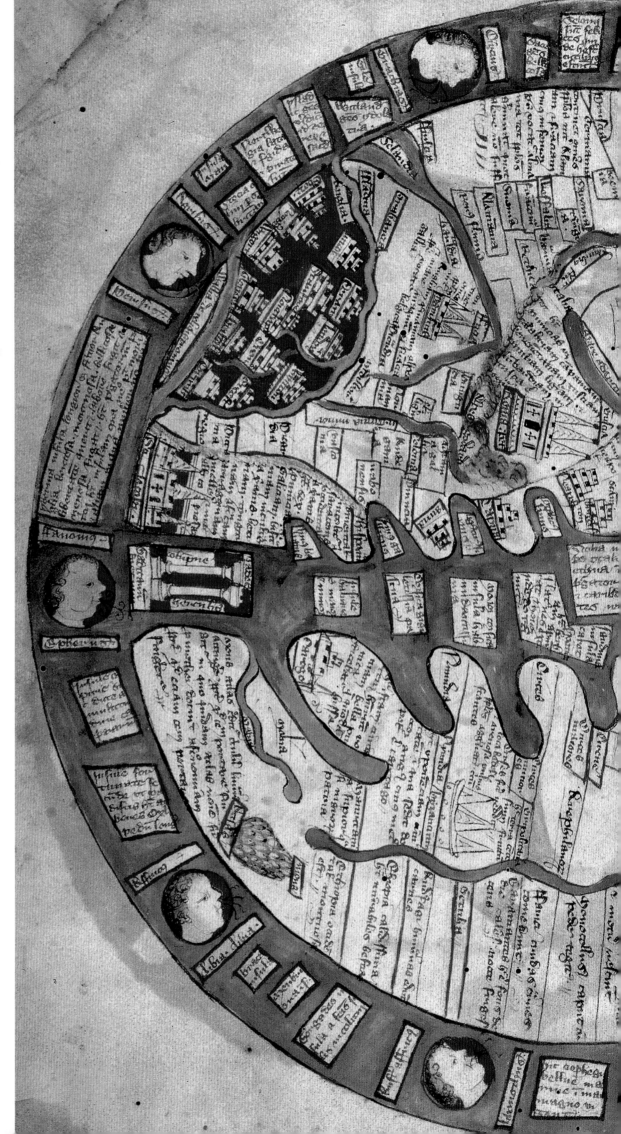

88-89 On maps influenced by Christianity, the Garden of Eden always appears as the center of the earth. Ranulf Higden created the map reproduced here in 1342 for the *Polychronicon* (British Library, London, United Kingdom).

90 In 1480, Hans Rust drew this elliptical map where the territory of "Vinland" also appears (The Pierpont Morgan Library, New York, USA).

90-91 The Venetian, Giovanni Leardo, created this circular world map on parchment in 1448 (Biblioteca Civica, Verona, Italy).

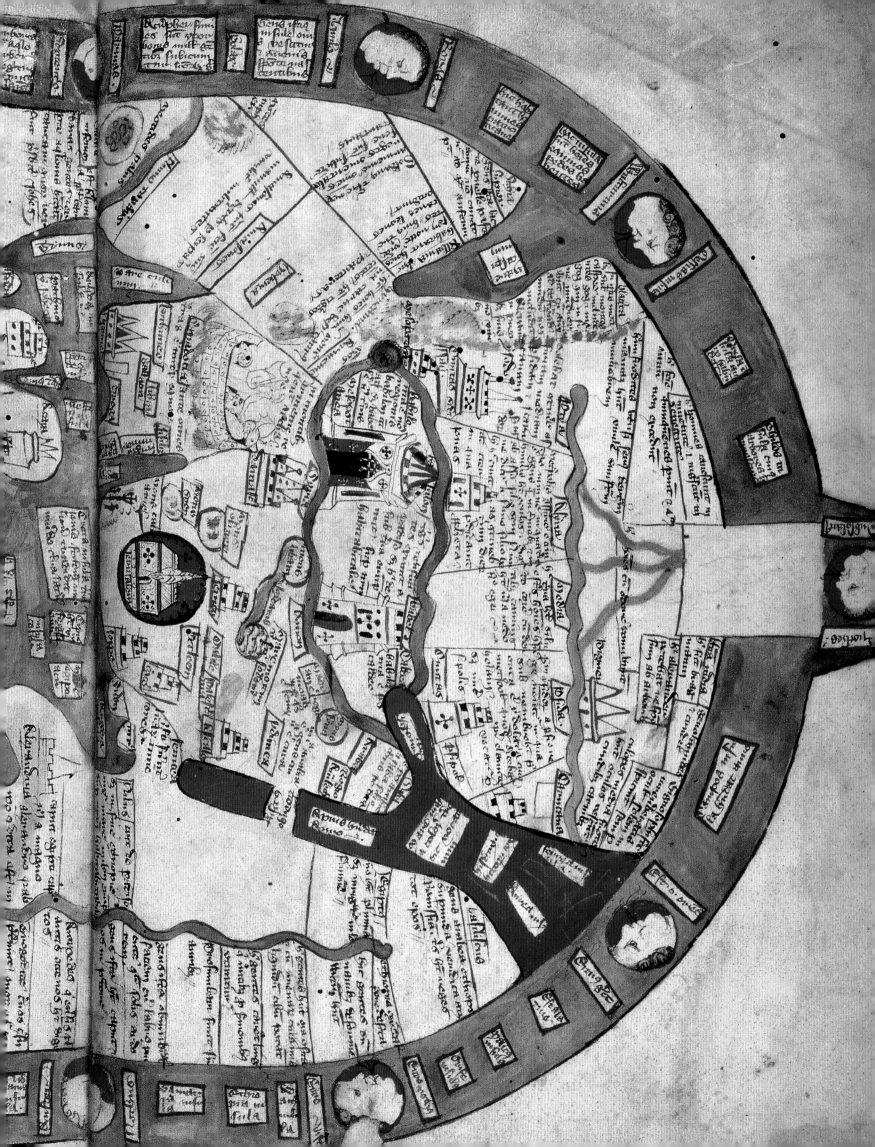

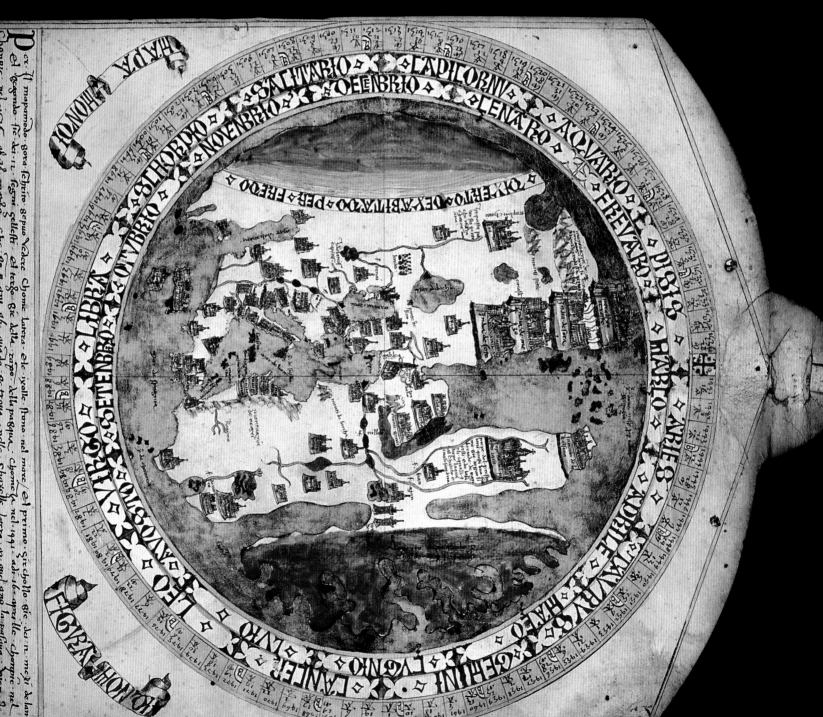

94 In Madrid, different scenes from the life of Christopher Columbus are represented on all four sides of the base of this Neo-Gothic style monument dedicated to the explorer. In this scene, he proposes his project to Queen Isabella.

95, 96 and 97 On 17 April 1492 the Agreement between the Catholic rulers and Columbus was signed at Sante Fe (Granada) thus establishing a Crown-Columbus monopoly for the exploitation of lands to be conquered. From 1499 forward, the king and queen broke the agreement by conceding new licenses to other navigators in spite of Columbus' protests. Was it a conditional compensation package or contract? If it were indeed a conditional compensation package, the royals would have been able to rescind it. If it were a contract, once default had occurred, legal action would have followed. Columbus' descendents and the Crown were in conflict over its terms for almost a half-century (General Archive of the Indies, Seville, Spain).

THE AGREEMENT AT SANTA FE

After waiting for seven years to obtain the needed authorization from Ferdinand and Isabella to undertake his project, Columbus finally succeeded in getting their signatures on his Agreement, a binding document that allowed him to complete his voyage. In January 1492, the Catholic monarchs had conquered the Muslim-held city of Granada and suspended any further operations of the Reconquista. Even though the monarchs resided in the Alhambra, their court was located in Santa Fe, Granada, the place where on April 17, representatives of the monarchs and of Columbus signed the contract.

In this document, an important series of privileges and considerations were conceded to Columbus. First, he was authorized to use the title of Don and was named "Admiral of the Ocean Sea" for his entire life and that of his heirs, with the same enormous privileges that other admirals of Castile enjoyed, including judicial jurisdiction over all of its coasts and ports. He was also granted the title of viceroy, governor of both the islands and terra firma that he would explore, thus enlarging the territorial and maritime jurisdiction that he already possessed as admiral. Among the financial benefits, he was granted the right to receive one tenth of all the material that would be acquired, developed, or obtained within the limits of his admiralty and the right to participate in one eighth of the cargo of the ships heading to new lands, consequently receiving one eighth of all profits made there from it. These privileges were later confirmed even thought the amounts varied over the four new concessions that were approved for his subsequent voyages. The Agreement, preserved in a single copy, was signed in behalf of the monarchs by King Ferdinand's trusted secretary, Juan de Coloma, and by the Franciscan monk Juan Perez, who represented the admiral.

Was the Agreement a contract or a compensation package? In effect, the document established a Crown-Columbus monopoly for the exploitation of lands to be explored. Therefore, the admiral protested animatedly when, from 1497, the monarchs conceded licenses to other ship owners. The enormity of lands in the New World, the complexity of colonial administration, and the viceroy's bad management as governor made a change in strategy absolutely necessary. After the admiral's death, his son, Diego, entered into the so-called "Columbus Disputes with the Crown." While Columbus' family maintained that the Agreement signed by their father and the monarchs was equivalent to a contract that, when rescinded, provided for payment, the royal court's attorney maintained that it was a conditional compensation agreement that could be revoked when the Crown thought it appropriate. After many years of litigation, the Columbus family must have settled on terms that did not appear equitable to them but that the family had to accept; it included the concession of Jamaica, the duchy of Veragua, and some parcels of land in Santo Domingo.

Las cosas suplicadas e que vras Altezas dan e otorgan a don xpoual colon en alguna satisfacion delo que ha descubierto enlas mares oceanas y del viaje q agora conel ayuda de dios ha de fazer por ellas enserviçio de vras altezas son las q siguen

Primeramente que vras al. como Señores que son delas dichas mares oceanas fazen dende agora al dicho don xpoual y Colon su almirante entodas aquellas yslas y tierras firmes q por su mano o industria se descubriran o ganaran enlas dichas mares oceanas para durante su vida y despues del muerto asus herederos e suçessores de vno en otro perpetuamente con todas aq̃llas preheminençias y prerogativas pertenesçientes al tal offiçio e segund q don alonso enrriquez q al myrante mayor de castilla e los otros sus predeçessores enel dicho offiçio lo tenian en sus distritos Place asus altezas Johan de coloma

Otrosi que vras al. fazen al dicho don xpoual su Visorey e gouernador gñal entodas las dichas tierras firmes e yslas que como dicho es el descubriere o ganare enlas dichas mares e que parad regimiento de cadauna e qualquiere dellas faga el eleçion detres personas pa cada offiçio e que vras al. tomen y escojan vno el q mas fuere serviçio, e assi seran mejor regidas las tierras q nro señor le dexara fallar e ganar aserviçio de vras al. Place asus altezas Johan de coloma

Jtem q de todas e qualesquiere mercadurias siquiere sean perlas piedras preçiosas oro plata speçeria e otras qualesquiere cosas e mercadurias de qualquiere speçie nombre e maña q sean q se compraren trocare fallare ganare e oviere dentro enlos lymytes del dicho almirantadgo q dende agora vras altezas fazen merçed al dicho don xpoual e quieren q haya e lleve para si la dezena parte de todo ello quitados los costas todas q se fiziere enello por maña q delo q quedare limpio e libre haya e tome la dicha dezena parte pa si mismo e faga dello a su voluntad quedando las otras nueve partes para vras altezas Place asus altezas Johan de coloma

Otrosi que si acausa delas mercadurias qu el traera delas dichas yslas y tierras q assi como dicho es se ganaren o descubrieren o delas q entrueque de aquellas se tomaran aqua deotros mercadores naçere pleyto alguno enel logar donde el dicho comerçio e trato se terna y fara q si por la preheminençia de su offiçio de almirante le pertenesçera conoçer del tal pleyto plega a vras altezas q el o su teniente y no otro Juez conozcan del tal pleyto, e assi lo provean dende agora Place asus altezas si perteneçe al dicho offiçio de almirante segund q lo tenyo el dicho almirante don alonso enrriquez e los otros sus anteçessores en sus distritos y siendo justo Johan de coloma

Jtem q en todos los navios q se armaren para el dicho trato e negoçiaçion cada y quando y quantas vezes se armaren q pueda el dicho don xpoual colon si quisiere contribuyr e pagar la ochena parte de todo lo q se gastare enel armazon e q tanbien haya el lleve del provecho la ochena parte delo q resultare dela tal armada Place asus altezas Johan de coloma

Son otorgadas e despachadas con las respuestas de vras altezas en fin de cada un Capitulo enla villa de Santa fe dela vega de granada

a xvij de abril del año del nasçimiento de nro señor Mil CCCClxxxxij

yo el Rey   yo la Reyna

Por mandado del Rey e dela Reyna

Johan de coloma

Este es traslado bien e fielmente sacado de una carta de capitulaçion de sus altezas, nuestros señores, firmada de sus reales nonbres e sellada con su sello de çera colorada e registrada e señalada de çiertos nonbres de sus oficiales...

Las cosas suplicadas e que vuestras altezas dan e otorgan a don Xpoual de Colon en alguna satisfaçion de lo que ha descubierto en las mares oçeanas y del viaje que agora con el ayuda de Dios ha de fazer por ellas en serviçio de vuestras altezas son las que se siguen:

Primeramente que vuestras altezas como señores que son de las dichas mares oçeanas fazen dende agora al dicho don Xpoual Colon su Almirante en todas aquellas yslas e tierras firmes que por su mano e industria se descubriran o ganaran en las dichas mares oçeanas para durante su vida e despues del muerto a sus herederos e suçesores de uno en otro perpetuamente con todas aquellas preheminençias e prerrogativas pertenecientes al tal oficio e segund que don Alonso Enrriquez vuestro Almirante mayor de Castilla e los otros sus predeçesores en el dicho oficio lo tenian en sus distritos. Plaze a sus altezas. Johan de Coloma.

Otrosi que vuestras altezas fazen al dicho don Xpoual su Visorrey e governador general en todas las dichas tierras firmes e yslas que como dicho es el descubriere o ganare en las dichas mares, e que para el regimiento de cada una e qualquier dellas faga el eleçion de tres personas para cada oficio e que vuestras altezas tomen y escojan uno el que mas fuere su serviçio e asi seran mejor regidas las tierras que nuestro señor le dexara fallar e ganar a serviçio de vuestras altezas. Plaze a sus altezas. Johan de Coloma.

Iten que de todas e qualesquier mercadurias siquier sean perlas preçiosas oro plata especeria e otras qualesquier cosas e mercadurias de qualquier espeçie nonbre e manera que sean que se conpraren trocaren fallaren ganaren e ovieren dentro en los limites del dicho Almirantadgo que dende agora vuestras altezas fazen merçed al dicho don Xpoual y quieren que aya y lieve para si la deçena parte de todo ello quitadas las costas todas que se fizieren en ello por manera que de lo que quedare limpio e libre aya e tome la dicha deçima parte para si mismo e faga della a su voluntad quedando las otras nueve partes para vuestras altezas. Plaze a sus altezas. Johan de Coloma.

os que yo ayusa delas mercadurias q̄ el traera delas dichas yslas y tierras que el
do como dicho es se ganaren o descubrieren o dellas que entrique de Castilla
se tomaran a ca de otros mercadres naçere pleyto alguno en el lo har
don del dicho comerçio e trato e terna y fara que oy porla preheminencia
de su ofiçio d almirante le perteneçera como oez d tal pleyto plazenⁿ aⁿbas
Al tezas qⁿel o su teniente e no otros juez conosca del tal pleyto casy
lo provehan dende agora plaze a sus altezas sy perteneçe al dicho ofi
çio de almirante segund q̄ lo tenia el dicho almirante don alonso enrriqⁿ
yles otros sus antecesores en sus districtos y seyendo justo Johan
de coloma.

Iten que en todos los navios que se armaren en el dicho trato e negoçiaçion
cada que y quantas vezes se armaren que pueda el dicho don xpoval
colon sy quisiere contribuyr e pagar la ochena parte de todo lo que se gas
tare en el armazon e quetan bien aya e lleve del provecho la ochena part
dllo q̄ resultare dela tal armada plaze a sus altezas Johan de coloma

Son otorgados e despachados con las respuestas de vras altezas en fin de
cada un capitulo en la villa de santa fe dela vega de granada a dies y
siete dias de abril del año del nasçimiento de nro salvador Ihu xpo de mile
e quatroçientos e noventa e dos años yo el rey e yo la reyna por mandado
del rey e dela reyna Johan de coloma e registrada calçena esto es trasla
do del dicho traslado dela dicha capitulaçion oreginal en la noble çibdad e
villa dela ysla española Martes todos dies e siete dias del dicho mes
de Salvador Ihu xpo de mile e Coçenta e no
venta e dos años a los quales fueron testigos que fueron llamados e ro
gados a ver corregir e concertar el dicho susodicho capitulo con los
dichos oreginal de çierto e verdadero yasi el mismo vezino dela çib
dad de Sevilla e Adan de mi quinel vezino dela villa de guerra
myz e pedro d Gelçedo vezino dela villa de fuen Aldoña e Fran
de madrid vezino dela villa de madrid q̄ a todo ello testigos fueron

E yo Pedro Ihu xpo vezino e notario publico en la dicha çibdad ysabela alande
del rey e la reyna nros señores en la dicha çibdad e traslado fize sacar
e aqui en fin d este traslado d este todos los dichos testigos al dicho
original e por ser pedro d la
verdad

Nº 2

VOYAGES TO THE NEW WORLD

Columbus made four voyages to the New World, all under the Crown's monopoly system and in keeping with the terms of the Agreement.

Reconnaissance Voyage

Departure: Palos, 3 August 1492. Return: Palos, 15 March 1493.

As he documented many times, Columbus' goal in this voyage was to reach Asia, Cathay, and India via a passage from the West, following a well-known route and itinerary that would first take them to the Canaries, supported by the eastern winds toward their destination. Today, this confirms that the Crown's primary objective was purely commercial, coinciding with its desire to restore the fragile Spanish economy and compensating for the sacrifice of their African trading activities to Portugal in the Treaty of Alcaçobas in 1480.

Three ships took part in the convoy: the *Santa Maria* and two smaller caravels the *Nina* and the *Pinta*. The crews totaled 90 sailors, the majority of whom were from Palos, Moguer, and Huelva (70 Andalusians, some Basques, Galicians (10 total), and several foreigners, including one Portuguese from Tavira; a Genoan, Giacomo il Ricco; a Calabrian, Antonio; and a Venetian, Juan Veçano. In addition, there was a black Portuguese, Luis de Torres, who was Jew who had converted to Catholicism; he embarked as the expedition's interpreter, having an expertise in Oriental languages, Arabic, and Hebrew. Despite there being no doctor on board, a certain Master Alonso, physicist, definitely took part in the expedition as well as a surgeon named Juan, and Master Diego took the role of pharmacist. In addition to coopers (barrel makers) and ship's boys, Columbus brought along a tailor, Juan de Medina, and a goldsmith, Diego Caro, who was given the task of analyzing and valuing the precious metals that he hoped to find in the Indies. Neither priests nor women embarked the ships – and four of the sailors were ex-jailbirds prisoners. Bartolomé Torres had been condemned to death for committing a homicide during a brawl, and Alonso Clavijo, Juan de Moguer and Pedro Izquierdo, had been found guilty of organizing the prison escape of a mutual friend.

Accomplished men accompanied Columbus on this voyage, such as the captain of the *Santa Maria* and its owner, Juan de la Cosa, the eminent cartographer who designed the first map of the Antilles in 1500. The participation of the Pinzón brothers, Martín Alonso and Vicente, was also decisive to the success of the voyage. Thanks to them and their prestige in Andalusia, were recruited most of the Andalusian sailors and, without their help, Columbus would not have been able to placate the mutiny of his sailors who, desperate when not sighting land, threatened to throw him overboard. In later expeditions, Vicente Yañez explored almost all the Antilles and a number of points on the South American coast, arriving in Brazil in 1499, months before the Portuguese voyage of Alvares Cabral.

The Crown employed all the members of the crew. The masters and the captains received 2000 *maravedì* per month, the sailors, 1000, and the ship's boys were paid 666 per month.

On October 12, 1492, Columbus and his men touched land at a small island in the Lesser Antilles, which the admiral christened San Salvador; its modern name is Watling Island. Their crossing from the Canaries had lasted 33 days. During

the months when the fleet remained at sea, they explored diverse islands including Fernandina, Isabella, Cuba and finally, Hispaniola (today's Haiti and Dominican Republic) where the admiral decided to remain until 6 January 1493, the date when he began his return voyage to Spain. The Spanish built a fort they called Navidad with the remains of the *Santa Maria* which, through negligence, was shipwrecked just off the beach. The 39 men of the crew were able to board the other two vessels.

On March 14, the *Nina*, carrying the admiral, arrived in the Tagus River estuary, near Lisbon. Off-course and detached from the convoy as a result of a storm, Martín Alonso and the *Pinta* arrived in Bayona, Galicia, Spain that same day.

The actual results of this voyage were reduced to the demonstration of a potential western route to "India," a return voyage, and the incomplete exploration of some Caribbean islands.

100 In this painting created by Antonio Cabral Bejarano in the first half of the 19th century, he depicted an idealized image of Columbus' departure from Palos de la Frontera on August 3, 1492. In the background, a considerably enlarged promontory with the La Rábida Franciscan Monastery appears (La Rábida Monastery, Palos, Spain).

101 Romantic painters thus imagined preparations for the voyage of discovery, and transport of food and supplies. The depiction of the Franciscan monastery where Columbus found support from the friars appears in the distance (La Rábida Monastery, Palos, Spain).

102 AND **102-103** DURING HIS FIRST VOYAGE, COLUMBUS SIGHTED MANATEES, CONFUSING THEM FOR MERMAIDS AND THIS IS WHY HE WROTE THAT THEY WERE QUITE "UGLY" IN HIS DIARY. THIS DRAWING BY JOANNES STRADANUS WAS PUBLISHED IN 1585 IN THE TOME *AMERICAE RETECTIO;* IT SHOWS CHRISTOPHER COLUMBUS ON THE DECK OF THE *SANTA MARIA* ALONG WITH A TRITON AND A MERMAID.

la ispaniola

104-105 In 1493 in Rome, Giuliano Dati published the first short poem dedicated to the "Discovery" where he cited King Ferdinand as sole sponsor of Columbus' voyage. For this reason, Queen Isabella did not appear in most of the other illustrations (National Library, Madrid, Spain).

105 Attributed to Columbus, this map of Hispaniola was drawn in his onboard diary. The admiral wrote the word, *Civao* as he asserted that he'd reached Cipango (Marco Polo's term for Japan) (Private Collection, Madrid, Spain).

Insula hyspana

106 USING PREVIOUS DRAWINGS, THE PRINTERS DESIGNED A MEDITERRANEAN GALLEY IN PLACE OF A *CARACCA* (CARRACK) OR CARAVEL FOR THE FIRST EDITION OF THE LETTER THAT CHRISTOPHER COLUMBUS SENT TO ANNOUNCE HIS DISCOVERY OF THE NEW WORLD IN 1493.

107 THE LATIN TRANSLATION OF COLUMBUS' LETTER REPORTS THE NAMES HE USED TO CHRISTEN THE ISLANDS: *FERNANDA, ISABELLA, SALVATORIS, CONCEPTIO MARIE,* AND *HISPANIOLA.* THIS IS WHY SOME AUTHORS STILL UTILIZE THE NAME "HISPANIOLA."

108-109 PRODUCED IN 1650, THIS MAP REPRESENTS THE ISLAND OF HISPANIOLA WHERE COLUMBUS STOPPED OVER DURING HIS FIRST VOYAGE (PRIVATE COLLECTION).

HISPANIOLA INSVLA.

Anuimane

Mons Christi

Isabella

P. Plat

C. Franco

C. Capris

S. Jago

Samana

Ioan

P. Quises

Vega

R. Funa

C. del Engaño

Zacheo

CAISCIMV

LA.

Orama fl.

San Dominico

Yguseÿ

C. de Ciguey

Asua

C. de S. Raphael

Punt. de Nigua

S. Catharina

Saona

Mona

ORI.

21

20

19

18

17

110 top left Accompanying Columbus on his first voyage, Vicente Yañez Pinzón was captain of the Spanish armada that descended upon the Brazilian coast in 1500 (Naval Museum, Madrid, Spain).

110 top right Thanks to Martin Alonso, Columbus succeeded in recruiting a group of 90 sailors to sail on his first voyage. In conflict with Columbus, Alonso returned to Spain ill, the day before the admiral's return (Naval Museum, Madrid, Spain).

110 bottom Various members of the Pinzón family traveled with Columbus to the New World. If it weren't for their help during a mutiny on his first voyage, Columbus would not have been able to achieve his goal. In the image, we can see the Pinzón brothers' family crest (La Rábida Monastery, Palos, Spain).

111 Juan de la Cosa (1460-1510), a cosmographer and sailor who accompanied Columbus during his first two voyages, he produced the first map of the Antilles in 1500 (Naval Museum, Madrid, Spain).

112-113 As one result from his voyages to the New World, De la Cosa drew this map to provide information to the king and queen (Naval Museum, Madrid, Spain).

114-115 Columbus was received by his rulers in the royal palace's Tinell Hall (throne room) in Barcelona, where they confirmed his privileges, conceded their permission for him to remain seated in the monarchs' presence and to accompany them on horseback throughout the city (Army Museum, Madrid, Spain).

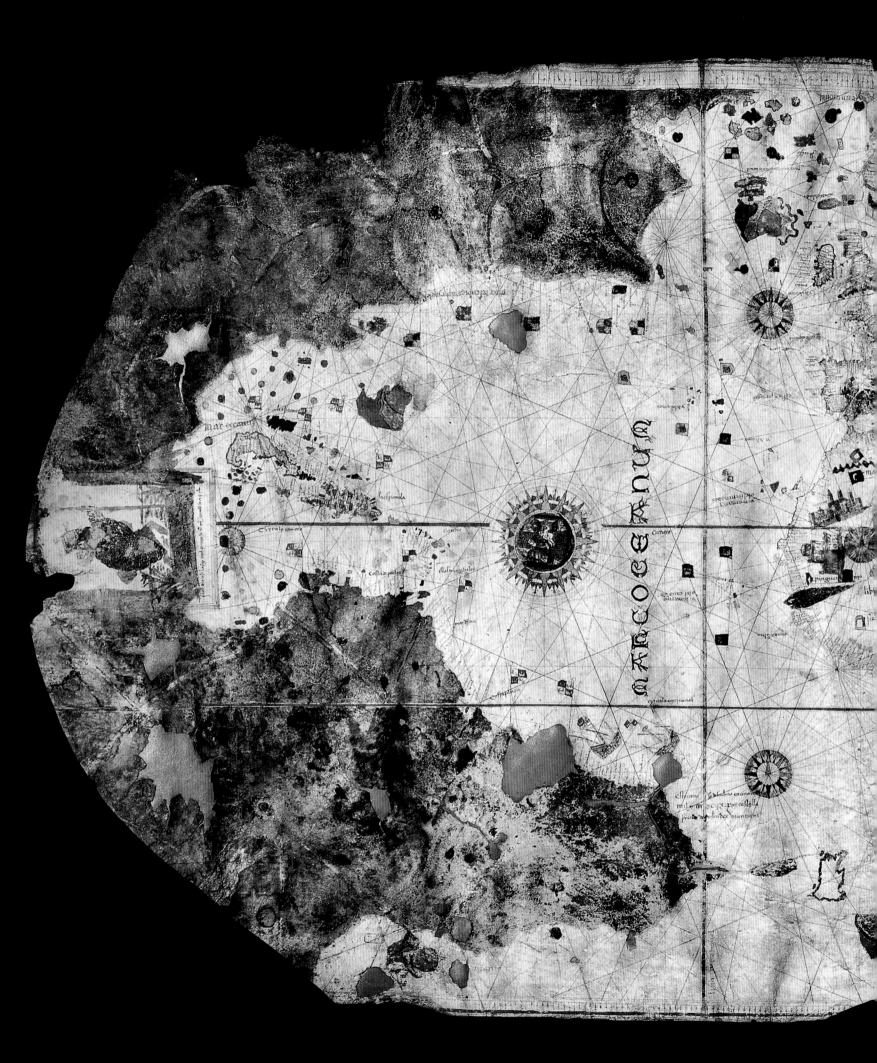

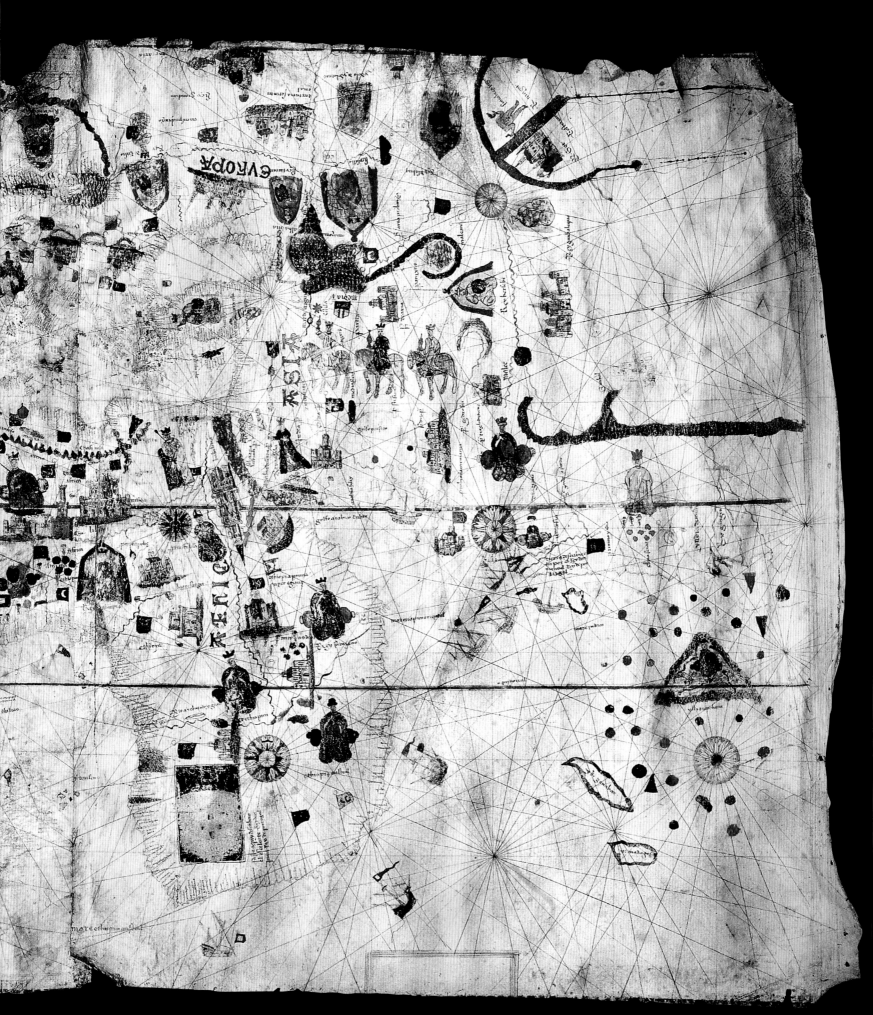

Second Voyage

Departure: Cadiz, 25 September 1493. Return: Cadiz, 11 June 1496.

Once Ferdinand and Isabella had obtained Pope Alexander VI's legitimation of the Castilian right to possession of the newly explored lands, the monarchs quickly arranged for the departure of Columbus' second voyage, designating the archdeacon of Seville, Juan Rodriguez de Fonseca, as administrator. The new venture would have the triple function of conquest, colonization, and evangelism.For their evangelistic policy, Ferdinand and Isabella requested and obtained from Pope Alexander VI the documents necessary to accredit Brother Bernardo Buil as apostolic vicar of the Indies. The hermit, Brother Ramón Pané, leading a group made up of at least four or five or Franciscan friars and three monks from the order of the Madonna of Mercede, was to found the first mission in the Antilles. Brother Bernardo, because of his hostility toward the admiral, quickly returned to Spain; Brother Ramón was the only monk who continued to live on Hispaniola. He learned various indigenous languages and wrote a kind of history of the native peoples of the Antilles for Columbus, recounting their traditions. Only one copy of this text was kept, which Fernando Columbus transcribed into his *History of the Admiral*. To implement civil, political, and colonial organization, concrete precepts were established for the formation of town councils and guidelines for the administration of justice, and the appointment of governmental officials, etc. Even though we don't have the *Books of the Armadas* available, which documented the expenditures made during this voyage, we know from other sources that the expedition included 17 ships: 3 *caraccas* (Portuguese armed ships), 2 large ships and 12 caravels. We don't even know the exact number of participants; however, there must have been around 1200, including both men and women. As far as preparations and costs, it was the most spectacular voyage to the Indies Columbus made. The admittedly false perception of the Indies had impassioned the hearts of Europeans; the whole world wanted to know and learn about its novelties. There was a solid group of Italians among the passengers, including the admiral's youngest brother, Diego, as well as Michele da Cuneo, a native of Savona who left us a report on the voyage, also describing his first impressions of this new land where he resided for only 6 months. Since it was a colonial voyage, a good number of civil servants, pages, officials, artisans, farmers carrying their own seeds, breeders bringing along their own livestock, and miners participated, as well as armed men, sent along as a means of defense against any potential attack by the Portugueses or simply because of the Spaniards' desire for conquest. Women also participated in limited numbers, given that the colonizers preferred that they arrive once everything had been organized. The most remarkable characteristic of this crew was its extraordinary combination of diverse passengers. Among these were the doctor from Seville, Diego Alvarez Chanca, the cosmographer, Juan de la Cosa (who had sailed on the first expedition), Pedro de Las Casas (father of the Dominican brother and historian Bartolomé), as well as Juan Ponce de León, the future explorer of Florida. Before arriving at Hispaniola, the fleet passed by the islands of Guadalupe, Dominica, Marigalante, Montserrat, Santa María de la Antigua, and Puerto Rico. On January 6, 1494, after the participants were settled in Santo Domingo on Hispaniola, the first mass in the New World was celebrated in the exact place where they landed. On that same day, they founded Isabella, the first European city in the Antilles. Despite his fragile health, Columbus voyaged constantly, traveling to Cuba and Jamaica. Once at Hispaniola, the admiral ordered his men to explore the island and to build a series of fortresses, from the North to the South. They were laying the foundations for Spanish colonization in these new lands. On June 11, 1496, Columbus set sail for Spain, in command of two ships, the *Nina* and the *India*, the first caravel built in the New World.

El Adelantado IUAN PONCE Des=
cubridor de la Florida.

7

Olumbus / demnach er die newe Welt erfunden vnd geoffenbaret / als er auff ein Zeit in einer herrliche Malzeit war / bey vielen Spaniſchen Edelleuthen / vnd vnter ihnen von dem neuwen India ſich ein Rede erhube / hat ſich einer gegen Columbum gewendt / vnnd ihn alſo angeredt: Wenn du ſchon Indiam nicht erfunden hetteſt / weren doch etliche in vnſerm Königreich Hiſpanien gefunden worde / die ſolchs eben ſo wol als du ſich vnterwunden hetten / dann Hiſpania wol ſo viel hohe vnd ſinreiche Männer hat: Darauff hat Columbus gar kein Antwort gegeben / ſondern ihm ein Ey vber Tiſch bringen heiſſen / vnnd zu ihnen allen geſprochen / ſie ſolten verſuchen / ob einer vnter ihnen diß Ey frey auff den Tiſch ſtellen köndte / daß es niergendt von gehalten vnd von im ſelbs auff dem Spitz möge geſtehen / Solches als keiner auß ihnen / ob ſie es ſchon verſuchten / hat treffen mögen / hat er ein Weiſe gezeiget / wie ſolches möge zu wegen gebracht werden / wie im 5. Cap. dieſes 1. Buchs zuleſen.

Columbi

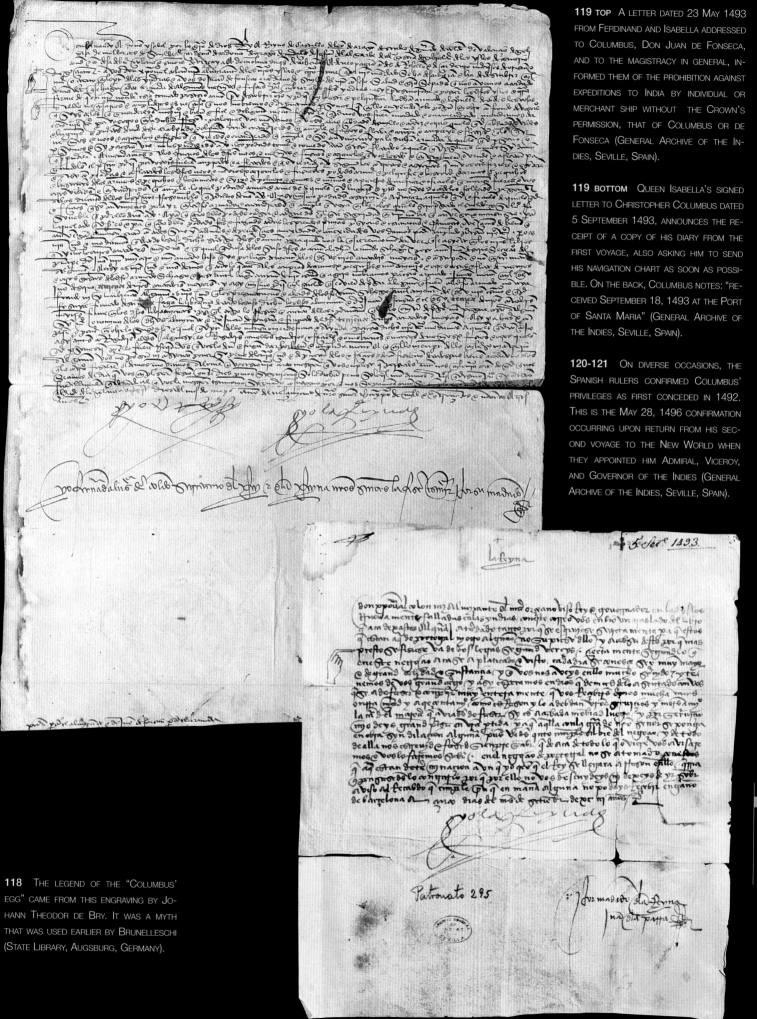

cosa alguna della que en ello ni en parte dello embargo nin contrario alguno vos non pongan nin consientan poner
ca nos por la presente carta dende agora para entonces vos fazemos merced de los dichos officios de almirante e
de visorrey e governador por juro de heredad para siempre jamás e vos damos la posesión e casi posesión
dellos e de cada uno dellos e poder e abtoridad para los usar e exercer e levar los derechos e salarios
dellos e de cada uno dellos a ellos anexos e pertenescientes segund dicho es. Sobre lo qual todo que dicho es
si necesario vos fuere e gelo vos pidierdes mandamos al nuestro chanciller e notarios e a los otros officiales
que están a la tabla de los nuestros sellos que vos den e libren e pasen e sellen nuestra carta de previllejo rodado la
más fuerte e firme e bastante que les pidierdes e ovierdes menester. E los unos nin los otros non fagades
nin fagades ende al por alguna manera so pena de la nuestra merced e de diez mill maravedís para la nuestra cámara a
cada uno de los que lo contrario fizieren. E demás mandamos al ome que les esta nuestra carta mostrare que los
emplaze que parescan ante nos en la nuestra corte do quier que nos seamos del día que los emplazare a quinze días
primeros siguientes so la dicha pena. So la qual mandamos a qualquier escrivano público que para esto fuere lla-
mado que dé ende al que gela mostrare testimonio signado con su signo porque nos sepamos en cómo se
cumple nuestro mandado. Dada en la nuestra cibdad de Granada a treynta días del mes de abril año del nascimiento de nuestro Señor Jhesu Christo de mill e quatrocientos e noventa e dos años. Yo el Rey. Yo la Reyna. Yo
Juan de Coloma secretario del Rey e de la Reyna nuestros señores la fiz escrevir por su mandado. Acorda-
da en forma: Rodericus doctor. Registrada: Sebastián d'Olano. Francisco de Madrid chanciller.
E agora por quanto plugo a nuestro Señor que vos fallastes muchas de las dichas yslas e speramos con la
ayuda suya que fallaréys e descubriréys otras yslas e tierra firme en el dicho mar Océano a la dicha parte
de las Yndias e nos suplicastes e pedistes por merced que vos confirmásemos la dicha nuestra carta que de suso va
encorporada e la merced en ella contenida para que vos e vuestros fijos e descendientes e subcesores uno en
pos de otro después de vuestros días podades tener e tengades los dichos officios de almirante e de visorrey e governador del dicho mar Océano e yslas e tierra firme que ansí avéys descubierto e fallado
e descubriéredes e falláredes de aquí adelante con todas aquellas facultades e preheminencias e prerrogativas de que han gozado e gozan los nuestros almirantes e visorreyes e governadores que han seýdo de los
dichos nuestros reynos de Castilla e de León e vos fuese acudido con todos los derechos e salarios a los dichos
officios anexos e pertenescientes usados e guardados a los dichos nuestros almirantes visorreyes e governadores o vos mandásemos proveher cerca dello como la nuestra merced fuese. E nos acatando el mucho riesgo
e peligro en que por nuestro servicio vos pusistes en yr a catar e descubrir las dichas yslas e en el que
agora vos poníades en yr a buscar e descubrir las otras yslas e tierra firme de que avemos seýdo e
speramos ser de vos muy servidos e por vos fazer bien e merced por la presente vos confirma-
mos a vos e a los dichos vuestros fijos e descendientes e subcesores uno en pos de otro e para agora e
para siempre jamás los dichos officios de almirante del dicho mar Océano e de visorrey e governador
de las dichas yslas e tierra firme que avéys fallado e descubierto e de las otras yslas e tierra firme
que por vos o por vuestra yndustria se fallaren e descubrieren de aquí adelante en la dicha parte de las
Yndias. E es nuestra merced e voluntad que ayades e tengades vos e después de vuestros días vuestros fijos
e descendientes e subcesores uno en pos de otro el dicho officio de nuestro almirante del dicho mar
Océano que es nuestro que comiença por una raya o línea que nos avemos fecho marcar que pasa desde
las yslas de los Açores a las yslas de Cabo Verde de septentrión en austro de polo a polo por
manera que todo lo que es allende de la dicha línea al ocidente es nuestro e nos pertenesce e ansí vos fazemos e
criamos nuestro almirante e a vuestros fijos e subcesores uno en pos de otro de todo ello para siempre jamás. E ansímesmo vos fazemos nuestro visorrey e governador e después de vuestros días a vuestros
fijos e descendientes e subcesores uno en pos de otro de las dichas yslas e tierra firme descubiertas e por descubrir en el dicho mar Océano a la parte de las Yndias como dicho es e vos
damos la posesión e casi posesión de todos los dichos officios de almirante visorrey e governador para siempre jamás e poder e facultad para que en las dichas mares podades usar
e usedes del dicho officio de nuestro almirante en todas las cosas e en la forma e manera e con las
prerrogativas e preheminencias e derechos e salarios segund e como lo usaron e usan gozaron e gozaron e gozan los nuestros almirantes de las mares de Castilla e de León e para en la tierra de las dichas

En granada a 30 de abril de 1492 años

Third Voyage

Departure: Sanlúcar de Barrameda, 30 May 1498.

Return: Cadiz, 20 November 1500.

Columbus' circumstances were completely changed by his second voyage. His popularity had diminished and, through new agreements, Ferdinand and Isabella had granted licenses to private citizens to undertake expeditions. Despite this situation, Columbus obtained the financing to make his third voyage to the New World.

While on the second expedition the turnout of volunteers was in keeping with need, recruiting the 330 people that the monarchs had anticipated for this third voyage proved difficult. The Indies had not yielded the promised wealth and life in the colony was difficult and unpleasant. Colonists had adapted neither to the new lands nor to the hunger and disease that ravaged their number. We have to resort to the availability of validated letters to verify the deportation to the Indies of prisoners to whom pardons were granted. However, despite what has been documented on the subject, we now know that of the 226 original members making up the expedition, only 10 appear to have been acknowledged as murderers. The crew was composed of a large host of 77 archers, 50 peons, 20 laborers and country folk, 18 officials, 15 sailors, 6 ship's boys, 4 Canaries natives (whose skills or professions we do not know), 4 domestics serving the admiral, 2 priests, 1 bombardier, 1 drummer boy, 5 unsalaried people, and at least 6 women. Everyone, or at least the majority, was of lower social status.

Of the eight ships that made up the fleet, Columbus sent two ahead from Sanlúcar under the command of his loyal friend, Pedro Hernandez Coronel, who carried most of the armed men. Without doubt, the admiral was anxious to deliver to his brother Bartolomeo, who remained as head of the colony on Hispaniola, the reinforcements necessary to fight and capture insurgent natives and thus supply slaves for work in the mines or to be sold in Europe. Instead of following the same route

as preceding voyages, Columbus chose to avoid the Canaries and head directly into the Cape Verde route. On this more southern passage, the crossing led the fleet to the island of Trinidad, sighted land for the first time on 1 August 1498. Four days later, on August 5, the first landing on the American continent took place. Columbus did not descend from the ship and it was his majordomo, Pedro de Terreros who, in the name of their Catholic Majesties, solemnly took possession of the territory. Until the end of August, the fleet continued to explore the northern coasts of Venezuela and Trinidad and, after crossing the Gulf of Paria, and also the Dragon's Mouth and Margarita Island, they arrived

at the Orinoco River delta. At the end of the month, Columbus and his men landed at Hispaniola to settle in the new city of Santo Domingo, founded in 1494 by Bartolomeo Columbus. It is said that Bartolomeo gave it this name in memory of their father, Domenico, even though others claim that the name reflects the fact that city's foundation stone was laid on a Sunday (*Domingo* in Spanish, *Domenica* in Italian). Until his return to Spain, Columbus endured difficult times. He had to suppress two uprisings (discussed later) and abandon the island as a prisoner in chains, following a court proceeding where he had to submit to Francisco de Bobadilla, whom Ferdinand and Isabella had sent out, with sweeping judicial authority. In addition to the important first landings and territorial claims on the South American continent, the colonial system was perfected during these years. From the administrative viewpoint, the first allotments of land and allocations of indigent slaves were completed, giving rise to the famous *encomiendas* years later. Following the route of this third Colombian voyage, so-called "minor voyages" were organized where expert sailors and businessmen explored neighboring new lands that were gradually annexed to the Spanish Crown. Among the men who participated in these other ventures, Amerigo Vespucci took part in the voyage organized by Alonso de Hojeda in 1499.

Fourth Voyage

Departure: Cadiz, 9 May 1502. Return: Sanlúcar de Barrameda, 7 November 1504.

After being pardoned by the monarchs for his alleged administrative failings in the new World, Columbus obtained permission to make a new voyage. His objective was to look for a strait that led to India. The discoveries of Hojeda, Bastidas, Pinzón, and Vespucci, among others, had prolonged the exploration of terra firma, but he still hungered for this as yet unknown gateway to Asia.

The fleet set sail with four ships; two caravels and two other vessels. The crew of this last voyage was composed of 140 men and, like the first, no women. For Columbus, it was hard work to recruit the crew, as demonstrated by the fact that very young men were enlisted as ship's boys and a specific number of Genoese men (the admiral's relatives), were in the majority. Among them were Bartolomeo Fieschi, captain of the *Vizcaíno*, and Diego Cattaneo. Also accompanying the admiral on this circumnavigation was his son Fernando, who also functioned as his father's secretary, his brother Bartolomeo, and his nephew Andrea Columbus, enlisted as ship's boy and responsible for accounting, along with Fernando. Among the Spanish, the figure of Diego Mendez emerges who, with Bartolomeo Fieschi, risked the dangerous crossing from Jamaica to Hispaniola to request the rescue of the rest of the crew, who had been shipwrecked in Jamaica for

a year, an incident described below. The fourth voyage was Columbus' most difficult one. Following the instructions he had received from the Crown, Nicolás de Ovando, the new governor of Santo Domingo, prevented Columbus and his men from entering the city and the fleet had to find refuge on a nearby bay to avoid the impending hurricane that their discerning admiral had predicted. Their misadventures did not end there. After heading to Guanaja Island, the armada skirted the southern coast of modern-day Honduras. From there, they headed to the Veragua section of the Panamanian isthmus coast, where Columbus tried to found the city of Bethlehem with the goal of leaving his brother, Bartolomeo, there and returning to Castile. The plan failed, so they took the route back to Jamaica. Hurricanes and fog had destroyed the four ships. The admiral had not recognized the isthmus at the point when he was nearing it and, when he had finally succeeded in redeeming himself to embark on the voyage to Spain, few men would accompany him. Of the 140 crew members who had left from Cadiz, fewer than half returned. A total of 38 remained on Hispaniola (some were sick, others refused to return to Castile), 35 were killed in battle, and at least 4 fled to other islands. The admiral arrived in Spain ill, plagued with debt, and completely lacking in prestige.

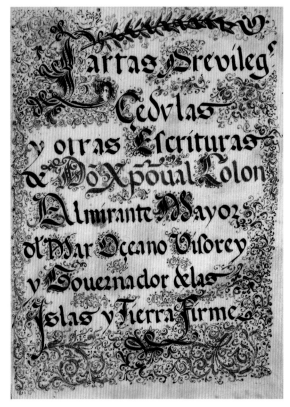

124 The title page of the *Book of Privileges* grants the permission of the Catholic King Ferdinand and Queen Isabella to Christopher Columbus. Columbus made this book for the purpose of combining all the privileges ceded him by his rulers in one volume. This is one of the copies that the admiral sent to Genoa (Galata Museo del Mare, Genoa, Italy).

125 On the first page of the *Book of Privileges*, the notary Martin Rodriguez certified that the documents contained in the book as presented by the admiral in his home in Seville on January 15, 1502, were authentic (Galata Museo del Mare, Genoa, Italy).

En la muy noble

E muy leal cibdad de Sevilla, miércoles ... días del mes de Enero (año del nascimiento de nuestro Salvador ihu xpo de mill e quinientos e dos años). En este dicho día e ora de bisperas de los poco mas o menos, estando en la posada del señor almirante de las yndias que es en esta dicha cibdad en la collaçion de Santa María, don Estevan de la Torre e xpoval ruys montero alcalldes ordinarios en esta dicha cibdad de Sevilla por el Rey e la Reyna nuestros señores. E en presençia de my martin rodrigue romano publico de esta dicha cibdad de Sevilla e de los testigos yuso escriptos que a ello fueron presentes, paresçio en ... presente el muy magnifico señor don xpoval colon, almirante mayor del mar oceano, viso rey e governador de las yslas e tierra firme. E presento ante los dichos alcalldes ciertas cartas e provisiones e cedulas de los dichos Rey e Reyna nuestros señores, escriptas en papel e pargamino e firmadas de sus Reales nombres. E selladas ... sellos de plomo pendientes en filos de seda de colores. E de cera colorada en las espaldas. E refrendadas de ciertos ofiçiales de su Real casa. Segund por ellas e por cada una de ellas paresçia. El thenor de las quales una en pos de otra es este que se sigue. —————— xxxx

El Rey e la Reyna

tierra de Soria lugar teniente de nuestro Almirante mayor de castilla. nos vos mandamos que le dedes e fagades dar. A don xpoval colon. nuestro Almirante de la mar oceano. Un traslado abtorizado en manera que faga fee. de quales quier cartas e mercedes e otras confirmaçiones/ El dicho almirante mayor de castilla tiene del dicho cargo e ofiçio de Almirante por donde el y otros por el lieve e cosen los derechos e otras cosas a ello perteneçientes a el dicho cargo. por que avemos fecho merced al dicho don xpoval colon que aya e goze de las mercedes e honrras e prerrogativas e libertades e derechos e salarios en el almirantadgo de las yndias que ha de tener e goze. segund nuestro Almirante mayor/ en el Almirantadgo de castilla. Lo qual faze e cunplid luego como fueredes requeridos con esta nuestra carta syn que en ello pongays escusa ny dilaçion alguna. E si asi no lo fizieredes ni cumplieredes. mandamos al nuestro Asistente e otras justiçias de la cibdad de Sevilla. que vos aprieten e apremie A lo asi fazer e cunplir. E non fagades ende al. fecha en la cibdad de burgos. a veynte e tres dias del mes de Abril de nobenta e seys años. yo el Rey. yo la Reyna. por mandado ...

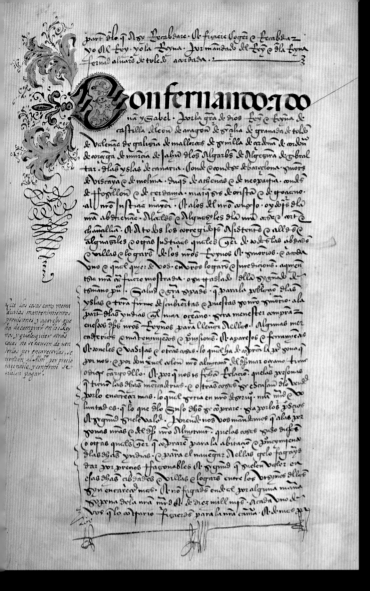

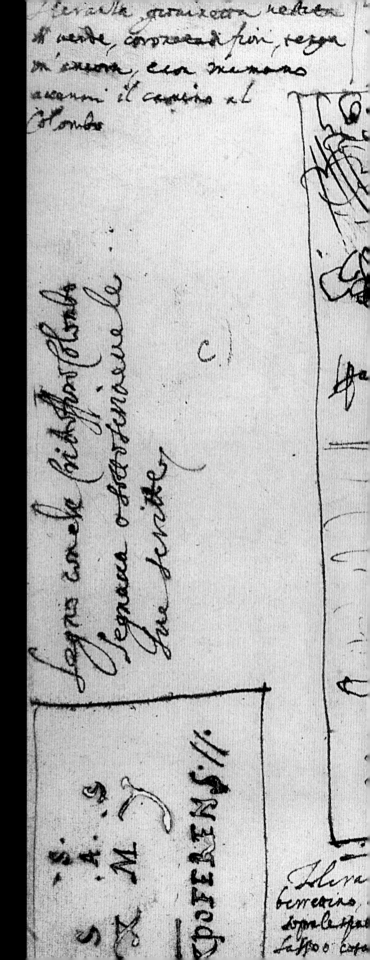

26 This page of Columbus' *Book of Privileges* bears the *Cédula de los Reyes* on April 23, 1497, decreeing that goods purchased by Columbus or other responsible person for delivery to the Indies, should not be marked up in price (Galata Museo del Mare, Genoa, Italy).

26-127 One further page was later added to the *Book of Privileges* where Lazaro Tavarone (1556-1641) made the ink drawing, *La Gloria di Colombo* (*The Glory of Columbus*). The figures represent Providence, Constancy and Tolerance, Justice, the Christian Religion, Victory, Reputation, and Hope. Columbus guides his ship and places his foot on the globe (Galata Museo del Mare, Genoa, Italy).

28 Pope Alexander VI's *Bolla Inter Cœtera* dated 3 May 1493 was transcribed into the *Book of Privileges*, deeding Columbus' explored lands to the Catholic king and queen (Galata Museo del Mare, Genoa, Italy).

29 The first pages of the *Book of Privileges* contained a list of letters, privileges, authorizations, and other text (Galata Museo del Mare, Genoa, Italy).

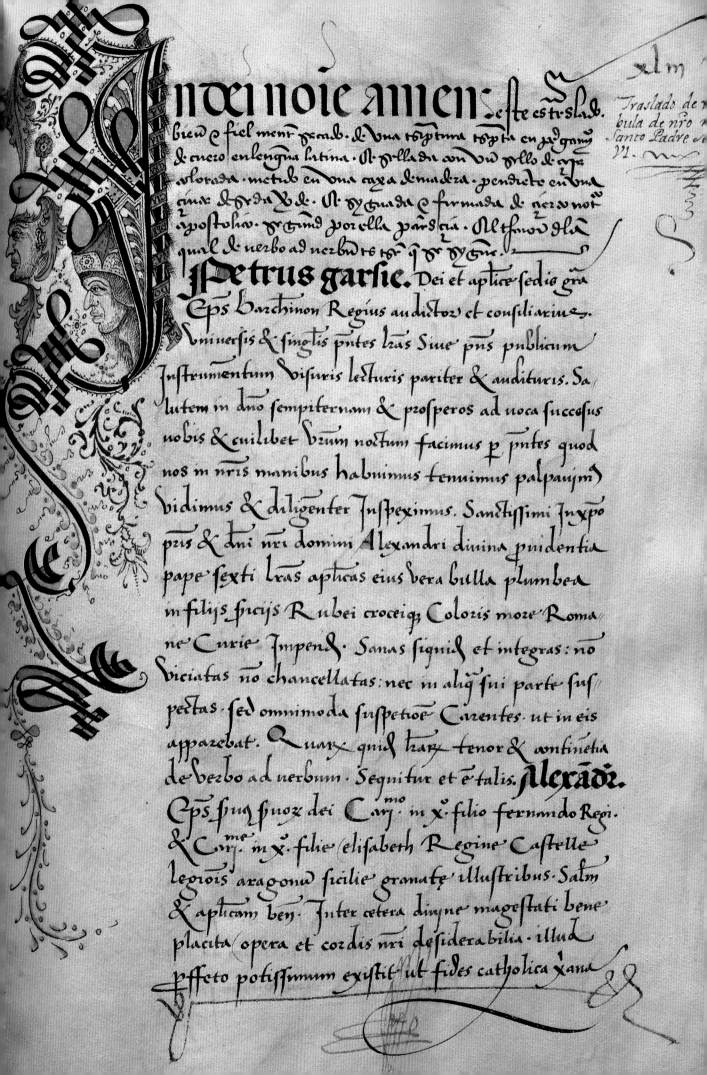

In dei noie amen: este es tr̄slad.
bien y fiel ment p̄cab. d̄ vna scriptura scrip̄ta en p̄gamino
d̄ cuero en lengua latina. Il sellada con vn sello d̄ cera
colorada metido en vna caxa d̄ madera pendiete en vna
cinta d̄ sed̄a V d̄. Il p̄guada y firmada d̄ cierto no̅
apostolico p̄ciend por ella p̄te su̅a. Il tenor d̄la̅
qual d̄ verbo ad verbu̅ es tr̄ q̄ d̄ p̄cie̅.

Petrus garsie. Dei et aptice sedis gr̄a
Ep̄s barchinon Regius auditor et consiliarius.
Vniuersis & singlis pntes lr̄as Siue pns publicum
Instrumentum Visuris lecturis pariter & audituris. Sa
lutem in d̄no sempiternam & prosperos ad voca successus
vobis & cuilibet v̄rum notum facimus p pntes quod
nos in n̄ris manibus habuimus tenuimus palpauim̄
Vidimus & diligenter Inspeximus. Sanctissimi Inxp̄o
prıs & d̄ni n̄ri domini Alexandri diuina pruidentia
pape sexti lr̄as apticas eius vera bulla plumbea
in filıjs scicıjs Rubei croceiq̄ Coloris more Roma
ne Curie Impend. Sanas siquid̄ et integras: no
viciatas no chancellatas: nec in aliq̄ sui parte sus
pectas. sed omnimoda suspetioe Carentes. ut in eis
apparebat. Quar q̄ quid trarz tenor & cōntinetia
de verbo ad verbum. Sequitur et e̅ talis. **Alexad̄z.**
Ep̄s ser̄ seruoz dei Car̄. in x̄. filio fernando Regi.
& Car̄. in x̄. filie elisabeth Regine Castelle
legiois aragonu̅ sicilie granatę illustribus. Salm
& aptıcam ben̄. Inter cetera digne magestati bene
placita opera et cordis n̄ri desiderabilia. illud
p̄ffeto potissimum existit ut fides catholica xana

Tabla delas cartas y prevjs y cedulas y otras escripturas q̃ ay en este libro

Primera carta de henrriqueso al almjrantadgo mayor de castj — fo i

Segunda carta de prevj del almj delas yndias cõ firmacion delo capitulaçio prim̃o cõ prevj alõso — fo viij

Tercera carta de prevj cõfirmacion al d̃ho almj Rodriguez naçion delas dhas yndias — fo x

cedula de m̃rd q̃ por qr̃ anos q̃ se aj pmero al ochauo q̃l diezmo del pvecho delas yndias — fo xv

carta q̃l almj pueda nõbrar una pona q̃ entieda enla negoçiaçio delas yndias jũtamiente cõ los qestã por s.a — fo xv

cedula de ynstrug̃o delas cosas q̃ pr̃ due p̃ a castjlla vja — fo xvi

carta q̃ las cosas q̃ pr̃ cõpraren para las yndias seles venda a prios rrazonables — fo xviij

cedula de memorial delas cosas q̃ pr̃ due llevar a las yndias — fo xviij

carta de ttesorero delo h̃e q̃ se a de dar a cr̃o para pr̃ de sancho lopz en qujen es encarno del almj — fo xx

carta p̃ a los arr̃os valmoxs q̃ no lleue d̃jo de la carga y descarga q̃ p̃ a las yndias — fo xxij

carta p̃ a los dezmo exportadgo e pote a los q̃ no lleuẽ d̃jo — fo xviij

carta de prevj grande a los del suprimeto q̃ fuere asjst̃e ala ysla — fo xxiij

carta p̃ a las justiçias q̃l destierre p̃ a la ysla españ̃ola — fo xxvi

cedula p̃ a el asiet̃ el q̃ e de prevj q̃ enuje los p̃sos al almj — fo xxvij

cedula p̃ a q̃ pueda tomar e flectar nauios — fo xxviij

cedula de q̃ re el de catjros de p̃ a p̃ a las yndias — fo xxviij

cedula p̃ a q̃l reçeu de del almj de castilla q̃ de q̃ pasado el prevj del almirantadgo al almj delas yndias — fo xxix

licencia al almj p̃ a tomar a sueldo çierta gente — fo xxix

cedula de librança del d̃hos sueldo cõ l̃ ttesor delas yndias — fo xxix

cedula q̃ haga pagar al almj lo q̃le due algunos pes̃nas — fo xxx

licençia para tomar a sueldo mas gente sj el almj q̃siere — fo xxx

carta de facultad al almj p̃ a dar y rrepartir tr̃ras a los q̃s — fo xxx

carta de m̃rd delas teras delas yndias de d̃ berrto colõ e colõ — fo xxxj

carta para q̃l almirant̃ pague la gent̃ q̃ tomare a sueldo p̃ a q̃ se anerse ẽ las yndias — fo xxxij

SERICA

serici montes

c de luna
R de finos

manaua
oaque como
bunaça

ASIA

tena baxa

p de confida

c della serpe
canal
c sammbaru

bile teragnia belporto
p gora
b
omgra retree
p de iustimentos

iammicha
caricura
bominica canibali
spagnota
guadelupa

C S viceric
SPAGNIA

o caria
canaria
c di cantin
c bosador

L CANCRI

c broncho popoli
Agena gi
c verde senegu
ganbria

c de palmas

boca dildragon
ofirs de canibali
CANKHIETE
CVRIANA
PARIA
mar de agua
dolce
Ins dle
verde

golfo formoso
s croce

L Equinochialis

MONDO NOVO

130 THIS SIGNED SKETCH BY BARTOLOMEO COLUMBUS EXPRESSES THE CONTOURS OF THE
COASTS EXPLORED DURING COLUMBUS' FOURTH VOYAGE (BIBLIOTECA NAZIONALE, FLO-
RENCE, ITALY).

131 FERNANDO COLUMBUS WROTE THE *HISTORY* OF HIS FATHER'S LIFE THAT WAS PUBLISHED
AND TRANSLATED INTO ITALIAN IN VENICE IN 1571 AFTER THE DEATH OF ITS AUTHOR. THE IM-

HISTORIE

Del S. D. Fernando Colombo;

Nelle quali s'ha particolare, & vera relatione della vita, & de' fatti dell'Ammiraglio

D. CHRISTOFORO COLOMBO,

suo padre :

Et dello scoprimento, ch'egli fece dell'INDIE Occidentali, dette MONDO NVOVO, hora possedute dal Serenifs. Re Catolico :

Nuouamente di lingua Spagnuola tradotte nell'Italiana. dal S. Alfonso Ulloa .

CON PRIVILEGIO.

IN VENETIA, MDLXXI.

Appresso Francesco de' Franceschi Sanese .

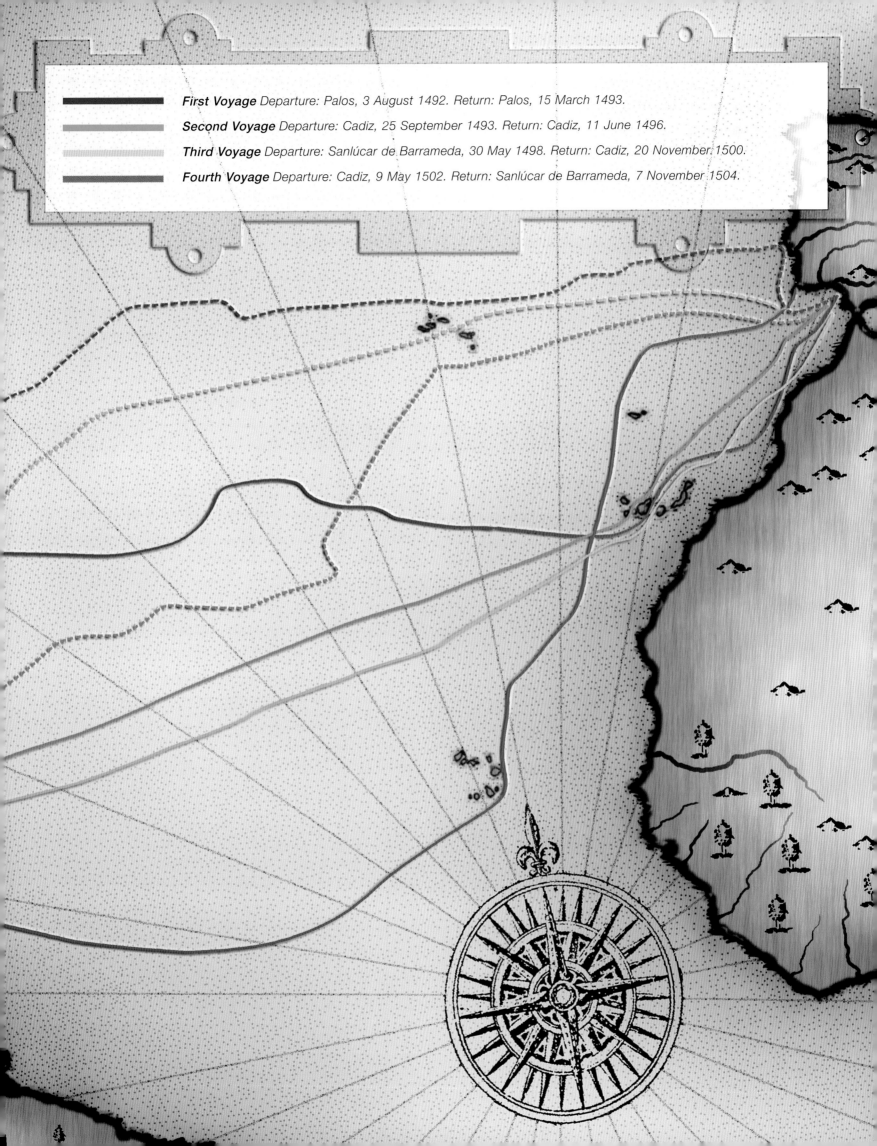

134 On two occasions, in 1494 in Hispaniola and in 1504 in Jamaica, Columbus witnessed an eclipse and on both occasions, attempted to measure its distance from Spain, but made errors in his calculations. The computation of longitude was not accomplished until the late18th century (Museo del Templo Mayor, Mexico City, Mexico).

135 Among the books that Columbus brought on his voyages were Abraham Zacut's *Almanach Perpetuum* and Regiomontanus' *Calendar* that he used to measure the longitude separating him from Europe while observing a lunar eclipse (Biblioteca Nazionale Marciana, Venice, Italy).

A SAILOR'S INTUITION

In addition to being a skilled sailor, which is one thing, Columbus also enjoyed a great measure of a sailor's intuition. His overall fame as a consummate navigator was not up for discussion, though his adversaries never failed to point out (regardless of those who subsequently assumed the responsibility) that he had lost his flagship during his first voyage and all four ships on his fleet on his fourth.

Columbus often displayed his nautical knowledge before Ferdinand and Isabella. In a typical display, Columbus told a tall tale that was probably true. It was 1497 and the court was at Burgos expecting the arrival of the adolescent Margaret of Austria, who was to marry their Catholic Majesties' son, the Infante Don John (who unfortunately died at age 19 on October 4th of that year same year). Bad weather and seemingly endless snowstorms convinced the royal advisers to move the court to Soria, anticipating the young bride's delay. No sooner said than done: the move began, sums of money were sent ahead, and it was agreed that the monarchs would depart a couple of days later to allow for completion of preparations for their arrival. Ferdinand and Isabella, worried that fate might have a hand in shipwrecking the princess's ship, asked the admiral to draft an urgent report with his impressions of conditions at sea. Late into the night, Columbus delivered the requested memorandum, which was so clear-cut and well documented that not only did it pacify the monarchs but even motivated them to "forgo the move to Soria, following the advice of the sailor." The admiral had triumphed, and two days later the child princess safely

1479	1479	1480
Eclipſis del Sole	Eclipſis de la Luna	Eclipſis de la Luna
12 23 47	28 12 ſo	21 21 40
Decembrio	Decembrio	Zugno
Meça duration	Meça duration	Meça duration
1 2	1 44	1 31
Puncti ſette		Puncti octo

1481	1482	1482
Eclipſis del Sole	Eclipſis del Sole	Eclipſis de la Luna
28 6 23	17 7 42	26 5 57
Maço	Maço	Octobrio
Meça duration	Meça duration	Meça duration
0 43	0 ſſ	1 39
Puncti tre	Puncti cinque	Puncti undecim

reached Laredo, accompanied by her entire retinue.

Columbus dedicated the summer of 1494 to skirting the coast of the isle of Cuba, that he then believed to be terra firma. On September 14, his ships still remained off Saona Island, off the southeast coast of Santo Domingo. There was a lunar eclipse that night. The admiral immediately consulted the Regiomontanus' *Calendar*, which indicated the time when the phenomenon could be observed in Lisbon. Considering that it would be visible in Saona five and a half hours later, Columbus made his calculations. The Saona-Lisbon longitude (or that of Cape St Vincent) was 82° 30'. Despite Columbus' erroneous calculations, given that the difference between the two points was not greater than 60°, he was nonetheless undoubtedly the first navigator to make an effort at measuring longitude, a feat that no one would accomplish until more than 250 years later.

In 1504, Columbus stayed in Jamaica, where the fleet had been shipwrecked. It was a horrible sojourn. There was an attempted mutiny that Bartolomeo Columbus had to suppress. Initially friendly, the Indies people quite quickly stopped supplying Columbus and his men with food. The situation became increasingly unbearable. Months passed and although everyone thought they would, Diego Mendez and Bartolomeo Fieschi were not able to arrange their rescue from Jamaica, and Columbus' men never reached Hispaniola, their intended destination. The natives then realized they had an opportunity to put an end to the Spanish occupation and decided to go to the admiral's tent with the intent of murdering him. Impassive, Columbus came out to receive them and made his threats. "My God will obscure the moon and a terrible catastrophe will fall upon your heads. Only when you repent, will I pray that He wipe away your sin." At first, they did not believe him however, once they saw the conveniently predicted eclipse, they all began to tremble. Columbus immediately appeared in front of them as they wept and pleaded with him, announcing that his God had pardoned them. It was obviously a great relief to everyone involved.

Columbus did not have the gift of prophecy. As on all his voyages, among other books, he brought along copies of Abraham Zacut's *Almanach Perpetuum* and the astronomy text, *Ephemeris*, by Regiomontanus. Both informed him that on 28 February 1504, there would be an eclipse of the moon. Thus, as he had done in 1494 when a similar eclipse was observed in Hispaniola, he immediately began calculating the distance that separated him from the Spanish Peninsula. On this occasion, he discovered that the difference between Cadiz and Jamaica was 108°15'. He made an error in calculation, as he made years before, increasing the difference of 39°. Was it the admiral's inability to make good calculations or the fault of inadequate instruments? We will give him the benefit of the doubt. As much as he was an expert sailor, and he definitely was, available tools in that era did not allow him to make the most exact measurements to adequately complete his calculations.

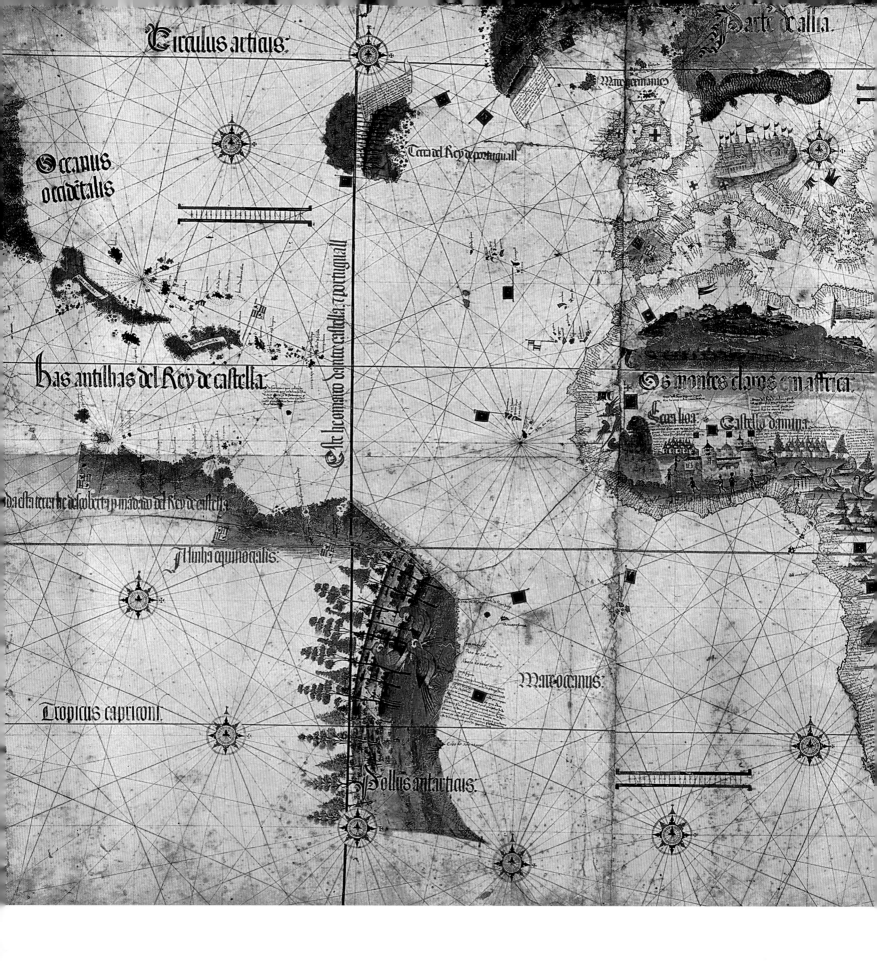

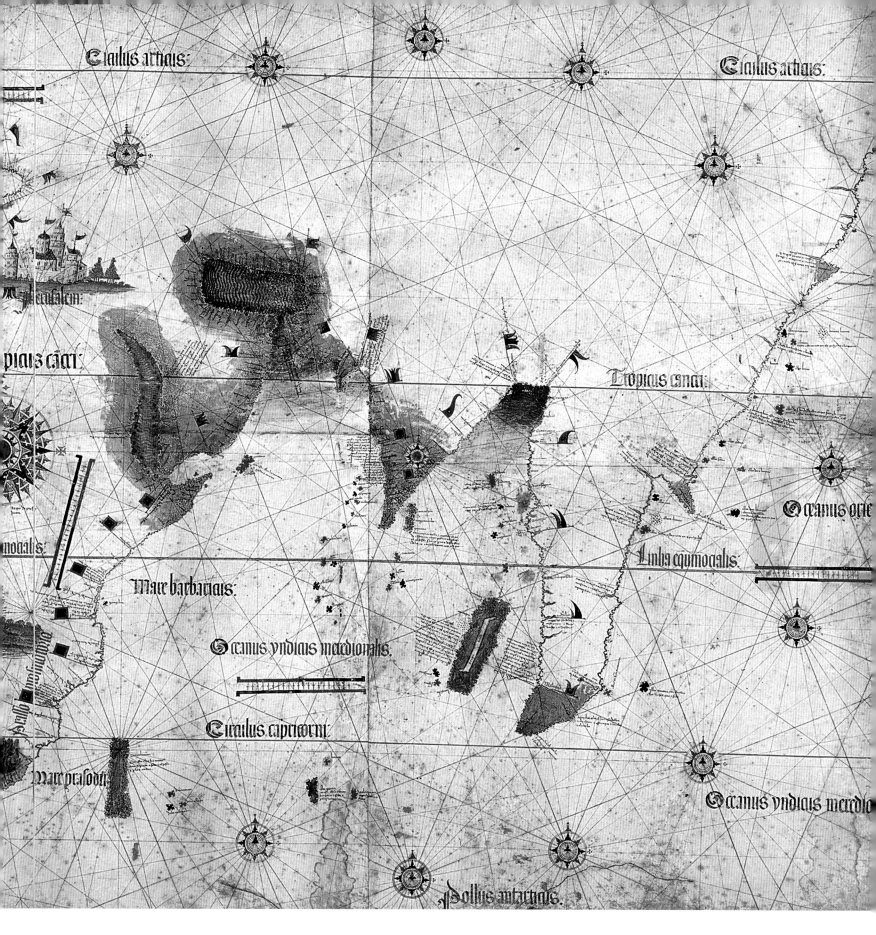

Circulus arcticus: Circulus arcticus:

Ierusalem:

pictis captis

Tropicus cancri

mortalis

Oceanus orie

Linba equinoctialis

Mare barbaricis:

Oceanus yndicus meridionalis.

Oceanus yndicus meridio

Circulus capricorni

Mare prasodu

Pollus antarcticus.

136-137 Later named for him, this Portuguese map was brought to Italy by Alberto Cantino in 1502. It demonstrated Portuguese progress and ignored the Italian John Cabot's exploration on behalf of England (Biblioteca Estense, Modena, Italy).

138-139 Due to this map representing both the New and Old Worlds incorporating both Vespucci and Ptolemy at the top, Columbus lost the honor of bestowing his name on the continent that he had been the first to reach (Museo of America, Madrid, Spain).

140-141 SHOWING THE COASTS AND IS-LANDS OF THE NEW WORLD, THIS MAP WAS PUBLISHED IN THE FOURTH VOLUME OF THE MONUMENTAL WORK, *AMERICA*, BY THEODOR DE BRY (KUNSTBIBLIOTHEK STAATLICHE MUSEEN, BERLIN, GERMANY).

142-143 ORTELIUS WAS THE FIRST CAR-TOGRAPHER TO CONCEIVE OF THE IDEA FOR CONVERTING A GROUP OF MAPS INTO AN AT-LAS. BASED ON THE NEWS RECEIVED IN HIS CITY OF ANTWERP, HE GRADUALLY IN-CREASED HIS COLLECTION. WHILE THE FIRST 1570 EDITION INCLUDED 53 MAPS, THE 1603 EDITION WAS PUBLISHED AFTER HIS DEATH, MERGING 119 MAPS IN ONE VOLUME (UNIVERSITY LIBRARY, SALAMANCA, SPAIN).

144-145 IN THIS PORTOLAN CHART (PILOT BOOK) CREATED BY THE MALLORCAN CAR-TOGRAPHER, JOAN MARTINES, AT THE END OF THE 16TH CENTURY, THE COASTLINES OF THE AMERICAN CONTINENT ARE WELL DE-FINED (PRIVATE COLLECTION).

THE VICEROY
chapter 3

149 THIS PANEL IS CONSIDERED THE OLDEST PRESERVED PORTRAIT OF COLUMBUS. THE ADMIRAL, WHO IS WEARING EXPENSIVE CLOTHING CONSISTENT WITH HIS ROLE AS VICEROY, WAS PRESENTED TO THE MADONNA OF ST CHRISTOPHER IN FRONT OF THE CATHEDRAL OF SANTO DOMINGO (LAZARO GALDEANO FOUNDATION MUSEUM, MADRID, SPAIN).

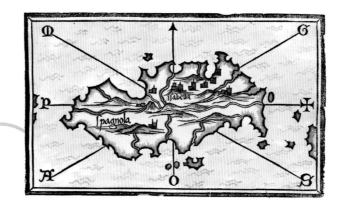

THE NAVIDAD DISASTER

On November 3, 1493 the second fleet transporting the first men, colonizing lands that had been explored for barely one year, arrived in the New World. Everything had been thoroughly prepared in advance. Commanded by Antonio de Torres, twelve of the seventeen ships in the convoy had to return to Spain once Columbus had determined the site for building their new city. Upon returning with good news, Torres' job was to captain the future supply fleets that would be sent to the Indies in response to advance requests from Columbus. Appointed administrator by their Catholic Majesties in Seville, Juan Rodriguez de Fonseca would take care of responding to the necessities of the growing colony. Columbus was faced with a new and unfamiliar challenge. He had to organize the settlement and select authorities to take his place during his absence due to either exploration of Hispaniola's interior or to the execution of new voyages using the five ships that remained anchored off the northern coast of the island.

Horror seized the explorers when they arrived in Hispaniola and found the corpses of the 39 men that Columbus had previously left at Fort Navidad. There was even a baby among them, perhaps the first mixed-race child born in the New World. In vain, Columbus' men searched the pit where theoretically, the Navidad contingent had kept any gold found on the island as per the admiral's orders. Cacique Guarionex, Columbus' friend, did not even appear to welcome them. Some of the natives justified his absence by saying that he was gravely ill. In order to uncover the truth, Columbus decided to send Diego Alvarez Chanca, the doctor that accompanied him. No one else but he could evaluate the seriousness of the cacique's illness. Chanca returned with the news that the cacique had a broken arm and he had immobilized it. A few days later, Guarionex recovered and Columbus had his first meeting with him.

The cacique told Columbus that the Spanish had devoted themselves to stealing and dishonoring the women there, and the natives had no other choice than to react. In his own defense, Guarionex also firmly asserted that it wasn't his people who had attacked the Spanish but rather people under another cacique with whom he was in disagreement. By punishing him, Columbus committed his first mistake as governor. Guarionex had been given not only the responsibility of feeding the Spanish, but also of defending them against any aggressive behavior. This was a demonstration of weakness on the part of the admiral, which the new arrivals didn't at all understand. Everyone must have been demoralized in comprehending the scope of the disaster that had happened at Fort Navidad. Because they were poor native people who were unarmed, how could they have so quickly eliminated within one year's time the 39 Spanish men that Columbus had left on the island, particularly as the Spanish had been well stocked with ammunition? What responsibility did Guarionex have, this cacique whom Columbus had trusted? These were difficult questions and answers that Columbus quickly resolved with his unique way of reacting. The Christians had dug their own graves not just by disobeying his orders, but also by violating the native people. Guarionex could not have defended them against the attack of Cacique Caonabo.

150 This map of Spain was sketched by the hermit, Benedetto Bordone, and dates to 1528. Compared with the sketch of the northeastern coast of the island executed by Columbus during his period of discovery, found then published in relatively recent times, this contour drawing of the island proves not to be very realistic (Biblioteca Nazionale Marciana, Venice, Italy).

151 This image was enclosed with the letter announcing Columbus' discoveries (1493), showing unfinished construction of buildings. The first city in the New World was founded in January 1494.

COLUMBIAN FOUNDATIONS

Everyone hastily searched for an adequate place to found a city. The 1200 men that made up the expedition had lived on ships for too long. Quite close to Navidad, on a bay that seemed suitable to everyone, Columbus decided to found the first European city in the New World: he chose to call it Isabella in honor of the Catholic queen.

The city had an ephemeral life. Site selection was an error in judgment caused by the rush and could never be considered a thoughtful solution. Was what Michele da Cuneo and Guillermo Coma said "not true," as in their opinion, Isabella was a splendid city with beautiful stone buildings? First of all, there was no stone available for construction, and secondly, during the six months the men remained on the island, there certainly were not enough workers to erect such magnificence in so short a time. Isabella suffered every kind of disaster, including a fire and hurricane that predicted its eventual abandonment. Ready to return to Castile, Columbus decided in 1496 to found a replacement city and he asked his brother Bartolomeo to find an appropriate new site. The proximity of the Cibao mines and the lands of the cacique Caonabo's queen, Anacaona, who had a relationship with Bartolomeo at the time, probably motivated the latter to choose the left bank of the Ozama River, in the southern part of the island, as the site for the new city. By 1500, the new city of Santo Domingo was already bustling with activity and Isabella was abandoned, becoming a pastureland for pigs and hunting grounds for the colonists. But Bartolomeo also erred in site selection as demonstrated by the fact that in 1502 the governor, Nicolas de Ovando, moved the city to the opposite bank of the Ozama River. The site is extant today, as a preserved monument.

In order to control the native population, Columbus had no fewer than seven fortresses constructed on the territories under the control of the caciques. The first was Santo Tomas near the Janico River where he left Pedro Margarite in command, with the task of building a fort to hold 25 men permanently. Diligent carpenters and masons followed the Catalan's orders and succeeded in constructing the fort in record time given that, as Columbus wrote to Ferdinand and Isabella, by April 1494 they had already dug a trench 18 ft (5.8 m) wide and 20 ft (6 m) deep that surrounded the fortress, which held diverse houses including a covered boardwalk through which they could reach the river. In the territory dominated by cacique Guarionex, 9 leagues (27 miles/43.4 km) from Santo Tomas, halfway from Isabella, and 3 or 4 leagues (9 or 12 miles; 14 or 19 km) from the gold mines, the viceroy ordered the construction of La Concepción (subsequently named St Christopher) in 1495, for which the initial command fell to Juan de Ayala and then to Miguel Ballester. A short time later, Magdalena was built at Vega Real in order to control the flow of the Yaqui River, whose command was entrusted to Luis de Arriaga and subsequently to Diego de Escobar. The construction of the fortresses of Santa Caterina, commanded by Fernando Navarro, La Esperanza on the Yaqui River on the Cibao side, and a last one in the province of Bonao on the Yuna River soon followed, remaining nameless (it isn't documented anywhere).

Among all the fortresses, La Concepción was the one preferred by Columbus. Situated in the interior of the island in a dry, healthy place, it combined the optimal conditions for alleviating his rheumatic pains. Columbus liked this place so much that he stayed there on May 21, 1499, writing a letter to its commander, ordering him to mark the boundaries of the best land that he himself would indicate, so that he could have a house built for his son, Diego who, Columbus thought,

was eager to reach Hispaniola. We do not know whether Don Diego succeeded in having his house constructed there.

In view of the position of the forts from north to south, from Isabella to the mouth of the Ozama River, where years later the city of Santo Domingo would rise, we can clearly understand the old admiral's intentions for colonizing this land, despite what has been said thus far, as it does not at all resemble the Portuguese model that positioned fortifications on the coasts. In fact, from April or May 1494, Columbus gradually moved toward the island's interior with the clear aim of controlling that territory. With every fort, each progressively nearer a river, he ordered that the structures be built to accommodate and maintain a permanent guard station.

As pointed out by Columbus in a letter to Ferdinand and Isabella in 1495, the construction of so many strategically situated fortresses demoralized the native population that, observing the Spanish building more forts than boats, realized their desire to remain permanently on the island. Columbus was definitely central to ordering the construction of these fortresses that served to dominate Hispaniola.

154 This letter dated 23 April 1497 was addressed to Columbus by Ferdinand and Isabella to communicate their instructions for the foundation of settlements in the newly discovered lands during his voyages to the Indies (General Archive of the Indies, Seville, Spain).

155 Theodor de Bry recreated traditional pearl fishing on Margarita Island, explored by Columbus during his third voyage to the New World, to illustrate Girolamo Benzoni's book on America (State Library, Augsburg, Germany).

Ls Columbus den dritten Zug in Indiam gethan/ ist er
an dem Meerschoß Para angefahren/ vnd in der Insel Cubagua angelen=
det/ welche er die Perlin Insel genennet hat/ auß den vrsachen/ denn als er
für diesem Meerschoß war hinaußgefahren mit seinen Schiffen/ hat er ge=
sehen etliche Indianer/ die fischeten Meerschnecken auß iren kleinen Schiff=
lein/ welche die Spanier vermeynten sie pflegeten sie zu essen/ als sie aber
dieselbe auffthaten/ stacken sie gantz voller Perlin/ darauß sie ein grosse Frewd empfiengen.
Wie sie zum Gestaden kommen/ seynd sie außgestiegen auff das Landt/ da sahen sie an den
Indianischen Weibern vber die massen schöne Perlin/ die sie am Halß vnd Armen trugen/
solche Perlin bekamen die Spanier von ihnen/ vnd gaben inen geringe vnachtsame Waar
dargegen. 2. Cap.

DIFFICULT BEGINNINGS

Upon his return to Spain in February 1494, Antonio de Torres brought alarming news. The second voyage to the New World had started off on the wrong foot. In addition to the disaster at Fort Navidad, the last new to arrive confirmed the scarcity of gold and spices and that, for the most part, sickness had started to wipe out the colonists. The *Memorandum* that the admiral sent with Torres to Their Catholic Majesties could not have been more explicit in that it expressed the colonists' shortages of everything, including medicines and food. However, despite that, all the men were working without break and Columbus did not hesitate to request an increase in stipends or compensation for them as they were doing a great job, including Pedro Margarite and Dr. Chanca. The latter added his complaints about the colonists' lack of funds, which prevented him from receiving any extra salary from his sick patients. Besides requesting the consignment of any foodstuffs for the colonists, Columbus insisted on satisfying the needs of Brother Buil and his fellow monks. Another serious problem, also outlined in his *Memorandum*, regarded the more than 200 people who had arrived without any salary and who understandably could not provide for their own needs.

The colonial venture had been established in the Indies for scarcely three months and many of these problems had apparently already begun – and had become worse over time. To begin with, the colonists' voyage proved longer than expected because they hadn't sailed directly from Spain to Hispaniola, but had stopped first at the island of Guadalupe, then at Montserrat, finally arriving at the first settlement site at Fort Navidad, having endured headwinds that had created further delay. Before they had even begun to settle, the men were exhausted and the livestock was dying.

The colonists quickly realized that their wine and much of their food had gone bad during their journey, and that their horses, brought along for farming support, weren't as robust as they had been told at the time of embarkation in Seville. Once the colonists set foot on Hispaniola, everything was revealed for what it was. Apparently, many people had been enlisted as artisans in a craft in which they were unskilled, and Columbus complained about all of this in his letters to the monarchs. There were carpenters that did not know how to use a handsaw and miners that were incapable of distinguishing gold from a base metal. In any case, he had to admit everyone's disappointment as Hispaniola was not at all what they had expected.

Not long after the departure of de Torres' fleet, Columbus had a first disagreement with his men when the accountant, Bernal de Pisa, wishing to return to Castile along with a group of dissatisfied colonists, tried to take one or more of the ships that were still docked and waiting at the port, ready to set sail. It seemed that the accountant had taken a written report against the admiral and had hidden it not very carefully inside a buoy where it was easily found. Subjected to appropriate legal procedure, Bernal de Pisa was sent to Spain and his accomplices were punished as well. To justify his actions to Ferdinand and Isabella, Columbus sent them a letter on October 14, 1495, accusing Bernal de Pisa of corruption. According to its content, Bernal had entrusted the other men with roles for which they were not prepared, whether in stealing or preventing the colony from prospering.

Insula Iamaica

Franciscus Poraz.

Chrystophorus Columbus

14

ALs Columbus die vierdte Schiffahrt in Hispaniolam für
genommen/ hat Bombadilla jhm die Anlendung deß Meerhafens verbot=
ten/ ist also in der Insel Iamaica angefahren. Daselbst hat Franciscus Pore=
sius ein Oberster vber ein Carauel mit sampt seinem Bruder vnd einem gros=
sen theil Kriegsleuten ein Auffruhr erregt wider Columbum/ vñ mit etlichen
kleinen Schifflein der Indianer die Flucht in die Insel Hispaniolam genommen/ Als er aber
mit den geringen Schifflein nicht kondte durch das vngestümme Meer kommen/ ist er wider
vmbgekehrt. Als baldt Columbus deß Poresij zukunfft höret/ hat er mit sampt seinem Bru=
der ein Schlachtordnung wider in gestelt/ vnd als es zum Treffen kommen/ wurden viel er=
schlagen/ vnd viel auff beyden Seiten verwundet/ vnnd ward Franciscus Poresius vnnd sein
Bruder gefangen. 14. Cap.

One month later, it was Brother Buil who opposed the admiral, confronting him with "the punishment that you inflict upon men and restrictions you impose on their share of food [...] or the fact that you don't give me and my domestic staff more provisions, as had previously been requested, is unacceptable." The viceroy's reaction was unexpected. He immediately ordered that the rations destined for the monks be reduced even further due to their refusal to continue administering the sacraments. We don't know anything about the letter that Brother Buil sent with de Torres to the monarchs; however we have their response on 16 August 1494, Ferdinand and Isabella thanked him for his commitment and were happy with the news he had provided them (which suggests that he was not yet in conflict with the admiral), and ask that he remain on the island despite a lack of interpreters to help convert the natives. We can infer that this was the definitive reason the monk adopted to allow his return to Spain. The king and queen categorically refused their authorization for his return unless he had a health problem, in which case he would have to appoint another monk to take his place. Obviously, Brother Buil suddenly became ill and returned just as soon as was possible.

Things were not even going well at the interior of the island. Mosen Pedro Margarite didn't know how to manage the situation at Fort Santo Tomas and, perhaps unaware of the admiral's wishes as confirmed by Fernando Columbus, instead of pacifying the Cibao zone as was recommended, he moved to Isabella by dint of heavenly command. We are unaware of the reasons why these people were hostile to Columbus, and only know that on 29 September 1494, taking advantage of the ships that had carried Bartolomeo Columbus to the Indies, he returned to Spain with the same fleet that returned Brother Buil and his three fellow monks.

According to Las Casas, the desertion of Margarite that left the 400 armada men alone at the fort, was one of the contributing causes to the colonists' demoralization and eventual abandonment of the island that, captain-less and free to do as they pleased, assaulted nearby villagers, committing every type of abuse. It is possible that Las Casas had reason, given that even Fernando Columbus made reference to the fact that the soldiers began not just to rob the indigents of their property, but also to abuse their women, "committing such horrors that the natives dared to vindicate themselves with whomever they found alone or without a captain." As he was on a reconnaissance voyage to Cuba and Jamaica when they set sail, Columbus could do nothing *in absentia* to prevent Buil and Margarite from leaving.

Fernandez de Oviedo left us another version of these conflicts. According to this chronicler, the disputes between Buil and Columbus began after the death sentence Columbus handed down to an Aragon man, Gaspar Ferriz. Such a horrible occurrence antagonized both Buil and Margarite who decided to join forces and confront Columbus to convince him they should return to Castile. Always well-disposed toward Columbus, Las Casas categorically confirmed that the admiral did not condemn anyone to be hanged and that Gaspar did not appear on the list of the condemned that he saw years later. Who are the condemned to whom he referred?

We don't know anything about the version of this event that Buil presented to the royal court, though we can assume that the envious monk complained about the admiral's behavior, which then motivated the king and queen to send some person

of authority to verify *in situ* the truth about the complaints they had received. A few months after the departure of Brother Buil and Margarite, Columbus went to Isabella after having made a long voyage to Cuba and Jamaica. He was quite sick. Food shortages and exhaustion had given him "a very serious illness with noxious fever and drowsiness that almost deprived him of sight, of his other senses, and his mind" notes Fernando Columbus in his *History*. His brothers, Don Diego and Don Bartolomeo, found him in this perhaps unconscious state when arriving on the island on 24 June 1494. Bartolomeo and Christopher had not seen each other in years so their encounter must have been quite emotional.

Once cured of his illness, Columbus dedicated himself to placating any potential deserters. An opportunity presented itself when in the following year on 24 February 1495, Antonio de Torres returned to Castile for the second time with a cargo of five hundred slaves destined for Archdeacon Fonseca of Seville (the crown's administrator of the second voyage), accompanied by his brother Diego, who was sent to deliver letters to the monarchs with Columbus' own complaints and explanations. Among these was a very long one that closed in accusing the Spanish, whether secular or religious, of being empty-handed people who came to the Indies with the sole intention of enriching themselves "with no hard work or dedication," rolling dice, lazy, having low morals, and being blinded by avarice. This was the same version that he gave to his friend, Peter Martyr d'Angheria, in Granada in 1500 and that the humanist did not hesitate to include in the fourth chapter of his first *Decades*, directed at Cardinal Luis de Aragon: "[Columbus] said that the Spanish men he brought with him had a higher propensity for sleep and laziness than work, and were more in favor of rebellion and the latest novelty than peace and quiet."

To justify himself, Columbus did not think twice about ordering the royal messenger, Sebastian de Olano, to write a letter, reassuring the monarchs that at no time had he prevented the Spanish colonists from fulfilling their roles and that every aspect of the colony's accounting was accurate and duly noted in its books in a timely manner.

The exchange of letters and contradictory information that had arrived in Spain obligated the Ferdinand and Isabella to intervene and in October 1495, they decided to send Juan Aguado to Hispaniola as an investigating judge. The judge had received precise instructions. He would have to verify the distribution of provisions, verify the validity of complaints that had come before the royal court, and authorize the return of some of the people who had complained about the admiral.

Delayed for more than five months awaiting receipt of his letters of authority, Aguado finally arrived in Hispaniola. He then surprised Columbus in the interior of the island while he was fighting in the Maguana against the brothers of cacique Caonabo. Heading directly to the area, Aguado scattered seeds of hope here and there that a new admiral would take the place of the tyrant. . . . Neither the happiness of the natives nor that of the Spanish lasted very long. With his enigmatic words, Aguado succeeded in further increasing the separation between the admiral's supporters and his opponents. Sources do not clarify Aguado's process, even when they lead us to believe that the judge, who looked down on Bartolomeo Columbus, confined himself to threatening theadmiral with a potentially unfavorable report that he might deliver to Ferdinand and Isabella, which might conceal the facts about the admiral's enemies.

Columbus announced his desire to return to Castile to deliver his own account of the situation. The explanation left by the chronicler Fernandez de Oviedo tells us otherwise, stating that Columbus returned by order of Aguado and that from then on, he grew a beard and dressed in the humble clothing of the Franciscan order. In his *History*, Fernando Columbus did not want to tell about this unpleasant episode in his father's life and limited himself to writing that Columbus, after reestablishing peace on the island, decided to return to Castile to give the monarchs an account of certain things that he deemed ap-

Olumbus von wegen daß er in ein Kranckheit gefallen / vnd alſo den Zug wider die Caraber muſte vnterwegen laſſen / iſt wider zu rück in Hiſpaniolam gefahren / da hat er ein groſſe Vnruhe darinn funden / von wegen der ſchendliche vngebürlichen Laſter / ſo die Spanier in ſeinem abweſen begangen. Er aber hat nach ſeiner Weißheit vnd Verſtande baldt einen Raht funden ſolchem Vnraht zubegegnen / vnnd alle die jenige Spanier ſo an dieſer Auffruhr / Vrſächer vnd Rädlinführer geweſen / ſampt den jenigen / ſo theilhafftig an den begangenen Laſtern / laſſen vmbbringen vnd hinrichten / die Cacicos aber hat er auff alle weg vnd mittel vnderſtanden zu Frieden zubringen / Durch dieſe Strengheit haben die Spanier ein groſſen Neidt vnnd Haſſz auff den Columbum geworffen / alſo daß ſie ſchier ſeinen Namen nicht mehr mochten hören nennen / vnnd auch ein Münch Benedicter Ordens den Columbum in Bann gethan: Dargegen Columbus gebotten / es ſolte den Mönchen auß ſeiner Speißkammer nichts dargereicht werden. Auß dieſen vrſachen iſt entſprungen / daß viel vnter ihnen falſche vnd vnehrliche Stück von ihm vnnd ſeinem Bruder an den König in Spanien geſchrieben: Derwegen Columbus als er wider zur Gſundheit kommen / wider zurück in Hiſpanien hat ſchiffen müſſen. 9. Cap.

C ij   Ein

propriate to clarify, "especially because of the many malicious and sarcastic people who, motivated by envy, did not stop bad-mouthing the Indies venture to the monarchs with great discredit and dishonor toward the admiral and his brothers." Like Fernando, Columbus didn't even lower himself to the level of documenting Aguado and his investigation.

Columbus and Aguado, who remained on the island only five months, returned to Spain together, reaching Cadiz on 11 June 1496. We do not know anything about the report that Aguado presented to the monarchs and the arguments that Columbus put forward in his own defense. We only know that, two years later, the admiral returned to Hispaniola.

In February 1496, Columbus appointed his brother, Bartolomeo, governor of the Indies. It was a job that gave him absolute military power. Columbus then left peacefully for Spain knowing that the island's government was in good hands. In spite of that, upon returning to Hispaniola on 31 August 1498, he received a very different welcome than he'd expected. His brother's government was a failure. Even if partially pacified, the natives were cruelly exploited, the Spanish were discontent, and the city of Isabella had been abandoned and the new city of Santo Domingo founded, with all of the problems that this event involved. Syphilis had stricken 30 percent of the population and the first colonial rebellion of the Spanish had added to all these problems.

A group of rebels under the command of Francisco Roldan, who had been appointed by Columbus as administrator and high judge of Isabella, wanted to introduce a new government on Hispaniola. A good number of crew members from an incoming Castilian fleet joined him, having mistakenly docked at Xaragua, a place south of the island where the rebels had set up their headquarters. Along with his rebels, Roldan's intention was to attack La Concepción Fortress, then under the command of Miguel Ballester, who quickly wrote to the admiral. Faced with this situation, Columbus sent two merciful letters to the rebels in October 1498, asking them to restore come to a mutual agreement while obtaining his own safe-conduct. The negotiations were long given that until September of the prior year, they had not succeeded in arriving at an agreement. After a series of agreements that Columbus could not respect, the viceroy found himself obligated not just to withdraw his accusations against Roldan, but was also persuaded to concede parcels of land throughout the island to the rebels.

There are some spoils in every war. Some rebels settled at Bonao, others at La Vega, still others at Santiago, and Columbus conceded cacique Beechio's region, with his people and vassals included, to Roldan himself. Roldan and his followers had won the battle: the whole island was distributed among the rebels

One year later, for a list of detailed reasons we are omitting, Adrian de Muxica started an uprising against Roldan, which the admiral then suppressed. De Muxica was sentenced to death and once dead, was thrown into an empty cell in the prison at Santo Domingo.

160 Confronting the look of surprise on Brother Buil's face, Columbus ordered the hanging of Gaspar Ferriz, thereby provoking the monk's animosity and that of many of his fellow monks. Three hanged men appear in this image, drawn for *America* by De Bry. It did not actually happen that way. In effect, it's an exaggeration by the engraver who wanted to demonstrate the cruelty of the Spanish (State Library, Augsburg, Germany).

162 Cacique Guacanagarí gave Columbus a belt very similar to this one (Museum für Völkerkunde, Vienna, Austria).

163 In this illustration drawn for *America*, De Bry depicts Columbus' first encounter with the indigenous peoples of the Caribbean. Cacique Guacanagarí offered his own treasured possessions in a gesture of welcome (State Library, Augsburg, Germany).

RELATIONS WITH INDIGENOUS PEOPLES

Obsessed with exploration of new lands, Columbus passed most of his time returning to nearby islands. During his absence his brother Diego took care of governing the colony through a reigning council, over which he presided. The younger Columbus brother was a weak man, incapable of managing the natives who had by then lost their fear of the Christians and who prepared to attack them whenever the opportunity arose. Guatiguana, cacique of Magdalena, ordered the execution of ten Spaniards who were found scattered throughout his territory, then he besieged the fort. At that very moment, the Spanish promised themselves that for every one of them that fell in combat, they would kill ten natives. The raids were constant, not just between the indigents and the Spanish, but also among the diverse indigenous tribes.

At the end of 1495, Columbus returned from his voyage to Cuba and Jamaica. When he ordered the capture of Guatiguana, the cacique successfully escaped. However, almost half of his one hundred loyal subjects did not flee, were captured, and sent to Castile as slaves with the fleet that set sail from Hispaniola on 24 February 1496.

Not even relations with the natives who were his allies went perfectly. The Columbus brothers imposed a tax in gold and cotton on all of the inhabitants of Cibao and Vega Real. All who had reached the age of majority at 14 years old had to pay a shell full of gold and one *arroba* (25.357 lbs) of cotton per person, every three months. Confronting this excessive demand, Guarionex proposed a change in the tax payment with the promise that his subjects would cultivate a *conuco*, a local name for a yucca plantation, as the distance between Isabella and Santo Domingo was great and they could easily provide cassava bread made from these plants to the Spanish. Columbus did not accept his proposal although he did consent to lowering the taxes by half, given that the tools necessary to acquire such goods were not plentiful.

At the beginning of 1496, the admiral realized that his fiscal system was not working. Since the natives were not paying taxes and not even cultivating the land, Columbus issued a public notice authorizing the number of natives necessary to work in service in their homes and fields with the objective of finding his way into the hearts of the colonists and satisfying their hunger. It was an initiative that the natives did not welcome, refusing to provide any service and deciding to flee into the mountains, abandoning their own plantations. The few seeds that the colonists had brought from Spain for planting had dried out, and they were not prepared to work themselves, yet they certainly didn't leave Spain for the Indies in order to work. Columbus took advantage of the situation to designate the earnings obtained from two plantations growing something called the "Brazilwood" to cover the colony's cultivation costs. As equity partner with the Crown, he flaunt-

ed his ownership of the plantations, most likely as the majority shareholder. Revenue from this dye-producing plant pro-

vided Columbus and his sons with a good income. Finally, to compensate the people whom he had not yet paid and to

compensate suppliers who were sending provisions from Spain, Columbus decided to send native slaves in lieu of cash,

an arrangement that deeply annoyed the king and queen.

THE FALL OF THE VICEROY

The news running through the royal court on the situation in the Indies was progressively more alarming and the monarchs began to lose faith in the Admiral of the Ocean Sea. According to many people, the venture was drifting off course and the general opinion in Castile was that the Columbus brothers should be removed from office. In spite of that, Ferdinand and Isabella never acted hastily, always tried to listen to their admiral's reasoning, wanting to compare all opinions on the matter. Whether issued by Columbus or by Roldan himself, the first reports about the latter's revolt were arriving in Spain in the fall of 1498, in addition to an important cargo of slaves. It was then, in consenting to Columbus' request that he urgently required a judge to aid him in administering justice, that the monarchs decided to appoint a trustworthy person who was truly equipped for the task. Their choice for such a delicate mission was Brother Francisco de Bobadilla.

Initially, his authorized powers were limited to the execution of a thorough examination of Roldan's revolt and to handle it as needed. Dated 21 March 1499 in Madrid, an official measure urgently requested that Columbus provide every available support. The monarchs did nothing other than fulfill their admiral's requirements.

Two months later on May 21st, after receiving substantive information from the Indies, the rulers issued two new measures. Directed at advisers, judges, government administrators, knights, squires, officials, and inhabitants of the islands and terra firma, the first measure communicated that Spain's representative, Francisco de Bobadilla, had been appointed as governor. Neither of the Columbus brothers, Christopher or Bartolomeo, were appointed to any office at all, although one clause did authorize them to send back to Castile those who asserted the Columbus brothers should not remain on Hispaniola. The second measure was aimed at Columbus who, for the first time, was not designated as anything more than "our admiral of the Ocean Sea," at his brothers, and others authorities in the Indies, ordering them to relinquish power over all the fortresses, houses, ships, arms, ammunition, horses, and livestock to Bobadilla. Five days later on May 26th, the monarchs wrote another letter to Columbus, to be personally delivered to him by Bobadilla upon his arrival in the Indies. A very brief missive, which even omitted the title of viceroy in its heading, it simply informed him that they had sent Bobadilla to carry out their orders.

Despite these official orders being delivered in 1499, the newly appointed governor had not yet received authorization to leave. Bobadilla was detained in Spain for an entire year because the rulers were anxiously awaiting good news from the Indies or perhaps because Roldan had been submissive and there was no longer any need for an investigating judge.

All of their doubt soon dissipated. The arrival of the caravels in Seville, bringing reports on the conclusion of the revolt wors-

ened the situation. Columbus sent the royals a letter asking their permission for him to cancel his agreement with Roldan that he had signed himself. This annoyed the monarchs and, with good reason, they considered it indignant and improper. The powerful Cardinal Cisneros had Roldan's version in his hands, a long and extensive letter accusing Don Christopher and his brothers of being despots. Other testimony of which we don't know the content contributed to stoking the fire. The slow process of dispatching Bobadilla increased the gossip in Castile as well as in the Indies. It was then when, for the first time, people said that Columbus and his brothers wanted to hand over the Indies to the Genoans, therefore to a foreign prince. It was a very harsh accusation but not true. Despite that Columbus – a Genoan – was surrounded by his countrymen, the idea of rebelling against his king and queen had never crossed his mind. And yet, the gossip took such a toll that Columbus himself, in a letter written in October 1500 addressed to the Infante John's tutor, refuted all claims that he wanted to hand over the Indies to another ruling house. The first claim stated that when returning from his voyage of exploration and docking at Lisbon, he had disembarked in Portugal to relinquish the lands to King John II. "While I don't have knowledge of many things," he said, "I do not see who could judge me as so stupid and scatterbrained as to not realize that even if the Indies were mine, I could not manage them one day without the assistance of a Prince. Be that as it may, where would I find firmer support and better protection than in the King and Queen, our highnesses, who raised me to such dignified titles from my low social status and who are the most powerful rulers in the world, over sea and over land?"

Was he sincere? Perhaps he was, however we shouldn't forget that from then on, the king and queen ordered that all of the representatives responsible for managing his personal affairs in the Indies had to be native Spaniards, something they must have automatically expected anyway.

Another question intervened to sully Columbus' reputation. The colonists in the Indies were not being paid. Complaints gave rise to a good number of notices simultaneously directed at the admiral and the governor, ordering them to pay the colonists. Out of his own pocket, the admiral had to pay the salaries of those who had come to the Indies and Bobadilla had to do the same for those people with royal appointments – who should have been at the monarchs' expense. Fernando Columbus recounts that in Granada during the time between July 21 and 31, 1500, a group of natives from the Indies, who were dissatisfied, used to throw grapes they'd received, as the Catholic king passed by, after crying out "Pay, pay." Fernando adds "if me and my brother, the squires of her royal highness, the queen, would pass by, the natives shouted to the skies, saying: look at the admiral's sons and at the monsters with whom he discovered new lands of vanity and deception, as a tomb and land for Castilian knights. And they added many other insults, so that with we would avoid any further contact."

The situation was so unbearable that the royals had no other choice than to finally send a new governor. New communications were sent ordering the governor to verify which people on the island were receiving a salary from the king, to liquidate the accounts, and to pay what was due them. Additionally, Bobadilla hand-carried some communications and other blank letterhead, ready to be sent with appropriate notices to locations in the Indies as he saw fit. Bobadilla embarked for Hispaniola in late summer of 1500. The fleet was made up of two caravels with 50 people in each, 25 contracted to serve in the Indies for one year, the remainder being domestics and various ecclesiastical personnel. Nineteen of the natives that Columbus had sent in 1499, returned to their homeland as free citizens.

Francisco de Bobadilla embió presos à Castilla al Almirante Don
Cristoval Colon ij à sus hermanos.

166 In 1500, Francisco de Bobadilla was appointed investigating judge and governor of the Indies. Once his investigation was completed, he sent the Columbus brothers back to Spain. The admiral was removed from his roles as viceroy and governor but retained that of admiral and its associated financial privileges.

LEGAL PROCEEDINGS

On August 23, 1500, Bobadilla arrived at the Santo Domingo port. The first sight he had from the ship was of two gallows with two white men hanging from them. Terrified, he asked for information from those who came to welcome him. They responded only that in that very week, seven Spaniards had been hanged and that five others were in prison, awaiting their execution. After asking after the admiral, the response Bobadilla received was not what he expected. The admiral was at Concepción de La Vega and Bartolomeo at Xaragua, each hoping to find and capture the rebels who were still in revolt, with the intention of hanging them because all had already made confessions to a priest. The new governor did not want to disembark until the next day, when he headed directly to the church. At the end of the mass, at the door to the church and in the presence of Diego Columbus, he publicly presented the documents specifying his responsibilities, which Don Diego did not want to accept. Quickly thereafter, he asked that they take him to the prisoners, along with their legal documentation so that he could render justice. Diego refused, indicating first that his brother's power was more binding than Bobadilla's and secondly that he was not the appropriate person to decide the fate of the prisoners, given that did not have the same level of power as the admiral. Therefore, Don Diego asked that the official letter be delivered to the viceroy. It was either Don Diego or the rest of the government officials on the island that resisted Bobadilla as incoming governor, trying to defer the inevitable with outrageous arguments. After some "push and pull," Bobadilla took authority and headed toward the fortress whose authorities submitted without great difficulty, thus liberating the prisoners. The removal of the admiral and happiness in knowing they would receive their back salaries motivated those primarily in service to the king to take the side of Bobadilla. However, Diego did not and resisted. Bobadilla was obliged to sequester him, probably in his own home. Sending emissaries to the admiral and his brother Bartolomeo commanding them to come before him, the governor began to execute his mission by questioning the chief administrator and treasurer. The Columbus brothers did not appear in Santo Domingo before September 15th, 23 days after Bobadilla's arrival.

We have knowledge of the content of the conversations between Bobadilla and Columbus while we know nothing about those with Bartolomeo. Columbus stated that he had not actually paid the required salaries but would have done so very soon and, as far as the judiciary proceedings for the men who had been hanged or incarcerated were concerned, he did not have the documentation with him as he had sent it to Castile. He added that the documentation would probably have been burned by that time, an excuse that Bobadilla did not accept to the extent that he ordered that the two brothers be confined.

The process took the following line of questioning. Only about 300 colonists lived on the island at that time yet we aren't aware of the governor's criteria for summoning the 22 who provided testimony. We can assume that all were people of certain importance or that, given their jobs or functions, they were presented with factual information, which they were then asked to clarify. Once Columbus complained that Bobadilla had called for testimony from those who had been rebels under Roldan. But, it just wasn't so. Two of them, Pedro de Terreros and Pedro de Salcedo, were very close to the admiral. At least five of them testified years later in favor of Don Diego in the *Columbus Disputes* and two others gave testimonies of another conflict that Bartolomeo Columbus had had with the Crown. Some certainly harbored a grudge, like

Valles or Montoya who were in prison at the time of Bobadilla's arrival, or Montalbán whose hand the admiral had ordered cut off. As for the remaining prisons, we are unsure. Their statements didn't demonstrate any affection toward the viceroy but did not manifest any aversion either. What proves interesting is that their statements do not differ substantially. The interrogation was comprised of three questions. The first required the establishment of whether or not Columbus had sought to meet with individual people, natives as well as Christians, in opposition to the governor. The second asked for final clarification on whether or not the admiral and his brothers had prohibited the natives' conversion to Christianity, and the third investigated various conduct of the Columbus brothers, as well as the "many other injustices and iniquities" that they had committed against inhabitants of the island. The testimonies given were numerous, perhaps motivated by the governor, and even added various details regarding other matters. It seemed evident that Colombus tried to meet with the natives and Christians when he knew that Bobadilla was coming to Hispaniola. Initially, the admiral thought that the arrival of a new fleet, as unexpected as it was to him, could be that of another exploration armada like Hojeda's fleet the year prior. It was demonstrated in the judicial proceeding that Columbus, when he found out that a new governor had just arrived at Santo Domingo, tried by any means possible to present himself in front of the new dignitary, supported by a significant contingent of both Christians and nativess. Columbus had organized his strategy quickly, writing to his brother, Bartolomeo, inviting him to join him and that is what he did. There was something ensuring the loyalty of the Spanish people in Bonao, crossroads to Santo Domingo, and there Columbus sent his faithful friend, Terreros. The 17 witnesses responding to this question stated without exception that Columbus wanted to get up, go to Santo Domingo, and put Bobadilla on a ship, sending him back to Castile. And, others added that he wanted to go before the court himself to protest against how his rulers had offended him. Did Columbus, by taking this attitude, want to start a civil war in the colony, as later someone insinuated in a more or less veiled manner? Columbus' lieutenant, Rodrigo Perez, stated that oftentimes when the admiral was talking about the Indies, he would complain by saying "We are the ones who must always consider the Indies, how we have profited and the land we've acquired here," and that at the end, he would tire and add "all on behalf of the king and queen."

Columbus knew that even when he had achieved his objective of assembling a good battalion around him, he would never have been able to maintain his power. He didn't have the profile of a leader. He knew neither how to command nor how to attract people toward his way of thinking. His only defense was to affirm his desire to return to Castile in order to explain Roldan's revolt to the monarchs so that he could return to the Indies and continue his exploration with the goal of locating that strait to the East that obsessed him so and that he felt so close to finding. The responses to Bobadilla's second question did not shed the slightest doubt on Columbus' religious fervor: it was an issue that could never be debated. The admiral was a man of profound faith, a sailor who, after reciting the Ave Maria with his partners, placed a cross on all the lands of which he took possession, a viceroy who constantly asked his rulers to send him experienced priests to indoctrinate the indigents and pray fervently for the corrupted souls of the colonists. Was it possible that he had prevented the baptism of the natives, when his monarchs had explicitly mandated evangelism? With the exception of that of Terreros, all of the testimonies asserted that it was Columbus who decided which Indies people could be baptized. In the letters the admiral sent to the rulers, he excused himself as his scruples prevented him from attending to the baptism of people who not only did not know the sacraments, but who did not even know how to recite prayers. Was that truly his reasoning? The testimonies accused the admiral of preventing their baptisms so that he could enslave the natives. The admiral and his brothers were presented negatively in the responses given to the third question in the testimony. All of them stated that

the admiral and his brothers imposed excessive punishment and sentences for motives of self-interest. They were accused of acting punitively without allowing any due process of law to take place. It is confirmed that the Columbus brothers permitted their own officials to make money from food supplies. All the testimonies reprimanded the admiral's greed for money. When he did pay the required salaries, he compensated those owed with slaves instead of money. He demanded that the colonists acquire gold for him, causing a certain disgust among the people. As demonstrated, Columbus had been quite an incompetent governor. Sworn statements in the testimony portrayed all of the cruelty of a "Wild West" frontier where no one felt at ease. Hispaniola was an island where hunger and disease reigned and, what was more, there were no advantages to being there. The colonists were for the most part impostors, lazy good-for-nothings, and scoundrels sitting in judgment on the viceroy, and the Columbus brothers were bloodthirsty despots according to Spanish opinion.

The five Franciscan brothers who had arrived on August 23rd in Santo Domingo with Bobadilla did not hesitate to stoke the fire further. Many of them were returning to the Indies for the second time and others, like Brother Francisco Ruiz, Cardinal Cisneros' majordomo, had gone there for the first time. They decided to send a series of letters and memos to Cisneros, giving their own version of the situation on the island. Without hesitation, they accused the admiral of wanting to turn the lands over to his Genoese partners and for this reason they begged the cardinal to prevent his return to the island. It was evident to them that the admiral wanted to rise up against Bobadilla and for previously committing such vile acts had unsuccessfully sought to recruit both natives and Christians. Yet, the Franciscans said nothing about Columbus' alleged prohibition against the baptizing of the natives; rather, they continually praised him, indicating that he had baptized thousands of souls in a very short time, no fewer than five thousand, a considerable though somewhat exaggerated number. There was such a large

amount of work to do that the Franciscans urgently requested that an additional batch of missionaries be sent. The Franciscans did not neglect to request monies so that their work could be more effective. And, as they needed money for their task, the brothers proposed that the Christians pay their 10- percent tithes and deliver them to the person in charge of their mission. The Franciscans obviously also recommended that their allowances be maintained so that they could continue to deliver gold to the new Christian converts because, despite it being very little, they asserted that something would be due them as a share.

The admiral's statement completed, Bobadilla ordered that the Columbus brothers be incarcerated. It is more probable that he had really decided to take them in the ship that would take them back to Castile a few weeks later. The new governor followed his orders to the letter. If he had thought that anyone should be deported from the Indies, he would have sent that person to court. So, it happened in this manner, and the three Columbus brothers would make the crossing together. Without any doubt, they were incarcerated, but would they also be put in chains? Las Casas recounts that when Bobadilla ordered that the admiral be chained, no one wanted to execute his order until a cook by the name of Espinosa offered voluntarily. Las Casas adds that Columbus kept the chains in order that his remains be buried with this testimonial of how he was thus rewarded for the services he had rendered the Crown. Las Casas reproduces Columbus' conversation with his jailer in detail, when he appeared at the fortress to lead him to the ship. "Vallejo, where are you taking me?" asked the miserable admiral. "Sir, you must embark on His Majesty's ship," responded Alonso. "Vallejo, is it true?" Columbus persisted and Vallejo responded, "I swear on the life of His Majesty that it is true and that you must embark on the ship." On his brother's behalf, Fernando Columbus adds: the admiral's enemies went to the harbor and rang the bell so that the prisoners can hear it from the ship, and a male nurse, named Diego Ortiz, read the libel against the admiral in the city square. What a horrible departure! In the first days of October the ships set sail for Castile. Bobadilla appointed Alonso Vallejo as captain of the fleet, whose pilot was Andres Martín de la Gorda. According to Las Casas, these two were very capable people. Andres was the owner of the *Gorda* (Fat Lady), the ship that had brought Bobadilla from Spain, and Vallejo was the domestic employee of Gonzalo Gamez de Cervantes (the uncle of Juan Rodriguez de Fonseca, archdeacon of Seville). Both men treated the admiral and his brothers well. Soon after departure, the two offered to remove their prisoners' chains. However, Columbus refused the offer: wanted to appear before Ferdinand and Isabella that way. Perhaps, upon their arrival in Cadiz on November 20th, the Columbus brothers were secretly removed from the ship so that they could reach the royal court before the arrival of Bobadilla's letters. Unfortunately, we don't know whether things turned out that way or not.

THE LAST YEARS
chapter 4

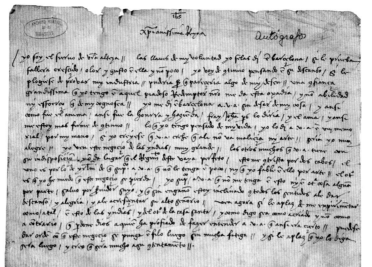

RETURN TO SPAIN

On November 20, 1500 the Columbus brothers arrived in Cadiz. We are unaware of any of the events that occurred during their crossing and when they disembarked. In Spain, no one knew who was on the incoming ships, as these were the first to arrive since Bobadilla had set sail for the Indies a few months earlier. It does not seem very probable that the Captain Alonso Vallejo, following the governor's instructions, delivered them to the governor of Cadiz; given that assumption, it is possible that the captain and pilot both opted to set them free. Columbus himself would have been anxious about going before the king and queen to give his version of the reports presented by Bobadilla. The brothers must have stayed together in some house in Cadiz or Seville, waiting to see how the reported information played out. Our sources for the subsequent events are very limited and do not concur. While Fernando states that his father wrote a letter to the monarchs announcing his arrival on the peninsula just after disembarking, Las Casas denies it. In fact, Las Casas states that Columbus, believing that his rulers had ordered his incarceration, preferred that others inform them of his imprisonment and arrival in Cadiz, so had arranged for the letters that he had written on the ship to be delivered to court before those that Bobadilla had sent, "believing that the king and queen would be motivated after reading his letters and would grant what was due to the admiral." Events might then occur as Columbus hoped they would. In any case, the only thing that we know with any certainty is that around December 17th, King Ferdinand and Queen Isabella received Columbus at Granada. Las Casas states that the monarchs were saddened to learn that Bobadilla had sent him from Hispaniola to Spain as a prisoner and that he had been mistreated, and had ordered his liberation and gave him 2000 ducats to allow him to make the journey to Grana-

da and come before them with dignity. According to what his biographers recount, Ferdinand and Isabella received him "with happy expressions and kind words," ensuring him that they had not approved his imprisonment and promising to judge his case in such a way that the guilty parties would be punished and he would be released, a satisfied man. Las Casas, giving a note of color to his "history," invented a meeting and narrated a moving scene, represented many times by painters, where the admiral appeared kneeling in tears before Queen Isabella. What interests us is the result of that meeting, which Fernandez de Oviedo summarizes with, "his favor was so superior that even when he erred about something, his royal majesty would not allow the admiral to be mistreated, reinstating all of the means and privileges that he had previously had here, and that they had been taken aback and suspicious at the time of his arrest. Yet, they did not permit him to return to his post as governor." And, so it was. Bobadilla's actions were, without doubt, excessive. Columbus and his brothers had committed crimes, some serious, exceeding the limits of their authority, but the sanction the governor had imposed was extreme. And Columbus missed no opportunity to tell his own version of the abuse he had endured to anyone who cared to listen.

The admiral had not only lost his position as viceroy but also his income and property in the New World, and after arriving in Granada, he spent his time struggling to recover these assets. He began to compile a comprehensive documentation against Bobadilla, something that could not have proved too difficult, given his successor's bad management practices. And, once Columbus had obtained all the negative evidence he deemed necessary, he prompted Ferdinand and Isabella to send a new governor to resolve the situation in Hispaniola.

Los altos Reyes don fernado y doña
ysabel y la   Real i fata
doña   Juana

DESIRE FOR REDEMPTION

On 3 September 1501, hardly 10 months after Columbus' arrival in Spain, Ferdinand and Isabella dismissed Bobadilla. The rulers appointed Brother Nicolás de Ovando, Commander of Lares (an officer of the military-religious Order of Alcantara), as new governor of Spain's new World islands and mainland, "except for the islands governed by Alonso de Hojeda and Vicente Yañez Pinzón by prior agreement." Columbus had succeeded in obtaining the removal of his adversary Bobadilla, yet he had already totally ruined his status as equity partner to the king and queen. By then, licenses for exploration were many and new conquistadors publicly flaunted titles similar to those that Columbus had been the first – and once the only – person to possess.

Ovando received precise instructions, enhanced by all of the reports considered necessary to finally resolve the grave situation that Bobadilla had created in the Indies. Some of these documents seemed dictated by Columbus himself. For example, one directive dated September 16th, 1501 ordered that he should not retain the designated portion of any gold that was found because Bobadilla did not have the power to authorize it – a fact Columbus had never tired of repeating. In the same notification, he was ordered collect all of the gold belonging to the royal treasury according to the agreement that the rulers had had with Columbus. At the same time, Ovando was instructed to verify whether Bobadilla had paid back salaries to whomever had not previously received them, a matter Columbus had complained about on many occasions.

With respect to the Columbus brothers' possessions and property, an edict of 27 September 27, 1501 gave orders on what should be done on their behalf. First, the Ferdinand and Isabella ordered that the men's right to the eighth share due them according to the Agreement between the Crown and Columbus be restored. They also ordered that all the personal belongings and household items that Bobadilla had taken away from the two men be returned or an amount equal to their market value be granted from whatever had been sold. The document also described in minute detail how two mares and their colts, as well as the horses that Columbus had in Hispaniola which were confiscated by Bobadilla should be returned to him, in addition to ceding him a specific quantity of gold nuggets. Furthermore, the admiral was authorized to take from Hispaniola 111 quintals (almost 12.25 tons) of wood "from the one thousand quintals due him each year."

Columbus was also permitted to keep one person on Hispaniola who would take care of collecting his rents. As his representative, he chose Alonso Sanchez de Carvajal who had to be present when the gold was melted down into ingots and stamped, as well as participate in the merchants' negotiations, attended by the royal attorney. Regarding any potential debts that the admiral could have accumulated and still had not yet paid, the monarchs ordered that the admiral's gold, jewelry, and movable property in the Indies or his rent revenues on Hispaniola should first cover back salaries with the remainder divided into ten shares, nine for the Crown and one for Columbus, as their Agreement had specified. And, the same thing must have been done with his livestock, once the costs of acquisition and transport were deducted.

At least Columbus' financial situation was secure. And, then the admiral was not a man who left things half done so he didn't stop fighting until his rulers sent a second letter to Ovando, ordering him to create a list detailing each item that would be returned to his brothers. The admiral's financial rights were again in order and the conditions of the Agreement were reinstated. Columbus had achieved the satisfaction that his rulers had promised him.

Columbus knew that he would no longer be viceroy of the Indies, yet he needed to remain active and continue to sail so he requested authorization for a new voyage. The admiral still needed to search for the strait that joined the two seas, allowing him to reach Asia, still wanting to achieve a new circumnavigation that he'd already called the *great voyage*. Finally, the king and queen consented and our man set sail yet another time for the New World, but this time with the sole title of Admiral of the Ocean Sea.

When Ovando arrived at Santo Domingo on 15 April 1502, the inhabitants of the island rushed to Ozama Beach. The arrival of the 32-ship fleet filled them with joy and all were anxious to know who the new governor would be. Immediately after his initial welcome, Ovando ordered Bobadilla to follow him to the fortress where he publicly displayed the official documents and took his oath of office. Without losing any time, the new governor began to instruct Bobadilla on the requisite investigation – and history repeated itself once again.

Bartolomé de Las Casas also arrived with the fleet. He wrote about the impression it made on him to see the ousted governor heading toward the new governor's house, alone and in disfavor with the Crown. Everyone had abandoned Bobadilla just as they had abandoned Columbus in the previous year.

By mid-June, the investigation had already ended and Bobadilla had to make his return to Castile. Columbus arrived in Santo Domingo on June 29th when the fleet was ready to set sail for Spain. Following the instructions he had received from the monarchs, Ovando would not let Columbus enter the port. It would not be advisable for Bobadilla and the admiral to encounter each other. The admiral had to take refuge in Puerto Hermoso, 16 miles (26 km) from Santo Domingo, where he sent a letter to Ovando, beseeching him not to allow the fleet to set sail, given that a storm of unknown magnitude was moving in. Ovando did not want to listen and gave the order to raise anchor. With Antonio de Torres already aboard, the captain had Bobadilla, Francisco Roldan, and the cacique Guarionex, as prisoner, embark. Besides the investigative team, the ship carried other passengers and 200,000 Castilian gold pieces in the hold, 100,000 designated for the king.

Just 40 hours later, as they were leaving the dock, a raging storm broke out as Columbus had predicted. Of the 32 ships, 20 sank, "without either small or large men even able to escape, dead or alive." One of the lost ships was that of the captain. Bobadilla died in the shipwreck.

From his safe haven, Columbus waited for clear weather to begin his voyage and would have proceeded, however his enemies had been defeated and the straw houses in Santo Domingo had been completely flattened. "It seemed," Las Casas wrote, "that a whole army of demons from hell had been loosed into the skies."

Columbus' last two years were particularly sad and lonely. Upon return from his fourth voyage, he was a defeated man. Not only had he lost four ships in an ugly situation in a sailor's environment in the Indies, the court atmosphere was even worse as Queen Isabella, his primary financier, died in 1504, a few days before he arrived in Castile.

Despite being discharged with full honors and a large income still coming from the New World, he knew quite well that his bright star at court had been extinguished. No one called upon him for anything. He was a profoundly exhausted man, feeling sick and tired, not able to accept that his sons' situation, predominantly that of his firstborn, Diego, had been compromised while he was away.

He thought the solution was to get in contact with Don Fernando and attempt, in any way possible, a meeting with him. He wrote

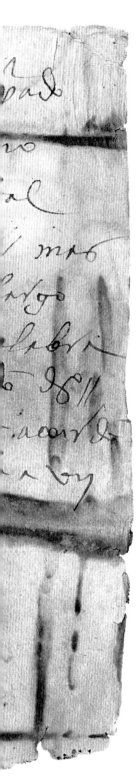

letters and tried in vain to pull a few strings. He went before the Dominican Archbishop of Seville, Diego de Deza, and took advantage of all the appearances his friends made at court to persistently verify whether he still enjoyed favor with the monarch. His friends did not respond and Columbus felt abandoned. Even his sons wrote to him less than he would have desired.

The admiral had another concern that deeply upset him. The men who had accompanied him on his last voyage were no longer receiving their salaries, justifiably pressuring him so that he would try to encourage payment. Only royal intercession would then be able to help them. The administrative machine was always slow and Columbus had to invest his own time in drafting long memoranda to the officials at the Contractation House, a ministry of Overseas established in 1502 that managed all facets of the voyages to the Indies. Though Columbus' rapport with the civil servants administering it were not good, "the old admiral," as everyone then called him, did not hesitate to meet with them to ask that his men be given their just rewards. His tenacity and persistence was fruitful and the salaries due them, even though late, were paid.

Becoming regent of Castile upon the queen's death, Ferdinand (who was king only of Aragon) had many problems to resolve and the situation of Columbus, who annoyed him with requests for appointments, was not foremost in this thoughts. Moreover, the soothsayers, to whom he was quite devoted, predicted ill omens. The king awaited the imminent arrival of his daughter, Joanna and her husband, Philip of Habsburg, to assume their reign over the kingdom of Castile. For Ferdinand, Joanna's arrival was a concern. The unity of Spain he had achieved with Isabella through so much effort and cost was at risk of falling apart with the accession of a king who did not feel Spanish and surrounded himself with a court of foreigners. And according to what Ferdinand's ambassadors in Flanders were communicating to him, his daughter had gone insane, confirming the suspicion that he and Isabella had had for a long time.

Columbus, realizing that he would not succeed in obtaining a definite appointment while living in Seville, decided to make the long journey to directly seek an audience with the king. As on other occasions, he thought his presence at court would make it easier to garner the support of courtiers, thereby allowing him to secure an audience with the king. On past occasions it had worked worked out just that way.

He was gravely ill and in the harrowing letters he wrote his son, Diego, at that time, he complained about his aches and pains. In mid-November 1504, he was feeling strong enough to travel across Spain. The royal court was then situated at Valladolid and the old Road of Silver was the easiest route to take from Seville. Determined to make the trip, he asked the Council of the Cathedral to lend him the stretcher used to transport the body of Cardinal Don Diego Hurtado de Mendoza to his sepulcher in the cathedral. On November 28th, after Columbus had made the all the right gestures, the canons acquiesced in his request. Two days later, Columbus decided to abandon his idea of the journey. He wrote to Diego that it was very cold outside and rained so much that the Guadalquivir River had overflowed its banks. The doctors advised complete bed rest and that is what he took.

DESPERATE LETTERS

The winter was harsh and Columbus, overwhelmed, could only write very little, receiving few responses in return: "I would like to receive letters every day that still do not come," he sadly wrote to his son Diego.

Desperate from inactivity, he inundated the royal chancery with memoranda and reports, asking that it pay him the percentages as contracted in the Agreement. The Indies business was growing and the amounts that he was receiving from his administrators were not enough to satisfy him, as well was not enough the commission on profits already collected. Columbus laid the blame for this situation on Ovando.

The admiral did not stop thinking about the Indies and wanted to be informed about everything that happened there. As a result, he lost his temper when he found out that at court they were thinking about creating two bishoprics in Hispaniola. He tried to get his son Diego, to speak with King Ferdinand, asking him not to appoint anyone before listening to his opinion. He, more than anyone else, knew the issues surrounding the venture and would have been able to advise the king. Receiving no response, he decided to write a letter to Pope Julius II, which we know little about, as well as another to the Bank of San Giorgio in Genoa and one to the Genoese ambassador to Spain Niccolò Oderigo. In his letter to this fellow Genoan, Columbus explained all of his problems. The bank had not responded to his request, therefore he would not be able to receive the interest due him, resulting in a serious loss. Columbus also asked Oderigo whether he had received the two packages he had sent him prior to his departure on the fourth voyage in 1502. The first, which Francisco de Riberol should have delivered to him, contained copies of some letters and the *Book of Privileges.* The second packet, sent with Franco Cattaneo, was identical to the first; he had sent for security's sake and in case the first might have been lost. Finally, Columbus had also enclosed one of the copies of his diary from the last voyage. Everything seems to indicate that this was the manuscript of the report on the fourth voyage, is known as the *Lettera Rarissima* and used for publication the next year in Venice. At least one of the copies of the *Book of Privileges* that Columbus sent to Oderigo is extant, preserved by the city of Genoa.

On 27 December 1504, the same day Columbus sent his letter to Oderigo, he sent another to an unknown person named Juan Luis de Mayo. The tone and complaints are equivalent to the contents of the previous letter. He also sent a copy of the *Book of Privileges* to this man, further expounding upon his problems. The money issue worried him even more than his delicate health, primarily because he needed to know whether his son Diego would inherit his responsibilities as he had promised him so many times. Just one paragraph differentiates this letter from the previous one. Columbus writes to his friend that at every moment, perhaps in the next week, he hoped to receive news from the Genoan bank. And yet, he never received any response. A curious detail of both letters is the signature that Columbus employed. Until 1500, he only signed with the words: *The Admiral.* From 1502, he eliminated the title and used an anagram, that is impossible to decipher unless we have the code, with the printed words *Xpo: Ferens*, and only on the most important letters did he insert the following closing: *The High Admiral of the Ocean Sea, Viceroy, and Governor General of the Indies*, etc. In the two letters cited above, he included this closing even when he was no longer viceroy or governor of the Indies. Was this due to the admiral's ego?

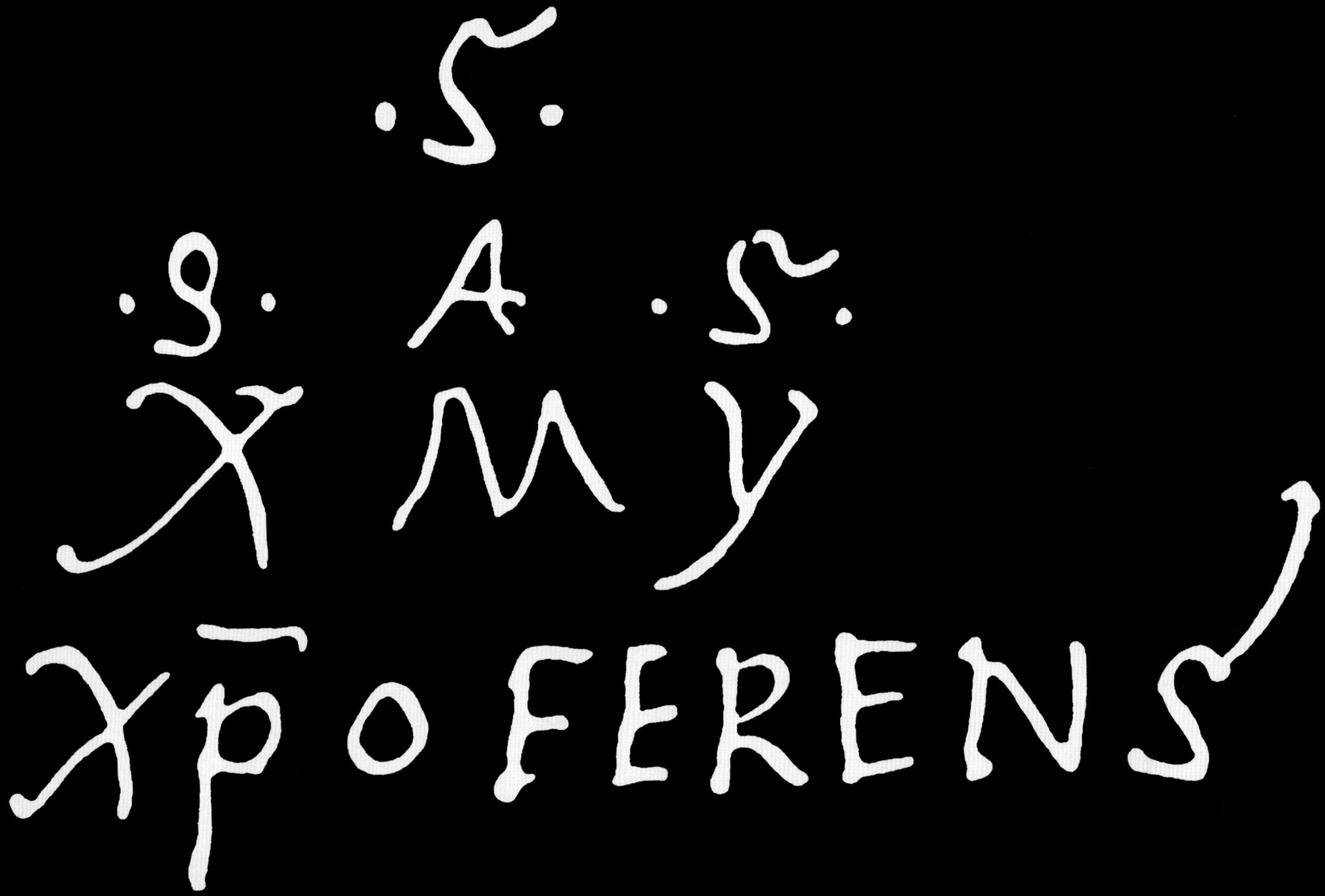
.S.
.S. A .S.
X M Y
Xpo FERENS

181 Over the course of his life, Columbus signed his name in diverse ways. Until 1498, he signed it as "The Admiral," and from then on, with this anagram, which has not yet been decoded to reveal its significance.

HIS LAST VOYAGE

183 COLUMBUS DIED IN A NORMAL CHRISTIAN SETTING IN VAL-LADOLID, ATTENDED BY HIS SON FERNANDO, HIS BROTHER-IN-LAW FRANCESCO DE' BARDI, HIS NEPHEW GIOVANNI ANTONIO COLUM-BUS, AND VARIOUS OTHER DOMESTIC STAFF. ALTHOUGH WE DO NOT KNOW PRECISELY IN WHAT HOUSE HE DIED, HIS BURIAL COSTS TO-TALED 50,000 *MARAVEDÍ* (COLUMBUS' HOME MUSEUM, VALLADOL-ID, SPAIN).

In the beginning of 1505 after the end of the cold season, Columbus started to feel better. Before setting off on his trip, he packed his bags properly as he had always done. He had to bring along all the required documentation so he wrote to Brother Gaspare Gorricio, asking him to make copies of some important documents and then pack them in a case of sugar, covering it with wax to avoid any unexpected rain from soaking the documents, rendering them useless. There still remained one matter to take care of. He required relevant authorization from the Asistente of Seville to be able to travel on a mule. Permission from this official was difficult to obtain, given that a royal order prohibited the use of these animals, except by monks or women, with the objective of protecting equine breeding. Finally, having obtained the requisite permission, the admiral took to the road.

Accompanied by his brother, Bartolomeo, Columbus then began a long journey that endured almost a year. On reaching Segovia, they were finally received by the king. Ferdinand did not want to respond to the brothers' requests and tried to delay his decision, despite the affection he had previously demonstrated for the admiral. Columbus persisted in going before the king again. He did not obtain a response and continued to travel, following after court. By December, he had already reached Salamanca. Supported by his faithful friend, Diego Mendez who was a part of the court procession, he gave his relative, Francesco de' Bardi, general proxy authorizing him once again to collect in his name all the goods, gold, etc. earned in the New World, simultaneously delivering all required account balances and payment orders as his administrator in Spain. From Salamanca, the party headed again toward Segovia where, probably experiencing a decline in his health, Columbus dictated a new will that has not survived. It seemed that a curse had fallen on the Columbus family. When they reached the site where the royal court was be held, the monarch had just left. Their journey continued from Segovia to Burgos, then from Burgos to Valladolid.

Columbus and King Ferdinand were finally reunited at Valladolid. The royal officials there, perhaps horrified by his appearance yet faced with his implacable persistence, assured him that he could soon go before the king. The admiral's joy lasted only a short while. Confronted with the sudden announcement of the imminent arrival of his daughter, Archduchess Joanna and her husband, Archduke Philip of Habsburg, Ferdinand had no choice than to leave Columbus to meet them. His audience with the king had ended. Unable to waste the opportunity of being among the first to welcome the incoming Castilian monarchs as they ascended the throne, Columbus quickly sent a letter with his brother, requesting that they depend on him as one of their most loyal subjects and assuring them that, despite being ill, he could still be of infinite service. He could do nothing else but await the return of the royal party and Joanna's response. The dreamer still had faith in his own good fortune!

Once again, his wishes were not fulfilled. Though we know very little about them, a series of complications aggravated his illness. The night before the royal coronation on May 19th, Columbus was in agony. Feeling that he was dying, he called the notary public, Pedro de Hinojedo, to his deathbed. In front of his most faithful supporters and a few unknown Valladolid inhabitants functioning as witnesses, he signed his will, dated 25 August 1505, and confirmed the 1502 documentation

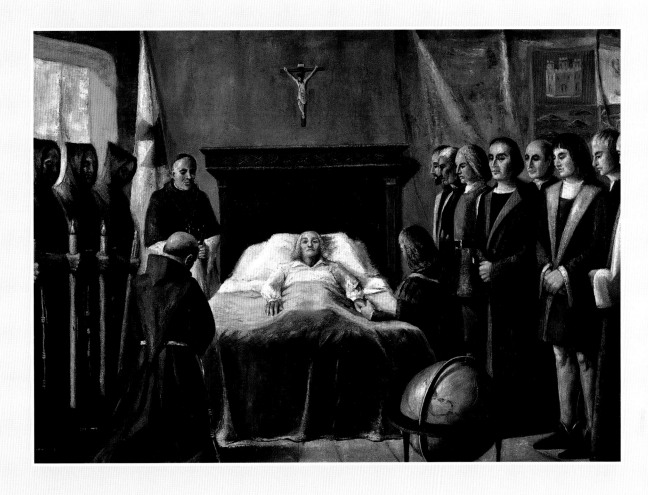

of his estate. We don't possess these original documents, however we do know their main points. By confirming clauses recognized by prior wills, he designated his firstborn son Diego as heir to all his property and contracts, also establishing the male line for future inheritance. If Diego had not had male offspring, his brother Fernando would have been his heir apparent and if the latter had not had any male descendants, his brother, Bartolomeo would be his heir, followed by his brother, Diego and so on, and so forth, ensuring that "no women would inherit anything unless there were no other male heirs."

The system that Columbus chose to protect the financial future of his family was quite complicated. Let's take a look at it. Rental income that Diego would inherit would be divided ten ways every year. His most needy relatives and charitable organizations would share 10 percent. The nine remaining shares would be divided into 35 parts, Don Fernando receiving 27 of them, Bartolomeo five, and Diego three. Diego would then have to give his brother, Fernando, 1.5 million Spanish *maravedì*, and 150,000 and 100,000 respectively to his uncles, Bartolomeo and Diego. As one can see, hierarchies were carefully observed. Finally, Columbus asked Diego to look after

Beatriz Enriquez de Arana, the mother of his son, Fernando, making sure that she lived "honestly" as a person to whom he owed so much. The rest of the family did not figure in the will, even though formerly mentioned in prior wills. Certainly Diego had been one of those who were previously named so that he could support his Portuguese aunt, Briolanja Muñiz.

The will that Columbus made at Valladolid included a peculiar postscript that contained the list of his former creditors in Lisbon. No friend or enemy appeared in this document, not even a gracious thank you to his faithful supporters or recriminations against his adversaries as one would have expected and given that such was the tradition. The Valladolid will seems to be more a confirmation of the disposition of his estate, annexed by a series of charitable provisions and, after the general text and signatures of the legal official and witnesses, a final designation where the dying man remembered a few foreigners. On May 20th, after asking to be dressed in a cassock like St Francis, Christopher Columbus died, surrounded by his son, Fernando, his brother-in-law, Francisco, and other faithful domestic staff. He was fifty-five years old.

Columbus passed away on his deathbed, convinced that he had respected the Agreement with Ferdinand and Isabella, and that he had found the route to the Indies, even when he could never have known that he had taken possession of the South American continent on this third voyage. He could no longer pursue exploration of the strait that he had worked so hard to find, and he had made certain errors on his fourth voyage. The letter in 1500 from Juan de la Cosa confirming that Cuba had already been discovered and documented as an island must have saddened him, that very beautiful "island" that years before he had believed was terra firma. The admiral died knowing he had been the first to successfully cross the Atlantic, the first to conquer it. What sadness his dismissal must have triggered when he had to relinquish control to Bobadilla, after being the conquistador who had opened the route to the New World and had given so much glory and wealth to his king and queen. From the beginning, the admiral's great power of intuition forecasted the profits that Spain could gain from those faraway lands. It is true that he tried to set the slave trade in motion and his Catholic rulers prevented it, yet it is also true he knew how to recognize other possibilities for wealth such as his forecast that sugar cane would prosper in Cuba. He died rich yet with the enormous regret that he would not see his privileges be granted to Diego, his son and primary heir. Years later, all honors would indeed be conferred upon Diego.

Columbus' death passed, completely unnoticed by his peers and nothing was mentioned in contemporary documents about the dwelling, certainly a leased property, where he died. A legend spread in the middle of the 19th century, attributing No. 2, via Ancha della Magdalena as his home in Valladolid, and today those walls bear a plaque from 1886 with the simple inscription and in the same tone as that period: "Columbus died here. Glory to the genius." The admiral's death seemingly struck his family hard as they found themselves in financially difficult times, not because they lacked means but rather liquidity, given that all their money was invested in Seville and they had been away from home for a long time. His most beloved brother and the monarch who could have lent him financial assistance for funeral costs both absent from Valladolid, the family took action. Diego went quickly to Villafranca de Valcarcel where he found King Ferdinand, who was irritated by Archduke Philip's change in schedule and missed appointment and did not give the slightest attention to Columbus' son until June 2nd, when he dispatched a royal instruction that everything regarding the admiral would be carried through to completion. Meanwhile in Valladolid, Francesco de' Bardi, in his official capacity as administrator and shrewd businessman, was given the responsibility of finding the money necessary to bury his brother-in-law and negotiate the return of his family to Seville. Once more, the Columbus family was obliged to turn to creditors to resolve its most urgent needs. The royal bankers and old acquaintances of the Columbus family, Tomas Calvo and Gaspar Centurion were located right there in Valladolid and it was simple enough to go and find them. No sooner said than done and just a week after the patriarch's death on May 27th, Juan de Porras and de' Bardi, accompanied by the Genoese bankers, visited the attorney and executor of Columbus' will. In the presence of the Valladolid clerk, Porras and Bardi accepted a promissory note in the amount of 50,000 *maravedi* that, according to what's written on the back of the document, would be paid to Seville five months later by de' Bardi and Giovanni Antonio Columbus.

Due on 9 October 1506, the promissory note was presented at the last moment for cashing at Francesco de' Bardi's Seville home, where he refused to pay it, saying that he did not have the funds to do so. Centurion felt obliged to protest the document via the Sevillian notary public, Bernal Gonzalez Vallecillo, among whose papers the original promissory note is still miraculously preserved today. According to an old tradition, the Columbus family chose the admiral's burial place as the church of San Francisco de Valladolid, holding his funeral ceremony in the church of Santa María de la Antigua. The body of Christopher Columbus was kept in that Franciscan monastery for three years, the time it took his descendants to find a suitable and more or less permanent tomb in Seville.

En la noble villa d[e] vall[adoli]d a dieze nueve dias del mes de mayo
año del nascimiento de n[uest]ro salvador ih[es]u xp[ist]o de mjll e qui[n]ie[n]tos e
seys años por ante mj p[edr]o de ynojeda escrivano de camara
de sus altezas y escrivano de pro[v]icia en la su corte e chancelleria
e su escrivano e notario publico en todos los sus reynos e
señorios e delos testigos de yuso escriptos el señor d[on] xp[oval]
colon almj[rante] e viso Rey e governador general delas yslas e tierra
firme delas jndias descubiertas e por descubrir q[ue] dizo que
estando enfermo de su cuerpo dixo que porque el tenia fecho su testam[en]to
por ante escrivano publico que agora retificava e retifico el dicho
testam[en]to e lo aprovava passo por bueno y que ne[c]es[ari]o era lo
otorgava e otorgo de nuevo e agora cria[va]el dicho su testam[en]to
el tenia escripto de su mano e letra b[...] escripto q[ue] ante mj el dicho
escrivano mostro e presento q[ue] dixo q[ue] estava escripto de su mano e
letra e firmado de su nombre q[ue] otorgava e otorgo todo lo
aten[id]o e[n] el dicho escripto por ante mj el dicho escrivano segu[n]d
e por la via e forma q[ue] en el dicho escrito se [...]tenia e todas
las mandas en el conten[id]as p[ar]a q[ue] se a[m]pla e valgan por su ul[tim]a
tymya e por su mera volu[n]tad e p[ar]a cu[m]plir el dicho su testam[en]to
q[ue] tenia e tyene fecho e otorgado e todo lo q[ue] en[...] co[n]ten[id]o
cada una cosa e[...] p[ar]te dello e[...] nobre[...] nobro por sus te[...]a
me[n]tarios e a[...]hidores de su a[n]i[m]a al s[eñ]or don d[ieg]o colon su fijo
e al d[on] bartholome colo[n] su h[erman]o e a s[...] de po[...] tesorero de vj[...]caya
p[ar]a q[ue] ellos todos [...] a[m]pla su testam[en]to e todo lo en[...]l co[n]-
ten[id]o e en[...] dicho escripto e todas las mandas e legatos e o[...]
o[...] en[...]l conten[id]as [...] por lo q[ue] dixo q[ue] dava e dio todo su
pod[e]r bastante e q[ue] otorgava e otorgo ante mj el dicho escrivano
todo lo aten[id]o e[n] el dicho escrito e a los p[un]tos dixo q[ue] rogava e
rogo d[e]llo fuessen testigos testigos q[ue] fueron p[rese]ntes llamados e rogados a todo lo q[ue] dicho es de suso el bachiller
andres mjñena e gaspar dela mjsericordia v[ezin]os desta dicha villa de vall[adoli]d e bartholome de fiesco e alvaro p[ere]z e ju[an] de
 billoria e andrea e fer[na]ndo d[e] vargas e fr[ancis]co ma[rtin]ez e fer[na]n-
dez criados de dicho señor almj[rante] e firmada de mi nombre
d[...]bo a[...] esta que[...] [...]

mercador que mo ves treynta mjll reaes
es de por tugal oclvo quales valen
ducados trezientos e oitenta que son
que son setenta e anos ñacados e por
mjnos e menos

r desos mjll maes herderos y aluuheres
ros de pablo de nepro que mo ves çent dua
dos e en valor de nasçer la mjtad
los unos herderos e la otra los e
dos

r de bautista e da mola os e en herde
ros e el es mmer do çynte ñaca dx
t debaptista tornuo la to yerno del sobre
huys en mjnon herochijo de mjz
y alao e tornuola dluoch de trona yos
senas el sro e dantz en lisboa el año
de mjll e quato aentos e oitrenta os
la ce chs memjra de e une ore
e de Ch bolonuno de fee de es
tro ue dhle ya i na fc es uto
mjnjno de chse dle e suo e dhr
e de chse dle e herna e mjo he
pedro lz
açaytra

They were difficult years for the whole family. However, this was definitely not due to any lack in conflict over Don Diego reacquiring his privileges, something that didn't occur until 1508 when he married Donna Maria de Toledo, first cousin to the Duke of Alba. Until that time, the Columbus family could not even take care of Columbus' remains which rested peacefully in the monastery at Valladolid. The situation changed only in 1509 when, close to their departure for the Indies, the Columbus family realized they were obliged to resolve some unfinished business. Diego was given the responsibility of governing the island of Hispaniola and then felt secure that they had taken care of everything in Castile.

In the spring of that year, all the family made their wills and, as Christopher Coumbus had done, left the related documentation in the monastery of Cuevas in Seville, in care of the venerable Brother Gaspare Gorricio. Doubtless it was then when they decided to place the admiral's body at that monastery. We are unaware of all the activities surrounding this event in Valladolid and know only that one fine day, April 11, 1509, Giovanni Antonio Columbus, then majordomo to Don Diego, came to the doors of the monastery of Santa María de las Cuevas, carrying a small chest, saying that it held the remains of Admiral Don Christopher Columbus. We don't know when the exhumation of the cadaver took place at the St. Francis monastery in Valladolid or who was responsible for taking his remains to Seville. Cuevas' registry of documents offers only minimal information about these facts and the provision that the monks not hand over his body to anyone unless expressly requested by Don Diego. Later sources indicate that he was interred in the chapel dedicated to Saint Anne, and there he remained for a number of years. Columbus did never specified where he wanted to be laid to rest, however it seems logical to assume that he wished to one day be buried in Hispaniola, the island of his dreams. Perhaps following Columbus' intention and the wishes of Diego, who died in 1526 and who was also interred at the monastery of Santa María de las Cuevas, Donna Maria de Toledo transported the remains of both of them to Santo Domingo in 1544. This is the date commonly accepted by traditional historiographers, based on literary texts, yet without any other documented evidence. No existing official documentation proves it and no cadavers appear on the embarkation list for transport, provided by Donna Maria when she set sail for the Indies.

Donna Maria made the voyage to Santo Domingo with a single crate that probably contained the two corpses, as it is seemingly absurd that the vicereine would be transporting two coffins. The funeral rites must have been performed there in the main chapel of the cathedral as the widow had already requested permission for this on June 2, 1537. The remains of both father and son, along with those of other family members that were buried subsequently, remained at that site until November 21, 1795. The Treaty of Basel, signed on that date, provided or Spain's cession of sovereignty over the eastern coast of Santo Domingo, and the remains were transported to Havana. Columbus' remains lay in repose in the Cuban cathedral until 1898. After the loss of Cuba, the Spanish government decided to repatriate the admiral's remains so that they could rest permanently in the cathedral at Seville. There they were interred in a monument on the Epistle side of the sanctuary.

So many transfers caused a series of nationalistic controversies that impassioned the hearts of people on both sides. Las Casas maintains that the admiral's remains never left Santo Domingo and that what was delivered and then transported to Havana were the ashes of someone else. The Cubans insist Columbus' body still rests in their cathedral, and the Spanish claim that what little remains of Columbus' bones are in Seville. One would hope that some new document would come forward to shed light on a question that has become political, making room for futile and almost senseless controversy. As proposed at a Columbian conference held in Seville in 1988, perhaps the solution is that the remains contained in three urns should be mixed together and divided again into three new and equal shares to be distributed among the sites that are squabbling over such macabre contents.

In any case, Christopher Columbus suffered much during his life and today, five hundred years after his death, he still cannot rest in peace.

THE BELL FROM THE
SANTA MARIA
chapter 5

191 THIS SMALL SHIP'S BELL, PARTIALLY CORRODED BY SALTWATER, PROBABLY RANG OUT ON 12 OCTOBER 1492, SIGNALING THE DISCOVERY OF THE NEW WORLD.

THE FASCINATION OF THE ABYSS

A world exists that is so close, yet so far from us, a world that is so mysterious, so fascinating that for thousands of years it was the object of countless attempts at discovering its mysteries. Yet, as impossible as it seems, we now know infinitely more about the immense void of these dark oceanic depths that hide immeasurable lost treasure and real time capsules of history. They lie imprisoned in the scores of shipwrecks lying idle on sea beds and ocean floors throughout the world.

How many of us wouldn't feel transported back in time at the surprise of discovering a buried treasure, an ancient wrecked galleon loaded with chests full of gold coins and magnificent jewelry studded with precious gems?

As for me, I was born in Castronno, a small village in the pre-Alps of Varese, Italy, so far from the ocean that enchanted me so much that I remained literally glued to the television when documentaries from Jacques Cousteau's "Old Man of the Sea" series were shown.

The sound track, the images – still in black and white – everything was so electrifying and magical but, more than anything else, mysterious. And, at the end of every episode, it was clear to me that the documentary had only skimmed the surface of a world that seemed to have no boundaries and had so much to give in terms of intoxicating emotion, the stuff of fantasy and imagination.

The passion that images of those first pioneers of the abyss kindled in me was so intense that every year, I anxiously awaited the arrival of the summer season when I could put on my mask and flippers to then plunge into Lake Monate. Thanks to a policy of conservation and ecological good management that small but very beautiful lake with transparent water is still the destination of many swimmers today.

To emulate the scuba divers from the *Calypso*, as Cousteau's oceanographic ship was called, I built quite a "professional" respirator by connecting two glass bottles, attaching old faucets to them with insulated tape and, even in such a basic form, this became my first scuba-diving equipment.

Years passed and, even if I can't provide details for security reasons, I can tell you that due to my military training, which was among the best in the world, I became a professional scuba diver and hydrodynamics engineer. Honorably discharged, owing to my technical knowledge and skills, I worked on the construction of diverse underwater robots (called ROVs), an acronym generally meaning "Remote Operations Vehicles" or more commonly, remote control vehicles. With these ROVs I was finally able to devote myself to "going where no man has gone before." It was a dream I'd had since I was very young.

At the beginning, I had to content myself with exploring the bed of Lake Maggiore, where I quickly located the remains of the *Milano*, a steamer that had sunk during World War II. And, after finding it with such ease, I embarked on a new and more difficult search.

My previous find had encouraged me to search for a mysterious shipwreck, which had taken place at the beginning of the 1900s, close to our border with Switzerland. We should note that the northernmost part of Lake Maggiore

extends for some miles into Swiss territory, and a surveillance service employing torpedo boats (motor boats about 66 ft/20 m) long) to combat the transport of contraband has been established in these waters.

One night, one of these boats and its whole crew disappeared without a trace.

The recovery of this particular torpedo boat, the *Locusta*, became my new goal and, with the help of a local business that offered me the use of a pontoon boat, I set out to search for the *Locusta* and, in just a few days, I located its remains at a depth of about 656 ft (200 m).

In the next years, while perfecting my ROVs, I deployed them on two recovery operations I would have been willing to accomplish even on my own. The first was in Lake Iseo and the second

in Lake Como, where I had to search and recover the bodies of two divers who, owing to unfortunate accidents, had drowned and drifted to such depths as to prevent their recovery by other divers.

Clearly, I had also been working on other diving projects in the area of archaeology, and treacherous, rather risky projects like the "reclamation of explosive devices." Through my military diving training, I had learned to locate and recover every sort of bullet or bomb that, during the two World Wars, had wound up in deep water and had to be removed to allow for the construction of a bridge or the dredging of a canal and to avoid accidental collision and explosion of such items of ammunition.

One day while I was busy assisting Erik, one of my divers who was looking for a very valuable watch lost by a lady as she was berthing her boat at the Laveno dock on Lake Maggiore. . .

FIRST EFFORTS

It was one of those sad and grey days when the winter had already removed the leaves from the larch trees along the lake near the Laveno dock and the air was cold. I almost envied Erik, who was underwater, thoroughly searching among the algae on the lake. I asked myself if it were possible that the lady had really lost the gold Rolex that had been on her wrist. . .

I was deep in thought when I heard my cell phone ring. It was Ennio, a friend and diving instructor from FIAS (Italian Federation for Diving) asking me if I had read the most recent issue of *Mondo Sommerso* (Underwater World) magazine. Ennio was quite familiar with my passion for searching lost shipwrecks and I could already imagine what he wanted to discuss with me. Every month, *Mondo Sommerso* published articles regarding more or less interesting shipwrecks, but this time had delivered something that was truly sensational. I stopped into a bookstore to buy the magazine and quickly understood what it was all about.

A certain Claudio B., who came across as an expert historian on shipwrecks, recounted the story of two Spanish galleons that, having returned from the Americas, became wrecked off the Portuguese coast in 1555, loaded with an enormous cargo of gold and silver. Despite the fairly accurate data on the locations of the shipwrecks, recovery expeditions of that period didn't have much luck and only one of the two was definitely located, with the recovery of only a small part of its cargo.

The two galleons were both named *San Salvador*. They were part of a fleet that set sail from San Juan, Puerto Rico in October 1555 under the command of General Gonzalo de Carvajal. By direct order of Charles V, Holy Roman Emperor and King of Spain, the fleet had the task of carrying to Spain a valuable cargo of gold and silver that had reached Puerto Rico a few months before, onboard a fleet led by Rodriguez de Farfán. It emerged from the archival documents examined by Claudio B. that only the flagship of the fleet, the *Santa Catalina*, had successfully reached the Portuguese port and city of Lisbon. Adverse conditions at sea had caused the wreck of the *San Salvador I* near the Portuguese town of Buarcos (now a suburb of Figueira da Foz) while the *San Salvador II* (also known as the *Condesa*) had sunk straight to the seabed, on the coast near the town of Carrapateira, in the Algarve.

After reading the magazine, I went to Ennio's house to comment that as interesting as the article was, it seemed more like a tale than true historical research. At that moment, I would never have dreamed that those two lost galleons would soon change my life. Ennio was enthusiastic about the article and conjectured about an expedition to Portugal to search for the two wrecked galleons. Nevertheless, my reservations dampened his enthusiasm. The Portuguese coastline was actually located more than 1200 miles (1930 km) away, making a potential expedition costly, without even considering whether or not the galleons had really been shipwrecked just off that coast. Not to mention the fact that they had to be located in a very difficult spot to investigate. In addition, big ocean waves constantly hit that stretch of the coast, making diving there almost impossible.

The evening passed pleasantly between the laughter and storytelling, but I have to admit that curiosity was starting to eat away at my brain, and I returned home to reread Claudio B.'s article very carefully. The historical research was quite meticulous and the original photographed documents, enlarged with a very powerful lens and then reproduced, were quite clear and readable. I had no doubt that the indications contained in these photos were quite precise.

Was it possible that no one had yet discovered these shipwrecks?

The temptation was strong and the more that time passed, the more the idea of going to Portugal piqued my interest. However, the fact remained that in order to organize an expedition to Portugal, I first had to find some absolutely trustworthy travel companions. This endeavor was about searching for a valuable treasure, and in a case like that, nobody could ever predict the reactions of a person confronted with such a discovery. Besides being absolutely honorable people, the other members of this expedition also had to be expert divers and, above all, free to accompany me to Portugal.

The more I thought about it, the more the logistics seemed insurmountable, but I decided to make the attempt anyway. The first person that came to mind was Erik, a French diver with whom I was working and who would not hesitate for a second to give me a yes. Unfortunately, Ennio had to be excluded since the expedition would take place in July when the ocean is fairly calm and peak tourist season of the August vacation period had not yet begun. And, Ennio just wasn't available in July.

I still had to find a third member who could stay on the boat while the other two would dive as well as share the driving over the length of our trip. The only person who came to mind was Luciano, an excellent diver with a great spirit of adventure whom I had met during the operation to recover the body of a diver who had disappeared in Lake Como a couple of years before. Luciano also could not leave town in July but suggested that I try to contact Silvio, a friend of his in the Cantù diving club. I met with Silvio a few days later. He was 35 years old and not very tall, but he had a kind face and, after some deep reflection about my plan, he accepted it.

The team was set and all we had to do was organize the logistics. In the following months, we prepared everything, the vehicle, the small trailer – and both of them wound up jam-packed. We even had a small rubber raft with an outboard motor.

I remember thinking: "We really have to be crazy to throw ourselves into an adventure like this as we don't have the faintest idea of what we might encounter upon our arrival." I felt a little like Christopher Columbus himself who, after struggling so much to assemble his small fleet, would leave for God only knew where, and would find only God knows what, out there in that immense body of water that carried the name of Great Sea Ocean in that era.

At last, we left for Portugal in search of one of the two lost galleons: the one shipwrecked off the coast of Carrapateira. The trip passed quite peacefully and, every once in a while, we stopped to check the tires and engine oil level. Each time we passed through a border, we needed to exchange lira, first to French francs, then to Spanish pesetas, and finally to Portuguese escudos. One of the most pleasant things was that every time we came into a new country, everything always cost less.

Once across the Portuguese border we found ourselves driving through orange groves whose flowering trees perfumed the pure and uncontaminated air, something that we were not accustomed to. In those places, everything had a different scent as if time had stood since the last century.

We arrived close to what must have been our destination at night; dark roads with almost no signs did not make things any easier. We decided to stay at a roadside rest stop to await the first light of dawn and then sum up the situation. In the morning we tried to figure out where we were. The evening before, we had taken the highway to Arrifana and, using a map, we ascertained that before arriving in Arrifana, we would have to pass Carrapateira. Off this point, our galleon had presumably sunk in 1555, at least that's what Pedro de Galarza's letter to the Spanish rulers had reported after the search for the shipwreck had proved fruitless.

"Year of our Lord, 1558, Your Majesties, [...] the ship going towards Lisbon was lost at Carrapateira, four leagues from Lagos, in line with the rock, at a depth of fifty fathoms and the divers sent by Your Graces are only searching the area where they dropped anchor."

There were no doubts that Carrapateira corresponded to the present-day village of Carrapatera and the rock in the document could be a cliff at the front of a rocky promontory. It was marked on the nautical map that I had brought with me, indicated as *pedra da galè*, which, translated from Old Portuguese, means "galleon rock."

We started back on the road and after just a few hundred yards a rusty signpost printed with "Welcome to Carrapateira" appeared in front of us. Less than three quarters of a mile (400 m) later, really old white houses came into view, so old that they were probably there before our galleon had sunk. Just after arriving in town, I saw a signpost in the shape of an arrow on the left, bearing the word "Pontal." It was the exact name of the promontory where the *pedra da galè* was located. Excited, we immediately turned onto the little road that, after a few hundred yards, ended alongside an impressive cliff, under which the ocean roared angrily.

It was an amazing sight. The cliff had to be at least 100 ft (30m) high and the ocean swelled rhythmically beneath it as if it were going to climb right up and then descend, transforming the rocks into countless foaming waterfalls. A bit further in front of us, a line of semi-outcropped rocks ended with what doubtless had to be the famous *pedra da galè*.

Looking at the imposing cliff, I quickly thought: "How are we going to get down that?" The beach was on the right side of the promontory but the waves wouldn't have allowed us to put our small rubber craft in the water. Here was a problem we hadn't considered. Was it possible that after so many preparations and miles traveled, we wouldn't even be able to get in the water? I took the binoculars and began to inspect the coast and, at a certain point followed the coastline north, and could just make out a marina lying beneath a tiny village. The town was so small that I wasn't at all sure what it was. It must have been Arrifana. In fact, by examining the nautical map, I discerned that Arrifana had a small fishermen's port and, with enormous satisfaction, I noticed that there was even a nearby campsite. Certain that we would have to navigate our little rubber craft for a few miles before arriving at *pedra da galè*, we were all more than ready to do so.

Arriving quickly at the campsite where we could detach the trailer and lighten the load, we ate something then went down to the port to check out the situation. Turning my eyes toward the promontory where the galleon must have sunk, I tried to imagine myself at the moment of shipwreck. I thought about the desperate shouts of the sailors trying in vain to avoid a catastrophe, of the merchants coming back from the New World to their families in Spain with the proceeds from their work, and about how they had lost everything, probably even their lives. I thought about how desperation felt when realizing that, after so much danger and sacrifice, all was lost just within reach of that final destination. In fact, Cape St. Vincent was so close that the shipwrecked had to know that, once they rounded this rocky promontory, they would be forced away from the coast and exposed to the whims of the open sea, then on to the southern coast of Portugal where they'd be sheltered from the winds and Atlantic currents. A few more miles of sailing would have been enough to secure their safety in the calm waters on the Bay of Sagres, yet the cruelty of destiny instead denied salvation to that ship and its crew. I asked myself how many ships and courageous sailors might have disappeared off that stretch of very beautiful, but very dangerous coastline.

While engrossed in thoughts I didn't realize that my compatriots in adventure had, in the meantime, started chatting with some fishermen from the port. The news they gathered wasn't good at all.

None of us would be diving around the Carrapatera promontory because the previous year, some Portuguese divers had reported finding some cannons just where we thought the *San Salvador* galleon had been shipwrecked. We had arrived too late.

At that moment, I have to admit that I was profoundly disappointed but, after a few minutes of silence, I turned to my traveling buddies and proposed that we dive anyway so that we could at least take a look at the galleon's cannons. We got ready for the next day.

After breakfast in the campsite bar, we returned to the port and, berthing the small rubber craft, we headed toward Pontal. The ocean was calm and the waves moved like the breathing chest of a sleeping giant. During our journey, we ran into a school of sardines that jumped out of the water as we passed, frightened by the noise of the outboard motor.

The trip lasted almost an hour and a half and, arriving near the cliff, we quickly realized that it was impossible to get any closer because the waves were truly daunting at that point. Probably, the presence of enormous underwater rocks, shaped by the rather strong currents, made the ocean swell even more, forming waves that were breaking against the cliff with a deafening and threatening uproar.

It proved correct that diving with oxygen cylinders would have been too backbreaking and very risky. I then understood why divers discovering wrecks have dived in without tanks. Without that burden, they could have easily fought hard against the current or waves.

Unfortunately, we hadn't prepared to dive without breathing apparatus as it differs quite a bit, not just in technique, but more so in the equipment used. It was clear then that we wouldn't be able to dive. So clear that we returned to the little marina at Arrifana and, once back at the campsite, reluctantly prepared for our return to Italy.

I arrived in Italy with the strong determination to return to Portugal. But alas, destiny wanted neither Erik nor, even less so, Silvio to return as my compatriots in adventure, even though I would always remember them with affection and gratitude.

THE *SAN SALVADOR* SHIPWRECK

The second galleon cited by the *Mondo Sommerso* article, the one that sank off the coast of Buarcos, also bore the name *San Salvador*. I gathered from the dates in the article that it had sunk in the first months of 1555 in the waters off the Portuguese coast, across from the place now known as Figueira da Foz, where at that time there had been only a small fishermen's village called Buarcos.

In 1993, I decided to go to Figueira da Foz to search for the ship's remains but the particular form and structure of the coast somewhat complicated any determination of where the *San Salvador* shipwreck site might be; there were no documented points of reference. Documents of that era did not refer to a specific area but just to the Playa del Lorical, a name that now must be obsolete given that no similar name appeared on my nautical map. Once in Figueira da Foz, I made contact with various people, but none of them were familiar with the Playa del Lorical. Discouraged by this first fruitless attempt, I left Portugal, ever more convinced that there was a great demand for scuba diving in Figueira da Foz. Given that it had not yet been developed by anyone else, I could personally start a lucrative business in scuba-diving equipment and training courses. So, I got organized, bought the necessary equipment, and returned to Portugal with the intention of setting up a new business – and with two goals in mind. The first would be to cultivate a passion for diving in that market, and second, to find a way to finance my *San Salvador* research in Portugal.

On the first trip, I had met a pharmacist in Coimbra, George, who was already passionate about scuba diving, and his brother Edoardo, who managed a sporting goods store with diving equipment and also manufactured surfboards.

They had offered me assistance. I arrived in Figueira da Foz, contacted them, and quickly began to arrange advertising for scuba-diving training courses. Meanwhile, I talked to them about the *San Salvador*, showed them maps, documents, photocopies, and the article published in *Mondo Sommerso*. We decided to find the *San Salvador* together.

Edoardo directed me to the library at Figueira da Foz where historical documents and shipwreck registries were kept. I dwelled on a particular passage in a letter written by a Pedro de Galarza. His letter talked about the *San Salvador* shipwreck and the place where he became a guest at the monastery of Nuestra Señora de Seiça in Casal de Marin, located right across from the beach where the galleon had been shipwrecked.

His letter also explained that the king of Spain had given him the responsibility of recovering any and all items surviving the shipwreck, also authorizing him to search the houses of local fishermen. It was quite normal in those times for neighboring inhabitants to collect anything that had washed up on shore after a shipwreck.

The monastery of Nuestra Señora de Seiça still exists; over the centuries it had been transformed into a factory that was later abandoned. Today, it is not much more than a ruin but it constituted a valuable geographical reference to aid me in finding the shipwreck site. I would just have to consult my map and the beach facing the monastery could be none other than the "famous" Playa del Lorical. Today, the beach is called Osso da Baleia, which means "whale bone" in Portuguese. The beach is a very long rectilinear strip of sand that starts almost right at Figueira da Foz and ends after about 43.5 miles (70 km) at a sort of small rocky promontory by a small town called Pedrogo.

I then had to concentrate my search along a little over 12 miles (19.3. km) of beach, and decided to comb it with a metal detector. Complicating things were the remains of a cargo ship that had wrecked in the area, leaving small pieces of iron, cast aluminum, screws, and bolts scattered all over the sand.

I decided to try anyway. With Edoardo one evening when it was starting to get dark, the metal detector emitted a sound and I, not really thinking I was mistaken, starting digging with my hands. I quickly found a rather large coin, cleaned it off, and realized that it was quite old: I recognized the coat of arms of the Spanish royal house imprinted on it. It was an 8-*reales* coin, consistent with the era of the *San Salvador* shipwreck. A very beautiful silver coin, blackened from seawater oxidation, the inscription was completely legible, "*Carolus* [Charles V] *et Johanna, reges*." Emperor Charles V was on the throne at the time of the *San Salvador* shipwreck and coins transported in that ship had to have been exactly the same as the one I was holding and admiring.

For the next few days we returned to the beach and I devoted at least two or three hours each time to combing continuously through the sand, but to no avail. One day while I was passing my metal detector over the sand, I encountered a fisherman who asked me if I was searching for coins. The man explained that he had found about one hundred very old coins in the same area years before, but maintained that they had no value and that he'd used them as decorative washers to adorn a fence around his home. He had me accompany him to his house and when I saw the fence, I immediately realized that he had drilled holes in more than 100 coins of 2-, 4- and 8-*reales* nominations that once must have been cargo aboard the *San Salvador*.

By then, it was quite clear in my mind where the galleon had become shipwrecked. However, finding its remains would not be easy because the strong ocean waves breaking on the beach would prevent me from diving in from the shoreline. I would have to take a boat from the port at Figueira da Foz, traveling farther offshore to accomplish any dive, and the port was quite a few miles from the shipwreck site. In 1994, I bought a rubber raft and equipped it for the task with a magnetometer, an instrument that plots magnetic changes due to the presence of ferrous or other magnetic metals. Certainly the *San Salvador* remains must have preserved nails, metal dowels or pegs, cannon balls, the cannons themselves, and anchors that were once on board the ship. I voyaged along that strip of coastline for days in my rubber raft without getting any signals from the magnetometer.

One day, almost at high tide when the ocean water was calm, I moved in closer to the coastline, much closer than I ever had before. At one point, the magnetometer needle began to frantically swing and it seemed that I had passed right over the *San Salvador's* cannons as the instrument gave off four very definite signals. I turned around, repeated the same route, and again received the same very strong signals. Looking around the seabed, I couldn't make out anything but sand. So, I then decided to drop anchor just over the exact spot where I'd received the strong signals and dive in. The only thing that I saw underwater was something dark in color pushing up out of the sand. It was wood and such an old piece of wood that when I touched it, it crumbled like ash. It was one of the *San Salvador's* sides. The ribs of the ship were so large that I had no doubt: I was right on top of the *San Salvador*, a galleon of almost 800 tons. When I examined the wood more closely, I saw a round object whose edge looked like some type of strange light grey-colored pot. I moved in closer and saw that it was the lower edge of a bell and with only a modest effort, I freed it from the sand. I had found a small ship's bell, easily recognizable due to its mounting, a thin flat piece of metal with a hole in it. Ship's bells are readily distinguishable from those used on land, primarily in the way they are used. Bells used on land rotate on an axis, swinging back and forth so that the clapper strikes the inside edge while ship's bells are fixed and you must pull on a cord attached to the clapper in order to ring it.

I pulled the bell out of the water and took it to Figueira da Foz. That same evening, I showed it to my buddies – who were not particularly enthusiastic about it. They thought it was an old bell with a hole in its side, and that it had been corroded over hundreds of years in the sea. I washed the bell in fresh water, leaving it in a closed container for several days to avoid potential permanent corrosion from the combined effects of salt and oxygen. My Portuguese friends were more interested in other finds that might still be onboard the *San Salvador* than the bell I had found. I was opposed to "looting" the ship's remains and more inclined to report any finds to the appropriate authorities, happy with any financial compensation deriving from my rights as finder. However, one day, armed with pistols, my "friends" ordered me not to report my find, strongly advising me to stand aside.

Deciding to leave Portugal, I took the bell with me. In Italy, I continued to reflect on the *San Salvador* and the bell. What was a "normal" ship's bell of that size and shape doing on the *San Salvador*, which was a large, important, and prestigious ship? A bell that was certainly manufactured in Europe could have perhaps gone to America, but not returned from America. On a galleon loaded with gold, silver, coins, and emeralds why would a simple bell be part of that cargo? It had to have some value, I thought. I then decided to do in-depth research on the *San Salvador*. In Lisbon in the "Torre do Tombo" archives, I found a document, which later mysteriously disappeared, referencing Christopher Columbus and saying that there were various objects on the *San Salvador* linked with "Colón's" flagship (Columbus had many flagships, but the most famous was certainly the *Santa Maria*).

I determined to have the bell analyzed by experts. Thanks to connections through my friend Albano, I first dropped it off for examination at the "Arqueolise" in Nice, an organization that restores archaeological artifacts found in the sea. Complete analyses established that it was a very old ship's bell and had been in the sea for hundreds of years. I had a second set of analyses done by a professor of archaeo-metallurgy at the University of Bologna and he also confirmed that the metal object had spent more than four or five hundred years in the sea.

These revealing analyses motivated me to do further archival research. I found other documents, which also mysteriously disappeared, confirming that the bell from the *Santa Maria* had traveled on the *San Salvador*. In one document, the sentence, "la Capitana Santa Maria por grazia dell'Amirante Colón" stood out with the monogrammed signature of Columbus right next to it. I took a photograph of the page and showed it to some experts who readily recognized that it was not an original document but more than likely the copy of an original document.

The forme of a fort wch was made by Mr
Ralfe Lane in a parte of St Johns Ilande
neere Caprosa where we toke in salt
the xxvj of May. 1585.

202 JOHN WHITE SKETCHED THIS FORTIFCATION ON THE COAST OF PUERTO RICO IN HIS 16TH-CENTURY DRAWING (PRIVATE COLLECTION).

203 TOP THE *SANTA MARIA*'S BELL FROM WAS KEPT IN THE FORTRESS AT SAN JUAN, PUERTO RICO, THEN LOADED ONTO THE *SAN SALVADOR* SHIPWRECKED IN 1555 WITH ALL THE REST OF ITS CARGO.

203 BOTTOM CREATED IN 1599 BY THE FRENCH EXPLORER, SAMUEL DE CHAMPLAIN, THIS MAP DEPICTS PUERTO RICO WHERE THE *SAN SALVA*... SET SAIL WITH ITS PRECIOUS CARGO (ROYAL COMMONWEALTH SOCIETY, LONDON, GREAT BRITAIN).

204 Roberto Mazzara recovered this small ship's bell in 1994 from the remains of the shipwrecked *San Salvador*.

205 Acquired by the city of Florence, this document quotes a list of shipwrecks in the year 1556. One listing refers to the cargo of the *San Salvador*, commanded by Guilherm de Lugo, setting sail from Puerto Rico and becoming wrecked off the coast of Buarcos. Emerging from this document, one detail stands out that in addition to large quantities of gold and silver, the "bell" from Fort Navidad, Hispaniola, was also on board.

206 and 207 Chemical and physical analyses performed on the bell recovered near the Osso da Baleia beach in Portugal have confirmed its antiquity, dating it to the same era as Christopher Columbus.

Luij.

ꝓ Otro registro dela nao nombrada na señora dela Ayuda
de que vino por maestre rodrigo madera de santo domingo
y aporto a cadiz

Lb.

ꝓ Otro registro dela nao nombrada san salbador de que venia
por maestre diego bernal de tierra firme En compania del
almiranta de que vino por capitan general fray fran° monten
 poral aporto a puertorico y el otro maestre conel
registro y oro y plata vino enuna delas naos del alm̄
on de don gonçalo de caruajal q aporto a lisbona

Lvj.

ꝓ Otro registro dela nao nombrada sant mortolina de
que vino por maestre Joannes de mota de puertorico
q es la almiranta de don gonçalo de caruajal q aporto
a lisbona

Lbij.

ꝓ Otro registro dela nao nombrada san Joan de que vino
por maestre Joan mynez de venian de puerto deplata
y aporto a villa nueua de portimar

Lbiij.

ꝓ Otro registro dela nao nombrada el espiritu sancto de
que venia por maestre lopegran de ysasa de honduras
la qual diz que contemporal aporto a las yslas delos
açores donde diz que descargo el oro e plata q trahia

LX°.

ꝓ Otro registro dela nao nombrada san salbador de que
venia por maestre guillen de lugo de puertorico la
qual diz que se perdio a burrios con mucho oro
e plata y el signo de villa de la marisena

LX.

ꝓ Otro registro dela nao nombrada ña señora dela luz
de que vino por maestre bartolo bello desanctosomyn
go el qual aporto a lisbona

Montados los registros de
venida deste año de JUDLb
años LX Registros

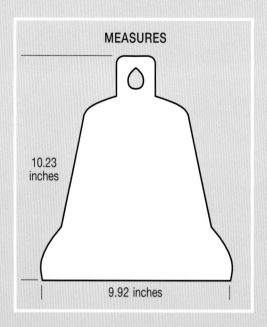

MEASURES

10.23 inches

9.92 inches

METALLURGICAL STRUCTURE OF THE BELL

Chemical composition of original metal

		%Cu	%Sn	%Pb
Global Composition	Media	75.02	20.30	4.68
	DS	2.32	1.66	0.80
α Phase	Media	86.17	13.83	
	DS	0.69	0.69	
$\alpha + \delta$ Phase	Media	67.83	32.17	
	DS	0.92	0.92	

Chemical composition of oxidized material (% of weight)

		%Cu	%Sn	%Pb	%Cl
α Phase corrosion	Media	36.19	45.81	11.34	6.30
	DS	13.86	10.58	1.80	1.31
$\alpha + \delta$ Phase corrosion	Media	19.34	66.08	12.32	2.27
	DS	7.74	6.15	1.69	0.61

MINISTERIO DE EDUCACIÓN Y CULTURA
Secretaría General Técnica

Madrid, 2 de Junio de 2000

Sr. Mazzara Roberto
Urbanización Aldea de Alguetares;
C/. Pégaso, nº 6
ALGECIRAS (Cádiz)

Estimado Sr.:

En contestación a su escrito recibido a través de la Casa de S.M. el Rey, y de acuerdo con el informe emitido por la Subdirección General de Protección del Patrimonio Histórico, le comunico lo siguiente:

En relación con los restos de un Galeón supuestamente localizado en las costas de "Portogallo", deberá ponerse en contacto con la Subdirección General antes mencionada (ubicada en Pza. del Rey, nº 1 28071 MADRID, Tfno.: 91-701 70 35), a la que deberá facilitar una información clara sobre los siguientes términos: lugar del hundimiento; pruebas que atestigüen que se trata de un Galeón español; entrega de los materiales recuperados a quien Vd. reconoce como legítimo propietario; y, a partir de ahí, establecer las conversaciones que este Ministerio considere legalmente convenientes para el interés de España.

Atentamente,

Fdo.: Juan Ignacio Cabo Pan.
Jefe del Centro de Información
y Atención al Ciudadano.

AL COMANDANTE MILITAR DE MARINA
DE LA PROVINCIA MARITIMA DE ALGECIRAS
SR. D. ARTURO CUÑA MIÑAN

De: Mazzara Roberto
Empresa: ABYSS
Nº TELEF Y FAX: 956-605146
Nº TELEF MOVIL: 619643694
C/PEGASO,6 ,URB. "ALDEA DE ALGETARES"
11.207-ALGECIRAS (CADIZ)

Estimado Sr.

Adjunto a esta carta la documentación que acredita mi descubrimiento del año 1.994, en la costa portuguesa, del hundimiento del galeón español San Salvador, documentación del sitio del hundimiento en el año 1.555, que demuestra además, que un objeto encontrado en el citado lugar del naufragio es la campana de la Santa Maria de Cristobal Colón.

Le tramito todo ello originalmente para que Vd. pueda informar a la Autoridad Competente.

Sin otro particular, quedo a su entera disposición y le envio un afectuoso saludo.

Mazzara Roberto

In 1998 I returned to Portugal with Albano to inform the government about my locating the *San Salvador* shipwreck site and finding a bell that had probably been on Columbus' *Santa Maria*, but they did not give me any consideration whatsoever. We then went and spoke with Francisco A., directing manager of the "Stass," the underwater archaeological services department of Portugal, a governmental organization with headquarters in Lisbon. This organization proved to be much more interested in finding out the exact location of the *San Salvador* wreckage than in hearing my detailed account of finding the bell and my subsequent analyses. I was prepared to give Francisco A. any sort of information on the condition that I receive assurances of some financial reward from him and the Portuguese authorities. The *San Salvador* had enormous historical and archaeological importance as well as value from the viewpoint of coin collecting, therefore also the potential for yielding a considerable financial return. However, in return, I received only a negative response from my contact in this organization. Meantime, *Mondo Sommerso* magazine decided to publish an article on the bell with a photograph of it on the first page. After the publication, I decided to get in contact with *RAI Radiotelevisione italiana* (Italian Radio and Television Network) with whom I participated in shooting a short documentary. Then everything just stopped right there. I forgot about the whole event for a while and went to Spain. In the meanwhile, the bell remained in Italy at my home, inside a special container that I had built, enveloped in argon gas that would prevent oxygen from further aggravating the condition of the bronze.

I then considered donating the bell to the Spanish royal family with the twofold goal of ensuring that it would be exhibited in a museum as well as receiving any appropriate and legitimate benefits from my important discovery. I wrote a letter to the Spanish royal residence and received a response from the public relations manager of Spain's Ministry of Education, Culture, and Sports. He told me that I would have to contact whomever I considered to be the legitimate owner of the object. However, I had contacted the Spanish crown directly as, of course, I considered them the rightful owners. . . . I then wrote a letter to the chief of the port authority at Algeciras, Spain to make an official report through the appropriate authorities. Again, I received no positive response. Even a follow-up meeting with an adviser to the Spanish royal family, the vice director and curator of the Naval Museum in Madrid, and a court counsel to the Spanish Military Marines resulted in nothing substantial.

208 In 2000, Roberto Mazzara contacted the Royal Residence in Spain and Spanish authorities to report the discovery of the bell from the *San Salvador* and to organize eventual donation of his find.
The letter on the left, dated 2 June 2000 and addressed to Mazzara from the Spanish Ministry of Education and Culture reads as follows: "In response to your document received at the Royal Residence of Spain, the King, in compliance with the report published by the Deputy Director-General for the Protection of Spain's Historical Heritage, I am forwarding you the following communication: In reference to the remains of the Galleon presumably located off the coast of "Portugal," you should contact the abovementioned Deputy Director-General, providing precise information relative to: location of the shipwreck, results of analyses certifying that it concerns a Spanish galleon, delivery of the found object to whomever is recognized as its legitimate owner, and it will then be necessary to establish any legally appropriate negotiations as mandated by the Ministry in the interest of Spain."
In the letter on the right dated 20 June 2000, Mazzara writes to the naval port authority commander in the maritime province of Algeciras: "I am enclosing documentation certifying my discovery in 1994 off the Portuguese coastline from the shipwreck of the *San Salvador* Spanish galleon, as well as documentation on the site of the shipwreck occurring in 1555 further demonstrating that the object recovered from the previously mentioned shipwreck site is the ship's bell from Christopher Columbus' ship, the *Santa Maria*. I am forwarding to you the originals of all this documentation so that you may inform the proper authorities.

After many futile contacts, I was convinced that the bell did not interest anyone so I could consider it my property and put it up for sale. I needed to complete all necessary scientific and historical investigations certifying that the bell was indeed from the very famous *Santa Maria*. Aided by my girlfriend Isabel, I found the money required to finance the research. I made an agreement with Claudio B. so that he would seek and acquire further documentation in exchange for a percentage of the sale proceeds of the bell. I also I contracted with an auction house in Barcelona that would support me with some financing.

My first stop was in Barcelona where collaboration with a specialized firm produced two 3D copies of the bell with a 3D photogrammetric system. From there, I moved on to the Technological Institute of Aragon in Zaragoza,, where I had a scientific analysis made of the metal in the bell. Then, I went to Portugal, back to the beach facing the place where I'd found the bell to collect sand samples, witnessed by a police officer. These samples were sealed in an envelope by a notary public in Figueira da Foz (an authority similar to an attorney in Europe) and taken to the university department in Zaragoza. There comparative analyses were made of the sand encrusted in the oxide on the bell and of the sand collected on the beach, authenticating the provenance of the bell.

At the same time, Claudio B. located in two documents some important information on the history of the bell. The first asserted that 32 pesos was paid for a bell to be packaged and stored at the fort of San Juan, Puerto Rico during the same period of time when my valuable bell was stored then loaded onto the *San Salvador*. This was quite an elevated price and more or less the equivalent of a year's salary for a sailor at that time. Therefore, the bell had to have had a significantly higher value than any normal bell in that era. The second document reconstructed the events tied to Luigi Columbus, Christopher Columbus' firstborn nephew, who had charged a trustworthy person to send him objects from his uncle in America. This person stored these objects at the fort of San Juan, Puerto Rico then loaded them onto the *San Salvador* himself. Yet, without even a definitive list of the objects designated to Luigi Columbus, the coincidence of Luigi Columbus' request and the presence of a bell at the fort of San Juan, Puerto Rico in the same period of time stood out.

However, the most important document emerged in Florence when I was able to buy an original 1556 manuscript that quoted a list of ship cargoes, arrivals, and wrecks in that year, with the *San Salvador* appearing among those shipwrecks listed. The text of the paragraph regarding the *San Salvador* read "*otro registro de la nau nombrada San Salvador*" ("on the register of the ship named *San Salvador*") "*qe venia por mestre Guilherm de Lugo*" ("coming from Puerto Rico with Commander Guilherm de Lugo") "*el qual diz que se perdió a Buarcos*" ("who states that the ship was wrecked at Buarcos") "*con mucho oro, mucha plata, y el signo de la villa de la Navidad*" ("with a lot of gold, silver, and the bell from the Christmas village"). The word, *signo*, in the old Castilian language is defined as a small-sized bell and the *villa de la Navidad* is the name of the small fort Columbus had constructed on the island of Hispaniola, using the wood recovered from the *Santa Maria*, which had run aground on a sandbank on Christmas night in 1492.

We had collected more than enough proof to demonstrate that the bell in my possession was the one that had saluted the discovery of the New World on 12 October 1492: in fact, the only object in existence from the expedition that had discovered the North American continent.

There was nothing more to do but arrange the auction, which would be held at the Hotel Ritz in Madrid on 17 February 2002. Three days before the auction, plainclothes policemen purportedly belonging to a special security unit impounded the bell, saying that the Portuguese government had reported my friend Albano and me to authorities for "robbery," requiring us to appear before the court of Algericas. I immediately set out to find a solution and contacted an attorney who accepted my case in exchange for my commitment to pay him 10 percent of any eventual profit when I had recovered and sold the bell. Making matters even worse, the management of Spanish auction house required me sign an acknowledgment of debt, witnessed by a notary public in Barcelona, equal to a very large amount, calculated at 3 percent of the estimated sale price of the bell.

Realizing that, despite so many battles and sacrifices, many people stood to profit from my precarious financial situation in order to submit me to their claims, I entered the Madrid courtroom hopefully.

The fact that I had already informed the Portuguese authorities in 1998 and the Spanish authorities shortly thereafter, offering the bell immediately and gratuitously to the king of Spain, largely demonstrated my good faith. In addition, more than one year had passed since I'd reported my discovery of the bell, the statute of limitations provided by European Community law regulating property rights for found objects had expired, and no one else had claimed ownership during that time period.

The court proceeding came to a close after many dramatic scenes and there was nothing more to do than wait for the judge's finding. What was really in my favor was the sanctioned statute of limitations on the Portuguese Republic's ownership rights. All I had to do then was to rearrange the sale of the bell. However, the Spanish auction house, to which I proposed arranging an auction in New York, would claim 80 percent of the sale price, taking further advantage of my already difficult financial situation.

At this point, I played one last card and returned to Italy. In an article published in 2007 in the *Prealpina*, a small newspaper in the region of Varese, and in the *Libero* daily paper, I promised 50 percent of the bell's net sale price in exchange for financing to cover my debts and arrange the auction in New York. I then started to receive telephone calls from people interested in discussing the project and was finally able to get some real assistance. Obviously, this is not the end of the story, just the end of the first part because, once sold, the bell would certainly be exhibited in a museum. After that, all of my efforts and all of the historical and scientific research would finally see light of day. At last, the public could admire this historical object of enormous value and great symbolic significance. Because I had not just found any object from the *Santa Maria*, I had found the *Santa Maria*'s bell, the icon, the heart and soul of this ship. It was this bell that echoed the legendary cry of "Land Ahoy" from Rodrigo di Triana when he sighted the line on the horizon that was the island of San Salvador on 12 October 1492.

It was this small, humble bell that signaled the moment that changed world history.

Ytenda por descargo deste tes xpto-
ual de alinas dozientos y ancora [...]
que gasto por la cuesta que la dicha y quatro nesgero nada Parte de la plata de sum
de los noveis e xviii pesos vii tomines
que segasto por la plata y ca-
ualdemas de estas personas pa-
ril areso vino parege por el iiii xx libro
iii con carta de pago la deсendio ——————

Ytenda por descargo deste tes qu-
ynienta e vni quedio e pago de
y eritando de libra con tre ynta e dos pesos
por la canpana questa en la fortaleza
y a m de canpos geri por la guarniçion
de ... caça para y çiertas aran-
decas yslanisas que hizo para la artiçeria y agrego un garço q que ... de
cierta madera hizo para pessar
la dicha artiçeria que son ... pesos on-
quenta unos di oli bramn con carta
de pago ——————

Ytenda por descargo deste tes
de dozientos e caturze pesos seys t
es e vi granos y son que se los dio e pago
a los e finançes de sum y aleço de
la fortaleza por el ti ... de quis
e a nquenta e anos as Colomen de
... de setienbre y se cun Julios
fin de diz del año e de los que
fatorio fieron e çtro veynte e
e gos e xx tomines ——————

Ytenda por descargo deste tes çro
a rquenta e ys y son glos ixo el
... a m juan lonbardo por los o
ille de aberpor el ti posto que o menz
e corner de soepro de setienbre de atiçi
e a nco el se cunplio fin de dize del año
di de libra mn con carta de pago ——————

212 AND 213 THIS ACCOUNTING DOCUMENT FROM THE REAL HACIENDA OF PUERTO RICO, DRAFTED BETWEEN 1554 AND 1573, MENTIONS A BELL KEPT AT THE FORT OF SAN JUAN, PUERTO RICO. THE TREASURER'S PRICE TO STORE THIS BELL WAS 32 PESOS, QUITE A LARGE AMOUNT FOR THAT TIME (GENERAL ARCHIVE OF THE INDIES, SEVILLE, SPAIN).

a la cota que esta coçiuimos gallegaub Una carauela que viene de sm Juan de puerto rico de que es maestre balta sar goncales que viene cargada de cueros y açucares de Aquella ysla y ha venid Enella pedro de colmenares por pasagero el qual Venia en Una delas naos dela flota de farfan y alli se embarco Enesta carauela

este pedro de colmenares quelas tres naos q faltauon dela flota de farfam Arribaron Aquella ysla donde Avian descargado todo el oro y plata que trayan y quelo an Avian puesto todo Xoy lo que trayan dela hazienda de V. mt como de particulares Enla fortaleza dela

214 AND 215 ON THE FIRST PAGE OF THIS LETTER DATED 4 APRIL 1555, OFFICIALS FROM THE CONTRACTATION HOUSE IN SEVILLE WROTE TO THE KING OF SPAIN, ATTESTING TO THE FACT THAT THREE SHIPS BELONGING TO THE FLEET OF COSME RODRIGUEZ DE FARFÁN HAD LANDED IN PUERTO RICO AND THEIR CARGO OF GOLD, SILVER, AND OTHER PRIVATE PROPERTY HAD BEEN UNLOADED AND WAREHOUSED AT THE FORTRESS IN SAN JUAN. THE BELL FROM THE SANTA MARIA WAS PROBABLY AMONG THOSE ITEMS, STORED FOR A BRIEF PERIOD OF TIME IN THE SAME FORTRESS (GENERAL ARCHIVE OF THE INDIES, SEVILLE, SPAIN).

S · C · C · Mt ·

a la ora que esta escriuimos ha llegado vna carauela que viene
de san juan de puerto rico de que es maestre baltasar goncales
que viene cargada de cueros y açucares de aquella ysla
y ha venido en ella pedro de colmenares por pasagero el
qual venia en vna de las naos de la flota de farfan y alli
se ha bareo en esta carauela y partieron juntas con
ella otras tress cargadas de açucares y cueros y vn
galeon del rrey de portugal que traen cargado de negros
de contratar e vendellos los quales vendio y cargo de
cueros y açucares y alli le tomaron fronça que vernia
al puerto de las muelas desta ciudad a hazer su descarga / dize
este pedro de colmenares que las tres naos que faltaron de la
flota de farfan arribaron aquella ysla donde descargaron
descargaron todo el oro y plata que trayan y questo a visto
puesto todo a buen recaudo lo que trayan de la hazienda de V. Mt.
como de particulares en la fortaleza della e asi mismo a visto
meter el artilleria de las naos para que estubiese
a mejor recaudo y los maestres que lo trayan a cargo se
metieron para que estubiese con mas seguridad y guarda
ya vnque la justicia della les quiso tomar el oro y plata
los maestres no lo quisieron dar y sobre ello les hizieron
cierto requerimiento y asi no solo tomaron y que daron
ello en la fortaleza / con esta biamos vn pliego de cartas
que este navio truxo para V. Mt. y asy mismo el dho
hemos tomado al dho pedro de colmenares el qual dize
viene con despachos para V. Mt. de nuebo rreyno de

x lo que esta se/o frece mas que dezir es que de buarcos nos hacesario pero suarez de castilla y
antonio corço quien algunos dias queçe tiempo ha hecho se bonança han hecho de el rrastro en la
mar y entrado los buzos en ella y no han podido hallar el lugar donde la nao se perdio ni sacar cosa
ninguna se de oro y plata/ dizen que es la costa tan perbersa y el arena tan libiana y mobediça que
ninguna señal se haze rrastro por donde se pasa que luego el arena lo torna a cubrir y en cui asmos mi
hbiese pasado por açi el rrastro convertir se hab se el arena çinco y seys palmos plazera a
dios que con las bonanças del berano que hasta agora ha hecho muy pocas aprouecharase trabajo
y costa que en ello se a puesto y pone.

Por otras hemos dado qta a V.mt delo que aqui se ofrecia y deque debiesemos dalla y hemos
respondido a todas las cartas de V.mt nos ha mandado escreuir estamos esperando lo que
V.mt enello nos embiara a mandar y hagamos./

x lo que en esta se ofrece mas que dezir es que de buzos nos ha escripto pero suarez de castilla y
antonio corco que en algunos dias que le tiempo a hecho de bonança han hechado el rastro ala
mar y entrado los buzos enella y no han podido hallar el lugar donde la nao se perdio ni sacar cosa
ninguna de oro y plata/ dizen que es la costa tan peruersa y el arena tan liuiana y mobediça que
ninguna señal de al rastro por donde pasa que luego el arena lo torna a cubrir y sin que al mismo
bbiese pasado por alli el rastro conentrar debaxo del arena cinco y seys palmos plazera a
dios con las bonanças del berano que hasta agora a hecho muy pocas aprouecharse el trauajo
y costa que en ello se a puesto y pone/ ala garrapatera hemos embiado a alonso de baça con
un rastro que hizimos hazer para alli y todos los aparejos necesarios/ y algunos buzos que
no sabemos que sean llegados./

x de zahara tenemos abiso del comendador Juan rrallon y de las otras personas que alli
tenemos como hecharon el rastro y conel sacaron quarenta y quatro marcos de oro y ochen
ta y tres mrs de plata los quales nos ymbiaron aqui abra siete o ocho dias y lo bendimos todo
y balio un quento y ciento y treynta y tres mill mrs y despues hemos tenido abiso dellos/ que
auian sacado otros treynta y tres mrs de oro conel rastro lo que mas se hiziere ya y en biaron
y garrapatera como en zahara daremos abiso a V.mt/

x las partidas que cada dia ba de barando el alld salazar de lo que e an sacado desta nao
y de lo que V.mt se mando seruir del oro y plata que truxo o lo peguaran ser asi son
muchas y asi mismo las que por cedula de V.mt nos manda bolber que aun que bbiesemos
obrado lo que se beel thesorero dela casa dela moneda no abria ya pon de se se cumplir y
pagar y asi estamos en mucho trauajo y confusion por no poder cumplir todo lo que V.mt
nos tiene mandado que paguemos y cumplamos asi delas partidas que tomamos prestadas
de mercaderes como para pagar las aberias de todo lo que V.mt se mando seruir de lo que
se tomo de pasajeros y particulares como delas aberias de lo dela florida y asimismo delas
partidas que V.mt manda que se buelban a sus dueños que no llegaron a tener cuidado
en lo dela florida/ y asi se quexan todos de nosotros pareciendoles que no se les paga ni
buelbe sus partidas por no querer se las nosotros pagar aun que en estas partidas dela
florida no se e a dexado de pagar a todos los que por ellas an benido y se les yra pagando
como V.mt nos lo tiene mandado/ y asi mismo ay mucha falta de dineros para probeer el

tenãna hũ qual de poys de acabar na Jndia ho seutpo da gouernança turnando pera
portugal ho mataraõ os cafres na agoada de saldanha, enesta pelleja morrerão
passante de 50. homes nobres, e que entrarão/ 12. capitaes, e os desta frota
erão. ∿deσ

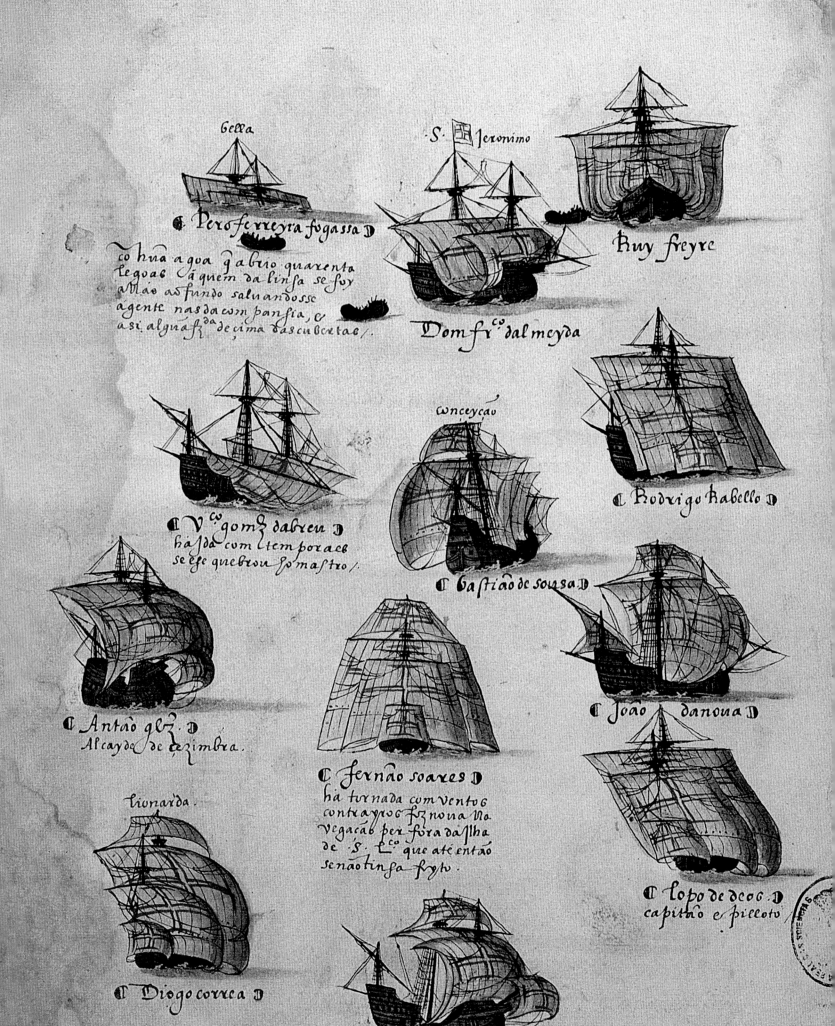

bella

S. Jeronimo

Ruy freyre

Pero ferreyra fogassa

co hũa agoa q abrio quarenta
legoas a quem da linha se foy
abrio ao fundo saluandosse
agente nas dacompanhia, e
asi algũafz de cima dascubertas.

Dom frco dal meyda

Vco gomz dabreu
há yda com tempo ael
se ele quebrou ho mastro.

conceycão

Rodrigo Rabello

bastião de sousa

Antão glz.
Alcayde de çezimbra.

fernão soares
há turnada com ventos
contrayros fznona na
vegacão per fora da Jlha
de .S. Lco que ate então
senaotinha fryto.

Joaõ danoua

lionarda.

Diogo correa

lopo de deog.
capitão e pilloto

S. Jorfe.

Janhomem.

Dom fr.^{do} deßa.

gonçallo de payua.

Antao Vaz.

lopo ysanoq.^a

gonçallo vaz de goes.

fellipe Roix.

taforea.

Bermu diaz.
hũ fidalgo caste ßano.

lucas da fonseq.^a
Jnd noui em moçambiqh

com temporaes q̃ leue eçabrio alta gñia
agoa, & pella naõ poder vencer verão
cõ ella em ceõ / cõo / Reyzão ...

carauellaõ.

A

Aegean Sea, 66
Aetna, Mount 61
Aguado, Juan, 25, 159, 161
Aguero, Jeronimo de, 43
Ailly, Pierre D', 77, 80c, 82
Albano, 201, 209, 211
Alexander VI, Pope, 39c, 46, 47c, 116, 126c
Alfraganus, 80, 82
Algarve, coast of, 67, 70, 195c, 195
Alonso, Martin, 98, 99, 110c
Anacaona, 152
Andalusia, 34, 47, 61
Anghiera, Peter Martyr of, 25, 47, 159
Anjou, René of, 66, 67
Antilles, 66, 74, 98, 110c, 116
Antonio (from Calabria, Italy), 98
Aragon, Cardinal Luis de, 159
Arana, Beatriz Enrìquez de, 28, 35, 183
Arana, Diego de, 35
Arana, family, 35
Arana, Pietro de, 35
Arbues, Pedro de, 40
Arriaga, Luis de, 152
Atlantic Ocean, 69c, 70, 71, 72c, 74, 80, 184
Ayala, Juan de, 152
Azores, 47c, 82

B

Baeza, Gonzalo de, 43
Ballester, Miguel, 152, 161
Barbary Coast, 60
Bardi, Francesco de', 35, 45, 182c, 182, 183, 184
Bargali, Marco de, 52
Bastidas, 124
Bayona, 99
Beaujeu, Anne de, 31
Beechío, 161
Behaim, Martín, 74
Bejerano, Antonio Cabral, 101c

Benzoni, Girolamo, 18c, 25, 154c
Berardi, Giannotto, 31, 33, 41, 45, 47, 49, 77
Bernal de Pisa 24, 156
Blanes, Jaime Ferrer de, 40
Bobadilla, Beatriz de (the *Cazadora*), 43
Bobadilla, Beatriz de (Marquise of Moya), 43, 45c
Bobadilla, Francisco de, 43, 45, 123, 164, 165, 166c, 166, 167, 168, 169, 174c, 174, 176, 177, 184
Bonao, 152, 161, 167
Bordone, Benedetto, 150c
Brazil, 98, 110c
Briviesca, Ximeno de, 45
Bry, Johann Theodor de, 18c, 98c, 119c, 140c, 154c, 156c, 161c, 162c
Buarcos, 195, 198, 204c, 210, 216c
Buil, Brother Bernardo, 25, 46, 116, 156, 158, 159, 161c
Burgundy, 34

C

Cabo das Palmas, 80
Cabo do Monte, 80
Cabo Roxo, 80
Cabo Verde, 80
Cabot, John, 53, 71, 137c
Cabral, Alvares, 98
Cabral-Bejerano, Antonio, 28c
Cabrera, Andres, 43
Cabrero, Juan, 39, 40
Calvo, Tomas, 184
Canaries, 74c, 82, 98, 122, 164c
Cantino World Map, 77c, 137c
Caonabo, 150, 159
Cape Creus, 60
Cape Mizen, 71
Cape Saint Vincent, 67, 135, 197
Cape Verde, 47c

Caprioli, Aliprando, 18c
Caribbean, 26, 35
Caro, Diego, 98
Carrapateira (Carrapatera), 195c, 195, 197
Carvajal, Alonso Sanchez de, 45, 46, 176, 194
Carvajal, Gonzalo de, 194
Casal de Marin, 199
Casenove, Guillaume de (Columbus the Elder), 69
Catai, 71, 98
Cattaneo, Diego, 124
Cattaneo, Franco, 180
Cattaneo, Francesco, 52
Cattaneo, Rafael, 45
Cea, Doctor, 42
Centurion, family, 47, 52, 70, 77
Centurion, Gaspar, 184
Centurion, Ladislao, 74
Cerda, Don Luis de la, 39, 42
Cervantes, Gonzalo Gamez de, 169
Champlain, Samuel de, 203c
Chanca, Diego Alvarez, 116, 150, 156
Charles I, 164c
Charles V, 194, 199c, 199
Charles VIII, 31
Chios, island of, 66, 66c
Chopin, 49c
Cibao, 152, 158, 162
Cipango (Japan), 82, 105c
Cisneros, Don Francisco de, 46, 47c, 164, 168
Ciudad Real, Alvar Gomez de, 43
Claudio B., 194, 195
Clavijo, Alonso, 98
Collantes, 43
Coloma, Juan de, 39, 94
Coloma, Mosen, 39
Columbus, Andrea, 33, 34, 124
Columbus, Bartolomeo, 15, 31, 33, 34c, 53, 122, 123, 124, 130c, 135, 152, 156c, 158, 159, 161, 164, 166, 167, 182, 183
Columbus, Bianchinetta, 15
Columbus, Diego (son), 14, 22, 28, 28c, 30c, 30, 31, 33, 35, 36, 39, 40, 42, 49, 53, 74c, 94, 152, 153, 178, 179, 180, 183, 184, 187
Columbus, Diego (brother), 15, 31, 33, 34, 116, 159, 162c, 166, 167, 183
Columbus, Domenico, 123
Columbus, Fernando, 12c, 14, 15, 18, 21c, 22, 28, 30c, 30, 31, 33, 34c, 39, 41, 42, 60, 65c, 69, 94, 116, 124, 130c, 158, 159, 165, 169, 174, 182, 183
Columbus, Giovanni Antonio, 33, 34, 45, 53, 182c, 184, 187
Columbus, Giovanni Pellegrino, 15
Columbus, Luigi, 210
Coma, Guillermo, 40, 152
Conceptio Marie, island of, 106c
Concepción de La Vega, 28, 152, 161, 166
Coronel, Pedro Hernandez, 122
Corsica, 61
Cortes, Maria, 40
Cosa, Juan de la, 98, 110c, 116, 184
Cousteau, Jacques, 192
Cuba, 22, 61, 99, 116, 135, 158, 159, 162, 184, 187
Cuneo, Michele da, 45c, 116, 152
Cyclades, 66

D

Dati, Giuliano, 43c, 105c
Day, John, 53c
Delleani, Lorenzo, 168c
Deza, Brother Diego de, 40, 179
Diego, Master, 98
Di Negro, family, 47, 67, 70, 77
Di Negro, Paolo, 66c, 74
Dominica, island of 116
Doria, Admiral Andrea, 15c
Doria, Francesco, 52

E

Enero, Juan, 45
England, 66, 67, 71, 80, 137c
Escobar, Diego de, 152
Escobedo, Rodrigo de, 35
Esdra, 82
Esperanza, fortress of, 152
Espinosa, 169

F

Falcon, Andres, 67
Farfán, Cosme Rodriguez de, 195, 214c
Fernandina, island of, 99
Ferdinand the Catholic, King of Aragon, 22, 25, 105c, 124c, 134, 154c, 158, 164c, 174, 179, 180, 184
Ferriz, Gaspar, 158, 161c
Fieschi, Bartolomeo, 52, 124, 135
Figueira de Foz, 195, 198, 199c, 199, 200, 201, 210
Florida, 116c, 116
Fonseca, Don Juan Rodriguez de, 116, 119c, 150, 159, 169

G

Galarza, Pedro de, 196, 199
Galicia, 99
Galindo, Beatriz, 43
Gallo, Antonio, 60
Galway, 71
Geraldini, Alessandro, 39
Geraldini, Antonio, 39
Gibraltar, Strait of, 47
Gil, Juan, 40, 80
Giovio, Paolo, 18c, 22c
Giuseppe, Master, 80
Giustiniani, 66
Giustiniani, Agostino, 15
Gomara, Francisco Lopez de, 25, 39, 42
Gomara, Lopez, 82c
Gonzaga, Vincenzo, 18c
Gorda, Andres Martin de la, 169
Gorricio, Gaspare, 52, 53, 179c, 182, 187
Granada, 36, 39, 59c, 94, 159, 165, 174
Guacanagarí, King or Cacique, 20, 21, 26, 35, 162c
Guadalquivir River, 179
Guadalupe, island of 116
Guanaja Island, 124
Guarionex, Cacique 150, 152, 162, 177
Guatiguana, Cacique 162
Guinea, 31, 77, 80c, 80
Gutiérrez, Pero, 35
Guzman, Don Enrique de, 39
Guzman, Don Juan de, 39

H

Havana, 187
Henry VII, 31, 53
Hervas, Alonso de, 45
Higden, Ranulf, 88c
Hinojedo, Pedro de, 182
Hispaniola, island of, 22, 35, 40, 45, 99, 105c, 106c, 116, 122, 123, 124, 134c, 135, 150, 150c, 153, 156, 159, 161, 162, 165, 168, 174, 176, 180, 187, 210
Hojeda, Alonso de, 49, 123, 124, 167, 176
Honduras, 124
Honorius, Philoponus, 122c
Hyères, 60

I

Iceland, 71, 71c
Indian Ocean, 46
Ionian Sea, 66
Ireland, 71, 80
Isabella (city), 25, 28, 116, 153, 158, 161
Isabella, island of, 99, 106c, 152, 159, 161, 162
Isabella I, the Catholic, Queen of Castile (Catholic queen), 25, 26, 28, 41, 43, 105c, 119c, 124c, 134, 154c, 158, 164c, 174
Izquierdo, Pedro, 98

J

Jamaica, 22, 61, 94, 116, 124, 134c, 135, 156c, 158, 159, 162, 179c
Janico River, 152
José, *maese* (astronomer), 74
Juan (master physicist), 35
Juan, Prince, 33, 134
Juan (surgeon), 98
Juan II (King of Portugal), 165
Juana, the Insane, Princess, 174c, 179, 182
Julius II, Pope, 52, 53, 180

L

Lagos, 196
Lamartine, 26c
La Rábida, Monastery de, 28, 28c, 34, 36, 101c, 110c
Laredo, 135
Lares, 176
La Roncière, 69c
Las Casas, Bartolomé de, 15, 18, 20, 21, 22, 25, 26, 31, 33, 34, 39, 41, 42, 60, 65c, 116, 158, 177
Las Casas, Pedro de, 116, 169, 174
Laveno, port of, 193, 194
Leardo, Giovanni, 88c
Leon, Gulf of, 67
León, Juan Ponce de, 116c, 116
Llanos, Pedro de, 45
Lugo, Guilherm de, 204c, 210
Lynn, Nicholas of, 53

M

Madeira, island of, 66, 74
Magdalena (fortress), 152, 162
Magona, 66
Maguana, 159
Maiorca, 67
Malagueta, coast of, 77
Marchena, Antonio de, 28, 36, 39
Marchioni, Bartolomeo, 47, 77
Margaret of Austria, 134
Margarita Island, 123, 154c
Margarite, Mosen Pedro, 152, 156, 158, 159
Marigalante, island of 116
Martines, Joan, 140c
Mayo, Juan Luis de, 180
Medici (il Popolano), Pier Francesco de', 47
Medina Sidonia, Dukes of 34
Mediterranean Sea, 15c, 49c, 59c, 61, 67, 69c, 70, 164c
Medina, Juan de, 98
Mendez, Diego, 35, 124, 135, 182
Mendoza, Cardinal Don Diego Hurtado de, 179
Mendoza, "Great Cardinal" Pedro Gonzalez de, 39c, 39, 40, 42
Moconesi (region, Genoa), 15
Moguer, Juan de, 98
Mollat, M., 71
Montalban, 167
Montemayor, Marquise of, 34
Montoya, 167
Montserrat, 116
Muliart, Miguel, 34, 35
Muñiz, Briolanja (Donna Violante), 28, 34, 35, 49, 183
Muxica, Adrían de, 161

N

Narbonne, Gulf of, 60
Navarrete, M. Fernandez, 36c
Navarro, Fernando, 152
Navidad, fortress or, 35, 99, 150, 152, 156, 204c, 210
Nina, caravel, 59c, 98, 99, 116
North Sea, 72c
Nuestra Señora de Seiça, monastery of, 199

O

Oderigo, Niccolò, 47, 52, 180
Olano, Sebastian de, 159
Orinoco River delta, 80, 123

Ortelius, Abraham, 71c, 140c
Ortiz, Diego, 169
Ovando, Brother Nicolás de, 124, 152, 176, 177, 180
Oviedo, Gonzalo Fernandez de, 25, 42, 158, 159, 174
Ozama River, 152, 153, 177

P

Pacheco, Duarte, 80
Pagano, Francesco, 59c
Palos, city of, 41, 98c, 98, 101c, 133c
Pané, Brother Ramon, 116
Pariah, Gulf of, 122
Paul II, Pope, 91c
Pedrogo (town), 199
Peña, E. Cano de la, 36c
Perestrello, Bartolomeo, 74
Perestrello, Filipa Muñiz de, 30, 34, 74
Perez, Juan, 28, 33, 36, 39, 94, 168
Petit, Juan, 22
Philip of Habsburg, 179, 182, 184
Piccolomini, Enea Silvio, 71
Pinelo, Francisco, 52
Pinta, caravel, 59c, 98
Pinzón, Vicente Yañez, 98, 110c, 124, 176
Piombo, Sebastiano del, 18c, 25c
Playa del Lorical (Osso da Baleia), 198, 199c, 199, 204c
Polo, Marco, 46, 47c, 53c, 53
Pontal (Pedra da galè), 196, 197
Porras, brothers 42, 46, 156c
Porras, Juan de, 184
Porto Santo, island of, 30, 74, 74c, 80
Portugal, 30, 31, 34, 40, 47, 49, 71, 74c, 77, 77c, 80, 82, 98, 165, 195c, 195, 196, 197, 198, 199, 201, 204c, 209, 210
Portugal, Don Alvaro of, 34
Ptolemy, 91c, 137c
Puerto Hermoso, 177
Puerto Plata, 35
Puerto Rico, 40, 116, 194, 203c, 204, 213c, 214c

Q

Quintanilla, Alonso de, 42
Quinto, town of 15

R

Regiomontanus Calendar, 134c, 135
Reis, Piri, 82c
Riberol, Francisco de, 52, 180
Ricco, Giacomo il, 98
Rio do Ouro, 80
Road of Silver 179
Rodriguez, Martin, 124c
Roldan, Francisco, 161, 164, 165, 167, 168, 177
Rondinelli, Piero, 49
Roselly, 26c
Ruiz, Brother Francisco, 168
Rust, Hans, 88c

S

Saint Bruno, monastery of, 53
Saint Christopher, fortress of, 152
Salcedo, Pedro de, 167
Salvatoris, island of, 106c
Samos Island, 66
Sanchez, Gabriel, 39, 40
Sand, Georges, 49c
San Fernando, 18
Sagres, Bay of, 197
San Jorge de la Mina, fortress of, 77, 77c, 80
San Juan del Puerto, 28, 34
San Juan, Puerto Rico, 194, 203c, 210, 213c, 214c
Sanlúcar de Barrameda, 53, 122, 124, 133c
San Salvador I, 195, 197, 199c, 199, 200, 201, 203c, 204c, 209, 209c, 210, 211, 216c
San Salvador II, 195c, 195
San Salvador (Watling), 98
Santa Catalina, flagship 195

Santa Caterina, fortress of, 152
Santaella, Don Rodrigo Fernandez de, 46, 47c
Santa Fe, 47, 94c, 94
Santa Maria, *caracca* or sailing ship, 3, 20, 21, 25, 35, 59c, 98, 99, 102c, 188, 201c, 201, 203c, 209, 209c, 210, 211, 214c, 216c
Santa Maria de la Antigua, 116, 184
Santa María la Blanca, hamlet of 28, 35
Santa Maria de las Cuevas, monastery of 28, 52, 187
Santa Maria, Port of, 119c
Santángel, Luis de, 41, 43c, 52
Santo Domingo, 28, 94, 116, 123, 135, 148c, 152, 153, 161, 162, 166, 167, 168, 177, 187
Santo Tomas, 152, 158
Saona Island, 135
Sardinia, island of 59c, 60, 61, 67
Sbarroia, family, 35
Schedel, Hartmann, 15c
Segura, Diego Mendez de, 43
Sicily, island of 59c, 61
Sierra Leone, 40
Soria, city of 134, 135
Spinola, family, 47, 67, 77
Spinola, Gaspar, 52
Spinola, Niccolò, 66
Stradanus, Joannes, 102c

T

Tagus River, 99
Tavarone, Lazaro, 126c
Tavira, 98
Terreros, Pedro de, 28, 122, 167, 168
Tiro, Marino di, 82
Toledo, Donna Maria de, 31, 35, 187
Tomares, Spain 49
Torre, Donna Juana de la, 43
Torres, Bartolomé, 98
Torres, Captain Antonio de, 21, 43, 150, 156, 158, 159, 177
Torres, Luis de, 98
Toscanelli, 74, 82, 85c
Triana, Rodrigo de, 211
Trinidad, island of, 21, 122
Tristan, Diego, 45

U

Ulloa, Alonso de, 65c

V

Vallecillo, Bernal Gonzalez, 184
Valle del Paraíso, 80
Vallejo, Alonso, 169, 174
Valles, 167
Vallseca, Gabriel de, 49c
Vassalle, Emile, 26c
Vega Real, 152, 161, 162
Veçano, Juan, 98
Velazquez, Juan, 42
Veragua, duchy of 94, 124
Verde, Simone, 47
Vespucci, Amerigo, 31, 45, 47, 49c, 49, 123, 124, 137c
Vespucci, Ambassador Guidoantonio, 31
Villafranca de Valcarcel, 184
Vizcaíno (ship), 124

W

Waldseemüller, 91c
White, John, 203c

Y

Yaqui River, 152
Yuna River, 152

X

Xaragua, 161, 166

Z

Zacut, Abraham, 134c, 135
Zamora (courier), 43
Zapata, Doctor, 42

SOURCES AND DOCUMENTS

BERNALDEZ, A. *Memoria de los Reyes Catolicos*, M. Gómez Moreno and J. de Mata Carriazo edition, Madrid, 1962.

CASAS, LAS, *Historia General de las Indias,* J. Perez de Tudela edition, Madrid, 1957.

Coleccion Documental del Descubrimiento. (1470-1506), J. Perez de Tudela edition, C. Seco Serrano, R. Ezquerra Abadía, E. López Oto, 3. Vol., Madrid, 1993.

COLUMBUS, F., *Le historie della vita e dei fatti di Cristoforo Colombo per D. Fernando Colombo, suo flglio (Histories of the Life and Deeds of Christopher Columbus by His Son, Fernando Columbus)* edited by R. Caddeo, 2 vol., Milan, Italian edition, 1957-58.

Cristobal Colon. Textos y documentos completos. Nuevas cartas, C. Varela and J. Gil edition, 3rd, Madrid, 1992.

FERNANDEZ DE OVIEDO, G., *Historia General y Natural de las Indias,* J. Perez de Tudela edition, 3 vol., Madrid, 1959.

GIL, J. AND VARELA, C. *Cartas de particulares a Colón y relaciones coetáneas,* Madrid, 1984.

LOPEZ DE GOMARA, F. *Historia General de las Indias*, Madrid, 1946.

MARTIR DE ANGLERÍA, P., *Decadas del Nuevo Mundo*, Madrid, 1989

Nuova Raccolta Colombiana (New Columbian Collection), Istituto Poligrafico dello Stato, Rome.

THACHER, J.B., *Christopher Columbus. His Life, His Work, His Remains as revealed by original Printed and Manuscript Records, together with an Essay on Peter Martyr of Anghiera and Bart. De Las Casas, the First Historians of America*, 3 vol. Kraus Reprint, New York, 1967.

GENERAL BIBLIOGRAPHY

AIRALDI, G., *L'Avventura di Colombo. Storia Immagini Mito (The Adventures of Columbus: History, Images, Myth)*, Fondazione Carige, Genoa, 2006

CARACI, I. L., *Colombo vero e falso (Columbus, True or False)*, Sageo Publishers, Genoa, 1989.

CONTI, S., *Bibliografía Colombina (Columbian Bibliography). 1793-1990.* 2nd, Genoa, 1990.

FERNANDEZ ARMESTO, F., *Columbus*, Oxford University Press, 1991.

GIL, J. AND VARELA, C., *Temas Colombinos*, Seville, 1986.

MANZANO Y MANZANO, J., *Cristobal Colón. 7 años decisivos (1485-1492)*, 2nd, Madrid, Cultura Hispanica, 1989.

Colon y su secreto. El predescubrimiento, 2nd, Madrid, Cultura Hispanica 1989.

Los Pinzón y el Descubrimiento, Madrid, Fifth Centennial, 1990.

MORISON, S.E., *Admiral of the Ocean Sea*, Boston. 1983.

RHAN PHILIPS, C. AND W., *The Worlds of Christopher Columbus*, Cambridge University Press, 1992.

TAVIANI, P. E., *I viaggi di Colombo (The Voyages of Columbus)*, De Agostini, Novara, 1991.

VARELA, C., AND AGUIRRE, I., *La caída de Cristobal Colón. El juicio de Bobadilla,* Madrid, Marcial Pons, 2006.

VARELA, C., *Colombo e i fiorentini (Columbus and the Florentines)*, Vallechi, Florence, 1991.

WHITE STAR PUBLISHERS

© 2008 White Star S.p.A.
Via Candido Sassone, 22/24 - 13100 Vercelli, Italy - www.whitestar.it

Translation: Erin Jennison

ISBN 978-88-544-0396-3

REPRINT: 1 2 3 4 5 6   12 11 10 09 08

Color separation: Pixelab, Novara (italy) - Printed in China